A Chorus of Readers and Writers Praise *Journey to Khiva*

"What I love most is Glazebrook's delightful blend of old-world romance with the prsent-day realities of Central Asia."
—Diana Wells, The Traveller's Bookstore

"This book is pure pleasure. I permitted myself small doses at a . . . time to prolong it, but still wanted more."
—Anne McElvoy, *Times* (London)

"Glazebrook intriguingly links his very contemporary travels in Russian Central Asia with fascinating accounts of the fates of solitary travelers who made this hazardous journey in former times. The result links past and present in a very personal narrative."
re

"Here's a travel book that . d memorable journey to Centr empires. . . . Glazebrook's pa decades of Soviet rule and Cold uone to the territory between the Caspia China. . . . The book [is] difficult to put down. It [is] eye-opening and truly educational."
—Thom Storey, *Nashville Tennessean*

"[This is] one of those wry, literate travel books that the British seem to specialize in. . . . Glazebrook notes that Central Asia remains for him 'a green oasis composed of many kindnesses.' An intelligent introduction . . . to a place only recently accessible, by a writer of disarming modesty and humor."
—*Kirkus*

Journey to Khiva

PHILIP GLAZEBROOK

JOURNEY TO KHIVA

A Writer's Search
for Central Asia

KODANSHA INTERNATIONAL
New York • Tokyo • London

Kodansha America, Inc.,
114 Fifth Avenue
New York, New York 10011, U.S.A.

Kodansha International Ltd.,
17-14 Otowa 1-chome,
Bunkyo-ku, Tokyo 112, Japan

Published in 1996 by Kodansha America, Inc.
First published in the United States in
1994 by Kodansha America, Inc.

Originally published in Great Britain in 1992
as *Journey to Khiva* by HarperCollins Publishers

Library of Congress
Cataloging-in-Publication Data

Glazebrook, Philip, 1937–
Journey to Khiva : a writer's search for
Central Asia / Philip Glazebrook.
      p.   cm.
"First published in Great Britain in 1992 as
'Journey to Khiva' "—CIP t.p. verso.
Includes bibliographical references and index.
ISBN 1-56836-074-6
1. Asia, Central—Description and travel.
2. Glazebrook, Philip. 1937–
—Journeys—Asia, Central. I. Title.
DK854.G54   1994
915.8'704854—dc20   93-2537   CIP

Printed in the United States of America

96 97 98 99 00 RRD/H 10 9 8 7 6 5 4 3 2 1

CONTENTS

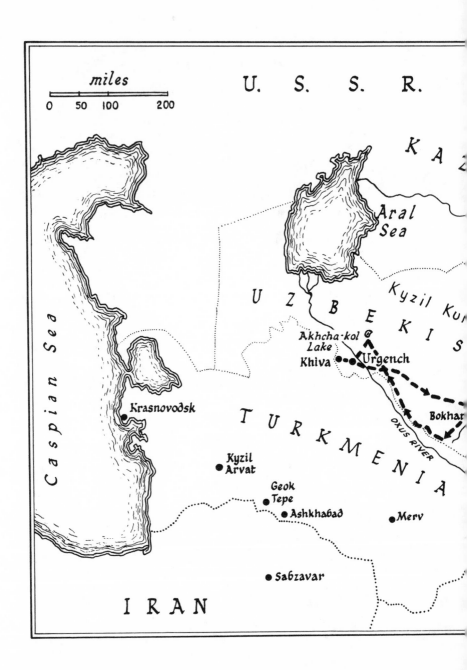

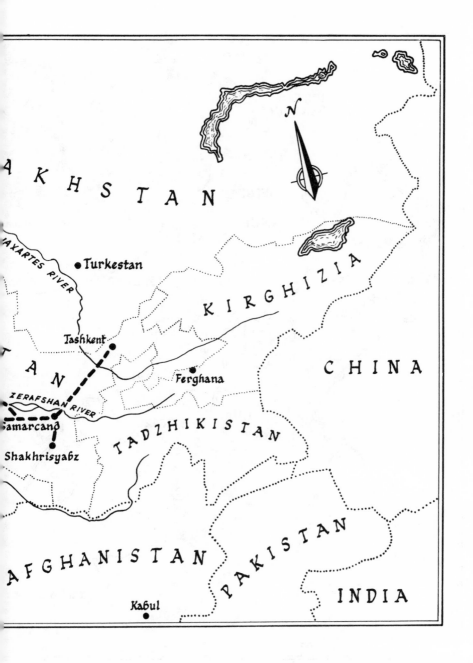

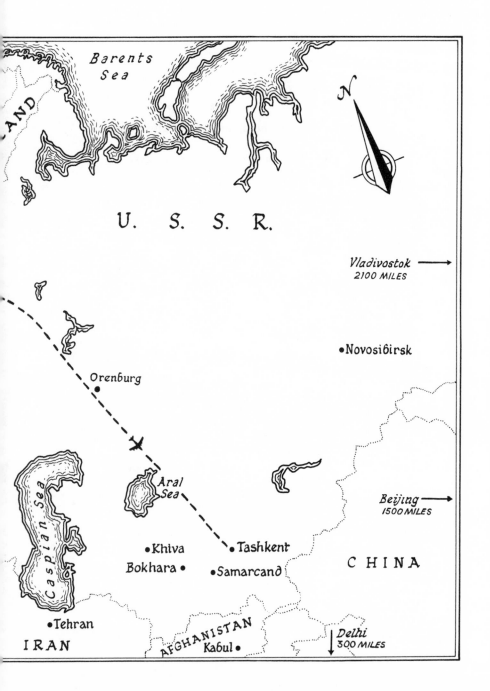

Russia may well fall to pieces, as many expect

CAPTAIN ARTHUR CONOLLY, 1838

Journey to Khiva

CHAPTER I

Train 237

I

A STRIP OF HOLLAND encased in concrete, which you cross by an iron footbridge, is all that lies between the quay at the Hook, where the Harwich boat docks, and the railway tracks which were to take me eastward into Russia. I was told that the Russian train was already in the station. The Russian train! I hurried across Holland with my couple of bags, eager to be off upon this vehicle of my dreams.

Train 237 was the usual line of dark green coaches, a medley of languages at its open doors, distressed faces at its windows, which forms any European express. But far down its caterpillar length, in sunlight outside the station canopy, an entity quarantined by its own shabbiness, waited the Moscow coach. There, only there, had a queue formed. On its grubby livery of cabbage-green and custard-yellow the sleeping coach carried the hammer and sickle, silver once but tarnished now. On its step, guarding its only unlocked door, stood a fat indifferent Slav, white as a slug, contentedly ignoring all pleas and arguments from the passengers at his feet. He had a peaked cap, vestiges of a uniform; he was a *chinovnik*, and he required a queue. I remembered what Russia is like. I remembered Russia clearly then and, despite my resolution to keep smiling throughout the indefinite extent of my Russian travels, my heart rather sank.

I don't believe there has ever been a European traveller (one or two of Stalin's English guests aside) who has made a journey into Russia sound any fun. A few – a Mr Cottrell in his *Recollections of Siberia*, Captain Cochrane in his *Pedestrian Journey* – set out full of good intentions, abusing other travellers who have abused Russia, smiling upon everything in their opening

I

chapter, even commending (through gritted teeth) the cab-
bage soup; but by page 24 we find Cottrell in the same fury as
everyone else, and thrashing the postmaster in the usual style;
whilst poor Cochrane, only one stage of his walk out of
St Petersburg, has already been stripped naked by a pair of
ruffians armed with knives, and left for dead tied to a tree.*
The source of the European's irritability, or worse, lies in his
expectation, fostered since Peter the Great's time, that he will
find in Russia the eastward extension of Europe; instead he
finds the westward extension of Asia, and flies into a rage.
Grattez le Russe, et vous trouverez le Tartare: this rather obvious
geographical truism was uttered viciously by Europeans as if
it was an insult, as if they had made a discreditable discovery
(and Captain Fred Burnaby added that the phrase was "une
insulte aux Tartares"). Finding the delays and corruption and
cruel indifference of Asia, where they had expected the con-
venience of modern Europe, upset these travellers' equanimity
beyond repair, so that they journeyed through the tsar's empire
at a high pitch of indignation, losing their tempers on every
page, enjoying themselves not a bit.

Not only from my reading of so many unpleasant tours in
Russia made by travellers past and present did I know of this
danger: I had learned it from the lesson of an excursion of my
own into the Caucasus eighteen months earlier. I didn't enjoy
it. I had seen a good many things and places that had interested
me, which I would not have come upon except by the chance

---

* "At about the ninth milestone I sat down, to smoke a segar, or pipe,
as fancy might dictate, when I was suddenly seized from behind, by two
ruffians . . . One of them, who held an iron bar in his hand, dragged me
by the collar towards the forest, while the other, with a bayonetted
musket, pushed me on, in such a manner, as to make me move with
more than ordinary celerity . . . Having appropriated my trowsers,
shirts, stockings and shoes (the last I regretted most of all, as they were
a present from Sir D. Bailey) – as also my spectacles, watch, compass,
thermometer and small pocket sextant, with 160 roubles, they at length
released me from the tree, and at the point of a stiletto made me swear
that I would not inform against them – such at least I conjectured to be
their meaning, though of their language I understood not a word" –
Captain John Dundas Cochrane, *Pedestrian Journey*, 1824.

of bumping about the mountains alone in a hired car, but I couldn't honestly have written an account of the trip which would have made it sound any fun. It wasn't any fun. The constant wearisome battle to keep going – for it is an Intourist pretence like that of Peter the Great, that the Western infrastructure of filling stations and meals and maps, necessary to the motorist, is to be found in Russia – this irksome struggle fretted away all joie-de-vivre. After a couple of weeks I was heartily sick of it, and so worn by care that I had to take in my watch strap a notch, let alone my belt.

How then, despite the Caucasian experience, was I now setting out for Central Asia on the Moscow train? Because no other quarter of the world attracted me half as much as the old khanates of Turkestan which lie between the Caspian and China. What child has not responded to the ring of those names, Bokhara, Khiva, Samarcand, and their images of cupolas and courts and shadows in the sand, images glinting with the scarlet thread of cruelty and spilt blood, names composed of syllables more haunting than the names of any other cities on earth? Such was the background of my interest, life-long but hardly sufficiently compelling to take me there for its sake alone. But into the foreground of my vision of these cities there had intruded, over the last ten or so years, a troop of adventurous figures, both Russian and English, whose activities had intrigued me more and more. These singular men were the players in what came to be called "the Great Game".

The Great Game was a cold war carried on from about 1830 till about 1900 between Russia and England over control of the approaches to British India, which the Bear threatened and the Lion defended. In those years, across Central Asia from the Aral and Caspian seas, the Russian Empire slowly advanced towards Afghanistan and India, the khanates of Kokand, Bokhara, Khiva and Merv falling successively into her power. England, depending as democracies must on the views of the government of the day, blew hot and cold. There was no open clash of arms between the adversaries. It was, as the Russian foreign minister Count Nesselrode said, "a tournament of shadows". On either side, though, agents were put into the

3

field to spy out the country or to influence a native ruler. These agents were the men who interested me.

Several of them wrote splendid accounts of their travels, which can be read with pleasure and interest. But there is more. In such narratives of adventure a Captain Burnaby or a Colonel Valentine Baker portrayed himself as the archetypal English protagonist – straightforward, chivalrous, brave as a lion and pure-hearted as a unicorn, dismissive of hardship and danger – and managed to paint this heroic self-portrait without ever appearing to boast, for modesty is one of the properties depicted. More than the action and events of their travels, more than the background of a cold war fought amongst fabulous cities, it was the true character and motivation of such men, concealed in their books, which began to fascinate me as a subject for speculation as I read.

I determined to go to Central Asia. I would see "the bumping pitch and the blinding light" where these men had played the game, and try to see if it illuminated their characters.* But I would only go on my own terms: alone, that is to say, and free to go where I wanted, but (because of my Caucasus experience) in the charge of an interpreter and general factotum, Russian or Uzbeg, who would look after me as a dragoman used to look after European travellers in Asia. The invitation

*   There's a breathless hush in the Close tonight –
   Ten to make and the match to win –
    A bumping pitch and a blinding light,
  An hour to play and the last man in.
    And it's not for the sake of a ribboned coat,
  Or the selfish hope of a season's fame,
    But his Captain's hand on his shoulder smote:
  "Play up! Play up! And play the game."

From "Vitai Lampada", by Sir Henry Newbolt. "Twenty years or so later [writes Mark Girouard in *The Return to Camelot*] 'Vitai Lampada' was adapted to celebrate the dead of the 1914–18 war:

    And though there is no need to tell
   Their answer to the call
     Thank God we know they batted well
   In the last great game of all."

4

from Uzbekistan, on which depended my visa, was fished for with inexhaustible patience and relentless telexes. A year passed.

I was leaning on the crook of a thumbstick in a glade in the midst of trackless woods in the midlands of England in late winter, March, at a time when it seemed to me unlikely that the invitation from Tashkent would ever come, when I realised suddenly and fully how much I counted upon making this journey. There was nowhere else I wanted to go. There was nothing else I wanted to do. About the idea danced a little skitter of excitement, and apprehension, like the ruffling cats-paw on water which makes the sail draw and the boat lean and the sheet tighten its clutch on your hand. In the midst of birch and oak and black-budded ash, caught in a close-drawn tangle of bracken and briar, the light still and hazy through mist and leafless branches, I recognised that the only way forward lay through Turkestan, and longed for that scud of wind to fill the sail. Aspiration, I've noticed, more often reveals itself by making all objectives but one seem pointless, than by any positive cutting ability to achieve that objective. Mere eager-ness doesn't get you there, but it stops you wanting to go anywhere else.

In April the wind from Tashkent suddenly blew fair. I got my visa. It was now May – May 2nd 1990 – and I waited under the hot Dutch sun to board the Moscow coach, made aware by the fact of queuing (behind us the sleeping cars for Warsaw and Berlin were being rapidly boarded by men and women whose names were struck off his list by an obsequious attend-ant) that the heavy hand of Russia, where all authority is always abused, had already fallen on my shoulder.

II

When I had thrown back the curtains of my bedroom high up in the Travellers' Club that morning about seven I found the sun already gilding the finials and curlicues of the elaborate

5

roof architecture above Pall Mall, and the sky behind these exuberant flourishes a deep and satisfactory blue. Planning was over: I was off. The cares of yesterday still cluttered the room with alternative books, additional shirts, an extra pair of shoes; but the decisiveness of today simply closed the bags as they stood, and took me downstairs to breakfast. Too late to worry, thank goodness.

At breakfast *The Times* carried a front page picture of President Gorbachev hurriedly quitting the saluting base by Lenin's tomb under the barrage of catcalls which had made the previous day's May Day parade in Red Square the most extraordinary one in Soviet history. I was certainly, if unintentionally, travelling towards the centre of the world's political interest. In the high-ceilinged silence of the breakfast room I read of Russia's misery and anger. Foodless shops, strikes threatened, the republics restless for independence . . . I had read and thought so much about old Russia that I half forgot that it wasn't to old Russia that I was travelling, but to this Russia of May 1990 which was so new and unpredictable that no one knew what to expect of it from one day to the next. That the Soviet president should be booed off his rostrum by the mob at a May Day parade would have been thought an impossibility by every Kremlinologist in existence a few months ago. What might a volatile mob of Russian malcontents do next? "Those who know Russia [writes a historian of the country] or who have heard of the revolt of Puchacheff, can well imagine how far the excesses [of the French Revolution] would most certainly have been transcended in Moscow or St Petersburg."

I took a taxi to Liverpool Street. In the light sharpened by imminent departure London flowed past with a lambency which is like a foretaste of nostalgia for those tall red buses and Englishmen in thousands crossing bridges over the sparkling river. I entered the station against the crowd to find the Harwich train. If I was to catch up with the men whose adventures in Central Asia so intrigued me – with Colonel Baker, say, starting out from Charing Cross in the April of 1873 with his ton of luggage, salmon rods included – the boat train seemed the proper way to begin.

6

I wanted to reach Russia slowly, to learn by experience how far away it is, and how many different landscapes separate it from England. The train split green England, emerged among saltings and wide estuary views. The sea! Once aboard the ferry I leaned on the rail to watch the cast-off hawsers splash into the widening froth between ship and quay. The throb and thrill of the quickening screw came shuddering through deck and rail to quicken my heart. Only an islander can have these dramatic outsettings from home and, ignorant as yet of life on a Russian train, I heartily enjoyed the boat's departure and its respectable restaurant in which I ate my lunch and drank a glass or two of claret looking out on the glittering North Sea.

I noticed that those in the queue for the Moscow coach whom I had seen on board the ferry had become curiously transmogrified, Russianised, by their coming again under the wing of Russia. There was a dapper sportsman in a short military-style overcoat, for instance, who had on the boat been rather an outré figure, buying up electrical equipment in the Duty Free shop, manoeuvring mountains of luggage and a large wife – this man, so alien in the free world, fell into place at once in the queue on the platform, a citizen of Russia returning home with all the spoil he could carry from outside the prison gates. What he couldn't carry he wore, the overcoat giving him a wintry Russian look despite the heat of the Dutch sun in which he waited with patience and docility.

At last we were allowed on board. In the attendant's cubby-hole a samovar was brewing as we trooped past and spilled into our compartments. Already in the bottom bunk of mine I found a student from Nigeria on his way to Moscow University, who had been stewing some hours in the heat of the train, for our rancorous attendant would of course allow no one off the coach once he was on. How uninviting Russia seemed! I thought of Edward Clarke emerging from the country in 1800 and writing in his first uncensored letter, "If you hear of anyone coming here, tell them to jump into Newgate sooner . . . we were like prisoners of war in a country of savages."

Unwilling to take to the top bunk and so miss the view from

7

the window till dark, I found a compartment so far empty where I sat tight and refused to budge. "Till Utrecht only," warned the attendant, a finger shaken under my nose. So, from this moving prison threading through the overcrowded landscape of Holland I watched and read as the country slid by and darkness came on. Turned out at Utrecht, as promised, I was soon in my own top bunk, comfortable in the sense of serendipity which makes you as snug in a berth in a train as a gull in a ship's rigging. At intervals in the night came and went those clankings and joltings and voices suddenly loud on platforms which waken you sufficiently to make you realise your luck, prone in your berth, before fading into the regular rhythm of wheels on rails bringing sleep. Despite a drenching in cold light at the East German border, when passport and visa had to be found, I woke as the train wound amongst Berlin's many stations with the feeling that I'd slept beautifully. I fetched some tea from the samovar but was obliged to breakfast as I had dined, off a couple of dried apricots from my stores. When my student companion awoke – he slept till nine-thirty wrapped head and all in a coloured blanket of his own – he reached for a large jar labelled "white spirit", an embrocation which he splashed eagerly over face and torso, rubbing it into his ebony skin with a kind of hopeful energy, and looking expectantly into his mirror to judge its effect. When awake he was a lively fellow, and made a long trip down the train in search of food, returning with two or three biscuits only, which he shared with me before wrapping himself up once more in his rug. I believe he slept most of the day.

The day between two nights on a train is a pretty long one. A society sprang up among the active travellers, who chatted in the corridor and lounged side by side at the windows. I talked off and on, when in the corridor to see a little life, with a Russian couple who had been holidaying in England. It was the woman, rather shrunken and wistful, who approached me – almost attacked me – with the tale of their journey. A life's savings had been put together for the holiday. The saved roubles had been converted into sterling and they had set out. But they had not reached London from Harwich before they realised that their life's savings, enough to keep them comfortably for years in Russia, would be spent in a few days in England. It was for the high cost of food and lodging in England that I was attacked so bitterly, though her husband, a cheery figure in black tights, made gestures of conciliation at me over her shoulder (he spoke no English, whilst she was voluble). "We lived like beggars," she hissed at me, "like beggars in your England." Her animosity roused her spirits and made her eyes glitter at me. In vain I told her that her hardship would have been the same in any Western country, and was caused by the rouble being virtually valueless outside Russia: it is curious to what extent national pride is concerned with the national currency, and she abused me and my sterling all the more roundly for having spoken disrespectfully of the rouble. What dodges they had got up to to extend their money she didn't tell me – the way she had spat out the words "like beggars" had made a picture form of the pair searching through bins and sleeping on pavements – but they had stayed out their full four weeks in England and were now returning full of resentment to Russia. Perhaps, I suggested, she would now like her homeland all the more; but at this she moved her hands restlessly on the rail below the corridor window and turned away from me.

Since there was no question of our attendant troubling to turn the sleeping berths into day coaches, or allowing us to do it for ourselves, there was nowhere to sit and read except on the bunk edge of the dormant Nigerian, so that I spent a good deal of time in the corridor. Here too there were drawbacks. A strapping great Dutch girl, rather inane, was forming a friendship with a German which took up a good deal of room. And then whenever our attendant walked down the corridor it was necessary for every passenger to retire into a compartment, so voluminous was the man's belly. Swept thus into strange doorways by the passing stomach I found that there existed a hidden majority on the train, listless faces peeping from their bunks like white mice from their holes, which remained supine, never appearing in corridor society. I returned to my piece of rail at the window and watched East

9

Germany's forests, the lightless forests of pine, sadly passing.

The idea of war, the thought of Russian armour devastating this landscape in 1944, dominated my view. Tanks, grey troops, shells. And none of the trees appears to be more than fifty years old, pines in ranks like no natural forest; it was perhaps my imagination which allowed me to see neither primroses nor white anemones in their darkness. I was aware of the Katyn massacre as if all the forest I saw was a mass grave. Yet in 1944 I was seven, hardly old enough to wrinkle my brow over news from the Eastern Front; nonetheless my view of Poland, of Eastern Europe, was then formed, and Europe itself divided for me by an Iron Curtain which it is hard for present-day events to raise.

For the nineteenth-century Englishman crossing Europe by train these countries made up a more or less seamless garment, all of them – short of the Russian frontier – governed in a similar manner, all of them considerably influenced by a class interconnected with the British upper class. They seemed a lot less alien than they do today. Because divisions were still between one class and another rather than between nations, Europe was comfortable to an English gentleman in a manner now unimaginable. It was true until 1914 sundered the ties. "I was the only first-class passenger in the Moscow train," wrote James Creagh in his *A Scamper to Sebastopol* (1873), adding dismissively, "and I didn't see anyone who looked like a gentleman at any of the stations along the line." What would he have made of the collection shelved in my first-class coach today? All the time, though, ahead of Creagh as much as ahead of myself, lay the enigma of Russia. Its outlandishness, despite a Western exterior wished onto St Petersburg, made him uneasy. Russia had only appeared among the European nations as a result of the defeat of Napoleon: before that (says the French writer de Lagny) "she was by her strange customs and form of government placed so far outside the sphere of the political action of Europe, that she was only spoken of as a country peopled by savages, inhabiting the holes in rocks, or the hollows of trees, and living on raw stinking meat".

On rattled the train across Poland. A train surprises people at homely tasks, and gives you intimate peeps into their lives, as a road does not: a house and garden is on guard against the road at the front, but not against the railway line at the back. In the suburbs of infinitely depressing concrete cities we ran amongst well-planted allotments, and in many an allotment stood a spacious shed, almost a summerhouse, on whose wooden steps sat Poles in their bathing dresses, reading the paper and smoking, or perhaps doing a little desultory hoeing amongst the vegetables. I wondered if they lived in the sheds, like country cottages. Then the train clattered past, and they were gone. It is this privilege of train journeys that I love, being carried into the unalerted heart of the place, and my own heart allowed just the time to beat with a pulse of sympathy, or understanding, before being carried on elsewhere. Probably it is a pulse of misunderstanding, but no matter: misunderstanding gives off as much warmth as the other, and the pictures I gathered of domestic peace gave me a happier impression of Poland than I'd carried in my head all my life.

It happens that I was reading *Praeterita*, Ruskin's autobiography, in the intervals of leaning at the corridor window, in which he attacks railway travellers. "Poor modern slaves and simpletons [he says] who let themselves be dragged like cattle, or felled timber, through the countries they imagine themselves visiting." (His own method of travel was by the already archaic private carriage which had been in use when he first visited Europe with his mother and father.) *Praeterita* is fascinating because the reader can watch whilst the mental arteries of a genius harden into senility. That brilliant susceptible mind lapses into ultra-conservative mutterings, and concerns itself with dressing up its own silly quirks, an old man's quirks, as general principles. "There is something peculiarly delightful [he says again] – nay, delightful inconceivably by the modern German-plated and French-polished tourist, in passing through the streets of a foreign city without understanding a word that anybody says." A great man talking such nonsense is a sad but interesting spectacle . . . and then occasionally, faintly, the marvellous gift of writing reasserted itself, and transported me

11

from the darkening plains of Poland to the Italy of his youth.

As dusk fell, and the Nigerian still slept rolled in his blanket – not unlike Ruskin's felled timber in appearance – I felt sure of the value of my thirty-six hours' journey across Europe. Nowadays the train can be compared as favourably with the aeroplane as Ruskin compared his private carriage with the train. But the journey, carefree whilst it lasts, will end in the disorder of a foreign terminus. Russia drew nearer. I put the confusion of arriving at a Moscow station out of my mind, and went to bed as comfortably as if the train had been my home for years.

CHAPTER II

Moscow

I

TO ENTER RUSSIA by train of course puts the passenger through all the usual hoops of currency declarations and the scrutiny of visas; added to these requirements, though, is an actual physical requirement demanded by Russia of the rolling stock, for each carriage entering the frontier must be picked up and dropped onto the wider set of wheels which will match the wider gauge of the Soviet track. What a performance! – the half-heard, half-felt hammering and banging of the operation – the lifting and shunting which spilled in and out of my dreams – all this work of the night formed a picture of a frontier really curtained in iron, through which the iron-wheeled train must be hammered so as to fit the dogmatic dimensions of another world.

I awoke into this different world to find the train just perceptibly moving across western Russia. I was thoroughly hungry, having eaten nothing beyond biscuits and dried fruit, and a square or two of chocolate, since that remote sunlit lunch aboard the ferry two days before. I determined to look for refreshments, especially as the train came so frequently to halt in the desolate silence of a provincial station.

Whatever the unfamiliar strangeness of Russia to the nineteenth-century traveller by train, and whatever its drawbacks, it was universally allowed that the refreshment rooms were wonderfully satisfactory – "Unequalled," said Fred Burnaby, making this same journey as myself on his way to Khiva in 1873, "anything you ask for ready in a moment". "After the gutta-percha pork-pies, mahogany cakes, and sawdust sandwiches, bolted standing in the English refreshment room, it is pleasant [says the author of *Sketches of Russian Life*], to sit down

13

comfortably when one is tired and hungry – napkin on knee –
to a half-hour quiet discussion of a well-cooked meal." It
would certainly have been a pleasant discussion. But I was not
allowed to leave the train to investigate today's refreshment
rooms, if any, in the stations at which we waited under the
catatonic stare of Russians waiting for other trains; and I wasn't
encouraged by our sluggish attendant tending his samovar to
seek a buffet elsewhere in our own train. However, I set off.

Somewhere or other we had shed all the coaches of the
European express which had stood waiting at the Hook of
Holland. Our Moscow coach, last in the line, had joined many
others as rusty and creaky as itself, and the whole long shabby
train fingered its way through the forests of Russia. I made
my way along the corridors of twenty or more coaches, all
sleepers and all packed, to find that the buffet car next to the
engine was closed. Back I walked through the clanking coaches
with their shelves of Slavs looking listlessly into my face as I
passed their doors. When I sat down in my own compartment
again, and made do with a biscuit, I was aware of belonging
not to the international express I had joined at the Hook, but
to a Russian crowd aboard a Russian train.

The landscape slowly passed the window. "The Russian soil
[says de Lagny in his unfriendly analysis of Russia published
just before the Crimean war] is nothing but an immense forest,
intersected with swamps, and lakes as large as seas, and steppes
the size of deserts, where the land that is capable of cultivation
is merely an accident." So it still looked. An unenclosed patch
of earth under cultivation for potatoes or grain, with here and
there a few cows tethered on strips of grass – such open spaces
are only clearings in an immense forest of birch. Now and then
a sluggish muddy river winding through a valley; now and
then a white road under aspen trees, and two girls walking
companionably along it with all the time in the world to talk;
or a man on a wobbly bicycle on a field track; or a woman
slowly pushing a pram in the shade of a line of poplars;
altogether a landscape which conveyed the slow idleness of
summer life. The may was everywhere in flower, and the
wood anemones, too, under the trees. The villages are pleasant

places, a compact group of dwellings on a hillside, the forest near, each homestead a one-storeyed wooden cottage within its picket fence, each with its woodpile, its chestnut tree, its rain barrel: altogether an appealing picture of domestic economy and a sociable community. But it is not a man-made or a man-centred landscape. Neither villages nor cultivated fields give the impression of having evolved through centuries of husbandry into what you see now, as today's hedgerow ash or cottage garden or Saxon church give to the landscapes of England their sense of a long descent in careful hands. That the Russians were not, until recent times, a settled race, seems reflected in their encampment-like villages in the midst of forest and swamp.

That this land, until 1861, was worked by serfs, contributed much to the European traveller's conviction of the outlandishness of Russia in those days. Slaves, ruled by the knout, owned body and soul by the apparently civilised French-speaking dandies met in St Petersburg! A hundred years earlier and the serfs had indeed been nomads bivouacked round the tent of their boyar (to whom they were bound for the purpose of military service), a band ready to strike their camp in the forest or steppe at an hour's notice to follow him under arms: it is these recent Tartar origins in much of Russia's society, a barbarous past resembling mediaeval Europe but concerning these nineteenth-century gentlemen's grandfathers – as may be seen in Aksakoff's account of his grandfather's country house – this was the frisson in Russian life which made the European cautious and curious when he entered Russia.

Given the frequency and violence of serf revolts – they averaged twenty-three a year between 1828 and 1854 – it is an astonishing passage in Russian history that carried through the emancipation of 1861 immediately, effectively and with sufficient goodwill all round for 285 million acres of land to be handed over peaceably to the freed peasants. But the whole of Russian society soon suffered a reaction. Not only did the ex-serfs discover that liberty meant also the freedom to starve to death; the "thoroughly Russian characteristic of profound despair [writes a historian] quickly succeeded confident enthusiasm, as each of the great reforms (emancipation, the army, the law) failed to bring about the complete regeneration of the whole Russian empire which its advocates had expected."* By 1866 there was a return to the autocratic repression of Nicholas I.

If the question is asked: What can it have been like to live in Russia under the tsar's autocracy? Under his secret police? Under the rule of an arbitrary will published in ukases? Under the terror of savage punishment and of exile to Siberia for a trifle? – The answer is: Ask anyone who survived Stalin's rule. Like visitors in the early 1860s, during Alexander II's reforms, we too see a people emerging from slavery and persecution, a press feeling its way to freedom, students beginning to voice dissent, provinces clamouring for independence. We see the beginning of the same kind of adventure which then culminated in *ochaiania*, profound despair, and ended in reaction. It is because of the notable way in which old accounts of Russia, and her attempts to liberalise herself, tally with what we can see today, that it is so hard now to expect Russia to break out of the pattern of her own past, and to develop into what she has never before been, a democratic nation.

I watched three elderly workmen idling beside the track, all of them old enough to have been grown men under Stalin, and wondered what their views were on turbulence and reform. "The character of the peasant is a profound abyss," wrote Aksakoff, "into which no eye can pierce. Is he aware of the enormity of the ill-treatment under which he is bowed down, and does he hoard up in his heart projects of terrible vengeance?" The three workmen spent much time peering one by one into the shopping bag of a fourth who, smoking a cigarette through a holder held between finger and thumb in the foppish Russian style, had come up to them on the tracks with considerable self-satisfaction. I had an hour or more to watch them, to "look into the profound abyss" and wonder, for at this point our engine had broken down comprehensively,

* Geoffrey Drage: "Russia and the Period of Reform" (*Cambridge Modern History*: Volume XI, Chapter XXII).

and here we waited amid a desert of grass-grown tracks whilst another engine, one of the old black long-bellied steamers which sidle about the shunting yards, was sent for spares. There was no question of the three workmen or their dapper friend having anything to do. When a stout and furious individual waddled up and roasted them with his tongue, they merely smiled at one another behind his back, only waiting until he had jerked angrily out of sight before resuming peeps into the shopping bag. What did it hold? Now and then one would put in a large hand as if to estimate the size or weight of what it contained. Under today's perestroika, or under Stalin, or under the tsars – or in a boyar's camp – I believe the four men might have been found similarly occupied. I concluded from the caution with which the owner opened his bag, and from something avid in the group's intentness upon its contents, that in it was trapped a living creature which its owner intended eating. Whether or not he would share it with the other three depended on how agreeable they made themselves to him.

We were close to Moscow when this last delay came about. I wasn't impatient. Last time I had come to Russia I had waited for my Aeroflot flight a whole day at Heathrow: I'd much rather wait in a Russian train a few hours. At last we crept forward, through suburban stations with crowded platforms, past plantations of dachas in their parcelled-out squares of garden, into view of the vast concrete cityscape of Moscow itself eating its way behind giant cranes into the surrounding forests. Bags were closed all round me, people gathered in corridors, all began to look anxious and to prepare for a rush. I didn't get ready to rush, because I hadn't any idea which direction to rush in. My Nigerian friend had folded up his blanket, packed away his cream pots, and vanished. The wheels groaned ever more slowly over the points, we sank amid concrete, the doubtful sun was shut out by a station canopy, and at length, with a final jolt which slammed shut my compartment door, the journey from the Hook was finished. I rather dreaded the chaos evident on the platform. Ruskin's "felled timber" railway passengers resent the need to come to life at journey's end and start taking decisions.

The train's final jerk had, as I say, slammed shut my compartment door on myself alone. It was flung open. In darted a porter. His eyes transfixed me. He kicked shut the door behind him and sprang at me, pulling a bundle of paper money out of a pocket. "Dollars, oh dollars!" he cried out in an agony of eagerness. "You change me dollars!"

I laughed. I showed him my two bags. "I'll give you a dollar if you'll find me a taxi," I said, concealing my own eagerness for this bargain. His eyes lost their wild shine. He looked doubtful, disappointed, then angry. "Okay." He seized my bags like the throats of enemies and dashed ahead of me onto the platform.

Chaos it surely was. People, families, women grasping children, all fussed and shouted amongst mountains of ill-fastened luggage and sacks and cardboard boxes heaped about the platform. That my porter had turned his barrow on its side before rushing aboard the train had preserved it like a magic charm from being commandeered; now that he set it to rights, desperate passengers begged a share of it, clamouring round him with anxious cries. He ignored them. He dumped my bags on his barrow and set off at a reckless pace, singing out at the top of his lungs "Eentooreest! Eentooreest!" which cut us a path through the crowd like an ambulance siren through the rush hour. Thus, by knocking aside the heavy-laden, he was able to wrap his disappointment at least in the rags of privilege.

The Intourist office, where he first led me, was besieged by a crowd of hundreds, so, since I was already on the wing with a porter, I wouldn't wait there in order to make use of my "station to hotel transfer voucher", and told him to find me a cab. This he rapidly did. Evidently I was a commodity being passed from hand to hand according to plan, for the taxi driver too held out his crumpled handful of rouble notes to be changed for dollars the moment we reached him. I promised him five dollars to drive me to the National Hotel, at which he flounced grumbling into his seat and started the engine. My porter too was grumbling and complaining, but I gave him his

dollar bill and clapped him on the shoulder like a spoilt child
you try to cheer up. It seemed that perestroika was making
scamps of them all.

By six o'clock, within half an hour of the train having
fetched up at the station – and fifty-odd hours from the Travellers' Club – I was alone in my tall airy room at the National,
the expected confusion of arrival having vanished like mist to
prove once again that it never is the problems you anticipate
which in the event come to pass.

II

It is, in a sense, "a great hotel", the National. Its huge, ponderous, reddish-flanked Edwardian bulk seems beached like some
wandering liner of the *Titanic* era driven ashore on an
unfriendly coast. Inside, the style is dilapidated Grand Duke;
wide shallow staircases, chipped ormolu, vast gilded clocks
which stopped decades ago on gilt consoles against the walls
of the corridors. Somehow mist and silence seems to enwrap
these dim passages, and the visitor is glad to pass through the
tall glass-panelled doors which lead through his apartment's
little lobby (for the furs and galoshes of a Russian winter) into
its bedroom. Stifled by fierce central heating, I had immediately flung open my window, which gave upon an inner courtyard where a number of idle cooks leaned and chatted at
opposite windows in the sun. This was a pleasantly human
touch. Hotels with any character are rare in Russia (rare
amongst Intourist hotels anyway) and the National is the nearest you can get to the eccentric pleasures of staying at, say,
Baron's Hotel in Aleppo or the Pera Palas in Istanbul.

I very soon went outdoors to walk in the strong evening
sunlight. Arrival in Moscow is an anti-climax; for what does
a traveller come to Moscow for? It is not in itself an achieved
goal, just to stroll in the streets, as it is a goal achieved by
strolling in Rome, say, or central Paris. You can say to yourself, Here I am in Moscow; but the wonder fades awfully soon.

There are the fantastic upper works of the Kremlin, and the famous cupolas of St Basil's, but that's about all. The scale is wrong; it is inhuman. Broad concrete thoroughfares pour traffic into the vast spaces under the walls of the Kremlin, where even a crowd is diminished to the insignificance of ants. Further off, true, are streets of pleasant neo-classical buildings, houses of the nineteenth-century merchant class, and there is the odd curiosity, the Pakhov mansion, for example; but there is no quarter which it is a pleasure to stroll through, on arrival on a fine May evening, so that a sensation of delight at being in Russia may invade you by the osmosis of its atmosphere. Put into my mind at once by the word "Moscow" is the image of the pinnacles of the six watchtowers which Stalin contributed to the skyline, those six thin and spiky ziggurats which, like secret policemen turned to stone, peer through their thousand windows into every house – every heart – in the city. But I wouldn't travel to Moscow to see them again. To me, Russia's capital is only a stepping stone to her provinces.

I walked past GUM and St Basil's towards the Moscow River. Long crocodiles of Slavs in wintry clothes looped and snaked about the sloping cobbles under the Kremlin wall. For them, the Russian tourists, this is the goal: to Soviet Russia's shrine, this cold and loveless tomb under the fortress's shadow, they come and wait in crowds the very image of dreariness, and are then content to start for home. I leaned on the embankment wall and watched the traffic crossing the bridges. At least I already felt a very long way from those tall red buses crossing the bridges of the Thames. A sense of his remoteness gratifies some instinct in the solitary traveller, and watching the chill grey river I felt remote; Moscow, and reaching it by train, had achieved that first objective, of severance from all that is familiar.

On the way back to the National I stopped at the Rossiya, a huge and terrible hotel, in order to exchange money at its bank and so obtain the documents without which you can't reconvert unwanted roubles into a hard currency when leaving Russia. I had no idea how many roubles I might need in Central

Asia, or whether I'd find in Tashkent a bank offering ten roubles for the pound sterling (as the Rossiya did) rather than one rouble to the pound which is all that Intourist at the National would offer, so I intended cashing a handsome sum. At a foyer desk I asked a girl with brass-coloured hair and painted nails where the bank was. In answer she stood up and joined me. Assuming that she was going to show me the way to the bank I followed her to the door. Nor was I surprised when she went through it into the street – the Rossiya has a dozen entrances – but I was a little taken aback when she laid her talons on my arm and said, "Bank is closed. I change you. Come wis me." As with the porter and the taxi-driver I felt she was a child trying out her tricks on a grown-up – and there has not been sufficient time for these people to become sophisticated racketeers – so I smiled and asked her when the bank would be open. She told me and clipped sullenly indoors.

The dining room at the National is on the first floor, its tall windows looking over the busy square at the fortifications and yellow palaces of the Kremlin. All this splendour the evening sun lighted magnificently when I sat down to dine at eight o'clock. It was a good dinner, too, red caviare, chicken Kiev, ice cream, all of which I ate with a hearty appetite. As I ate, and watched the low westering light flare on the walls and green-domed turrets of the fortress which was so recently at the heart of a secure, if evil, empire, I considered this incursion of petty criminality into Russian life which had not been notice-able on my visit eighteen months ago.

It clearly stemmed from a passion for hard currency. The black market existed before, of course – I could have changed dollars in any large Caucasian town on my last visit for five or six times the official rate – but it had not then been this universal and avid hunger assailing you on all sides. I had walked back from my attempt to cash a cheque at the Rossiya by way of the underpass, where two incidents in fifty yards had made this clear. First a family of gypsies, children a scav-enging pack filling the tunnel, young women with babies in their arms, all of them infinitely dirty, swarmed along the dim-lit subway. They accosted everyone, but they set upon me with particular vigour, children plucking at my clothes, the young women really snarling into my face. I held out two or three roubles, smiling as best I could. "Dollar! Dollar!" screamed the raucous mêlée. I hate having money bullied out of my pocket. Pinching the extraordinarily grimy baby's cheek as a gesture of goodwill I pushed my way to freedom through a net of clutching arms. But I hadn't gone twenty yards before a young fellow in a suit, haggard and white, blocked my path with a fistful of rouble notes. "You must change dollars," he insisted in a cracked shout, "you must change with me." Irrationally, perhaps because I half regretted giving the gypsies nothing, I held out a ten dollar bill. Quick as winking the roubles were pushed at me, the dollars snatched, and he had vanished in the subterranean shadows. His urgency, his relief – they were the desperate responses of an addict to a drug.

When I was in Russia last the touts had been sly and silent creatures given to looking over their shoulders. This insolent desperation of the porter, the taxi driver, the girl at the Rossiya and the man in the underpass was something new, which had come in with perestroika like a flea on the dove of peace. Approaching the National I had noticed the crowd of roughs round its entrance, under the trees, some of them drivers of the hire cars, all of them squarish, sallow, grubby young men in imitation leather blousons who stood joshing and smoking in a noisy group crowding the pavement at the hotel's doors. As I had entered after my outing I had been rather glad of the presence of the two other young men, on the inside of the National's street door, who had "Security Officer" on the lapels of their grey suits. It was their job to keep out the riff-raff to whom the National, with its foreigners and hard currency shop, was an Aladdin's cave, source of all they coveted.*

---

* I remembered from the accounts of Aksakoff and others that the grand houses of tsarist Russia were always thus besieged by a horde of impeding and useless "servants", whose aggressive activities alarmed Europeans, and this quieted my irritation with the riff-raff round the doors.

Upstairs I ate my dinner and drank some of the thinnish, sourish Russian wine with pleasure. The sun as it sank threw beams of ever richer light upon the gilt cupolas of the Kremlin, heightening the radiance of grass and trees, blazing on green copper roofs and yellow façades, whilst in contrast the background faded into sober dusk. As years pass, the greater is the part played by the light itself in forming my idea of beauty. The sudden glory which lifts the spirits and brings happiness resides in light: the sun's early rays dispersing mist in woodland, its chance and fleeting effects, its evanescence, all express the poignancy of beauty to ageing eyes. For light is the sole defence against the onset of night. To happen to dine at that window in the Russian capital, and to watch such splendour stream out of the west to light its citadel, was an experience worth the journey so far.

III

Arriving, you come into the roadstead like a ship in the dark, and whatever happens that day is all happening at the end of a journey. A night's sound sleep – oblivion after the rather restless amusement of two nights on the train – separates yesterday off, and gives you vigour and interest to make plans for the future. The ship has docked in the night, and in the morning you throw out lines to the quay.

Russian offices are a crumbling quay, and the Russian telephone system forms a warp as weak as thread. Whilst my own affairs were edging forward – overseeing progress meant waiting about downstairs – I watched the skippers of far grander vessels attempting to proceed ashore for business. At breakfast, amid sunny tablecloths and surly waiters, I had noticed one of those fleshy and superficially jovial Englishmen of the business community, silver-haired, prosperous-looking, breakfasting with a thin smart wife. Also at their table – though constantly afoot to bring them yoghurt, eggs, waiters – was a younger man, darkish, glossy, with a wealth of obsequious bounce in his manner. His suit, though a blue chalkstripe like his boss's, hadn't quite the Huntsman snugness or smugness of the senior man's outfit. He kept his briefcase in evidence as if to show that business trips, though fun with the right people, were no picnic. But he was apprehensive, glancing at watch and door. At a late stage of breakfast they were joined by the source of his uneasiness, his wife. She was an extremely handsome thirty, trim and dark and disdainful, a Home Counties heiress I should guess, who thought herself a match for anyone. She didn't apologise for being late; but her husband did, with an anxious glance at the thin lips of the skipper's wife. By chance at that moment the sun, or its light through a breeze-lifted net curtain at the open window beside them, lit the two older faces just as they sketched smiles at the late-comer, revealing in the eyes and crows'-feet of each a hardness and tiredness not superficially apparent. Anyway, these interesting shipmates were early downstairs after breakfast, their captain smoking a cigar by this time, all of them awaiting the smooth activation of London-made plans. An hour later they waited still. Icy-faced, the skipper's lady sat very upright on a plush banquette. Beside her the younger woman stared straight ahead, her husband's jacket carefully folded on her knees. He, stripped to his shirt sleeves, frantically sought to telephone. The boss paced the foyer, all pretence of joviality collapsed into rags of rage mottling a mulberry-coloured face. The Russian defence had drawn him out of his ground and defeated him.

I too found that the numbers I rang were either engaged, or a wrong number, or that the person I wanted was said to be out. It mattered very little. I never care for ringing strangers in foreign cities anyway; and most of the people I tried to ring knew that I would be in Moscow by now and would therefore get messages to me if it was their intention to be helpful. The result of so many calls failing was a free day. I had never been inside the walls of the Kremlin (which can only be entered in a group): accordingly, more to conform with universal custom than from any craving to see the place, I bought a ticket for a tour starting immediately and hurried out into the sun to join it.

24

I now fell into the company of a delightful American. As our Intourist crocodile, like many similar reptiles, wound round the perimeter of Red Square, he had made some slight enquiry of me; and in a matter of moments we were deep in talk, eyes on the pavement, the urgings of our tour leader to cross roads behind her unheeded. He was a well-tanned sixty-five, hair sparse and sleek, with wise warm eyes, who told me he had retired from the retail trade in Chicago to live in the South. There he had become fascinated by the phenomenon of Mikhail Gorbachev. It had struck him that suddenly, after decades of malignant incompetence in the Kremlin, there had appeared upon that most powerful throne a *deus ex machina*, an individual of immense capability with the intention of doing good. But he hadn't just read a few magazine articles in his Georgia retirement; my new friend had gone to college. He had put himself through the Russian History degree course and had sat the examinations. (But first, before joining the students on an all-square basis, he had asked the professor to sound out the youngsters in case they objected to having him in with them.) We walked under the trees of the Alexandrovski gardens without looking up, we passed the Kutafia tower without giving it a glance, and at every turn of our discussion his knowledge of Russian history showed itself. Henry James would have been proud of him: enquiring, sceptical without losing his enthusiasm, thoughtful, modest. I liked his practical clothes, too, the blue button-down shirt under a worn linen jacket, the chinos. This Russian trip of his, to Siberia and Tashkent after Moscow, was to look into Russia physically after reading her history. "I would tackle it alone," he said a shade wistfully, watching a regiment of women gardeners resting on their brooms whilst we waited to enter the Kremlin gate, "but I don't have commănd of the language."

Amongst the press of other tours, other guides, we crushed into the Armoury. Our guide steered us among the lighted display windows, her voice high, excited, anxious, as she explained and expounded in an English soused in the rich sauce of her accent. In her hand, dog-eared and nervously squeezed, she concealed an *aide-mémoire* to which her eyes slid when she feared forgetting an English word. From the shows in the vitrines, like shop windows you walk past, I caught an impression of half-barbarous grandeur in Ivan's ivory throne, or the gleam of his skull cap of a crown on which so many terrified men must have looked their last, or the great shabby golden coaches mixed up with the scimitars and yataghans. Though there is much English silver, many things bought from or given by Englishmen, the only British arms ever shown off in the museum as trophies of war (says *Murray's Guide* for 1849) proved to be cannon taken from an English merchantman wrecked on the Finnish coast, not a *prix de guerre* at all, and in consequence protested against by the British and removed from display. I wished that I, instead of trivia of this kind, and a mere sense of accumulated plunder, had in my mind my American friend's general knowledge of Russia's history which made sense of things for him, linking the objects in the windows to one another in a coherent way that I envied.

He had prepared himself with a thoroughness which ensured the success of his tour, for his present knowledge meant that he knew what further questions he wanted answered by his journey. What he saw in the Armoury filled in gaps, illustrated texts. Those who, like myself, aren't altogether sure what they are looking for – but hope to recognise it when it turns up – have to spend their time less purposefully.* I remember an example of this in Kutaisi, in the Caucasus. I had driven into the town, and been caught up in a traffic system circling the suburbs until I despaired of finding the town's centre at all, and had at last parked in an alley and walked. Again I was lost amid stained grey canyons of concrete. But then I suddenly emerged under a cloudy sky on the banks of the Rion, a fast, wide river flowing under stone-piered bridges over limestone

* "After I came home from St Petersburg and tried to instruct my mind by every book I could get hold of about Russia, I found my travels had been much more interesting than, from the very intensity of my ignorance, I believed them to be at the time." Augustus Hare makes this candid admission about his Russian journey of 1883. Perhaps more travellers than care to admit it will find in their hearts that the same fact has been true of their own journeys.

rocks. Without knowing what to look for in Kutaisi, or what I had wanted from it, I had stumbled upon this satisfactory scene. Along the riverside stood pretty stone cottages and terraces with shady verandahs; further into the town I came upon a whole quarter of handsome town houses, their ashlar façades decorated with pilasters and plasterwork window-cases, the streets planted with plane trees. Here was a town built for the Russian rulers of their newly conquered province of Caucasia about the middle of the last century. Only when I walked into it did I know it was what I wanted to find. Across an iron river bridge, and climbing by cobbled lanes overhung with fig and pear, I reached the half-ruined Bagrati Cathedral above the town and could sit and rest where the clamour of the river came up to me, and the mountains rose steep through fir woods into mist and rock above me. My journey had a point. But it had been a rewarding hour amongst many trying scenes in my weeks in the Caucasus. Hence the dragoman awaiting me at Tashkent. Would his presence (if he materialised at all) rule out the chance rewards as well as the trying scenes?

My American friend was rather appalled, I could see, that I had come twice to Russia on my own without learning the language. I had no excuse, except that it is not Russia that attracts me but Russia's Asiatic provinces, where Turki would be the more useful language. Talking, and half-listening to our guide's discourse on the history of its various buildings, we walked about the square outside the Armoury, the square amongst the churches. As we stared at the Great Bell and the Great Cannon I told him about the gloomy and pessimistic poet Tchaadayev, whom Herzen quotes as saying, "Every foreigner is taken to look at the Great Cannon and the Great Bell – the cannon which can never be fired, and the bell which fell before it could be rung. A strange town in which the objects of interest are distinguished by their absurdity; or perhaps the Great Bell without a tongue is a hieroglyph symbolic of that immense dumb land, inhabited by a race calling themselves Slavs* as though surprised at the possession of human

* The Russian for "word" is *slava*.

27

speech." Our guide just then was speaking of the cathedral bells, and, having told us that they never would be rung save on some earthshaking occasion, added with an earnest appeal in her voice, "But I hope, I hope, that I will hear them in my life."

"They'll never put these seventy years behind them," my friend said as we walked away together. "The satellites will maybe; they can blame it all on Russia, wash their hands of Communism, say it was imposed on them against their will, go back to the way they were, have palaces and kings even. But not Russia. The whole damn system was their invention. Russia can't duck out."

In the National after lunch I was called to the telephone. First a man's voice asked me who I was, then a woman's voice came on the line, faint and soft, telling me in good English that she had been asked in a message from London to "help" me. What did I plan to do that afternoon? I told her that I'd perhaps go and look at the Tretyakoff Collection, closed when I was last in Moscow. "My husband will be at your hotel in an hour," she replied. "How will I know him?" I asked. "He is Jewish," she said.

I had no trouble spotting Isaac in the National lobby. There were the businessmen, the foreigners, the thugs who had managed to penetrate the hotel from their bivouac outside, and there was Isaac. A careworn thirty-odd, in a blue denim suit, there was a hapless and downtrodden look about him, an air of humility expecting, at best, the cold shoulder. He cradled a tote bag and moved gingerly, as if his shoes were too small, all the while groaning out his English very slowly. We set out together on foot for the Tretyakoff.

It is an immensely long walk. Because of traffic noise, and the crowded pavements, and Isaac's muttered English, I couldn't fathom his plan or purpose as we pushed on over bridges and through ever drearier back ways and rutted streets. Kindness, or perhaps advice from his wife, made him think that I required an account of every building we passed, to which conscientious stream of information I listened as best I could. By the river a gaunt monolith – a block of flats I believe – is almost encased by the plaques and bas-relief portraits of writers and statesmen affixed to its walls. Had all of them been murdered in the Terror? That was what I gathered from snippets of Isaac's voice filtered through the roar of traffic as we stood above the grey river. Forty million was the toll of deaths allotted by him to Stalin. On we tramped, he murmuring out facts and grievances, myself at his elbow trying to catch his murmurs, all of them gloomy.

I had been a bit startled by his wife's frank assurance that I'd recognise Isaac in a crowded hotel lobby once I knew he was a Jew, yet it was an adequate and even comprehensive description of my companion. Are Jews as distinct a race in Russia as they once were in Europe? Time out of mind they have not been safe in Russia: the very word "pogrom" with its ominous syllables is said to represent the hoofbeats of a Cossack attack on the ghetto. And I knew that upon this coming evening a demonstration against Russia's Jews was planned for Red Square. Isaac's shoulders were understandably bowed.

At last we reached the shabby grass and broken kerbs of the Culture Park, and within it the vast oblong of the art gallery. A contagious depression similar to Isaac's now bowed my own shoulders. In the Caucasus I'd been able to stave off this gloomy mood, always at hand in the Soviet Union, by saying to myself, "You're in the middle of *Russia*, think of that and cheer up." I remember it working like a charm to raise my spirits in a grim sort of park much like this one, in which I had passed some despondent hours at Tskhaltubo. It was enough, then, to be alone in the midst of the Soviet Empire for the sense of interest and excitement to revive. But what had then seemed unthinkable – the breaching of the Berlin Wall – events in Prague, in Bucharest – the end of the Cold War which had been a central fact of my life since childhood – had in the past eighteen months become a commonplace we all lived with. The place had opened up. It was no longer forbidden ground, and to walk in a Russian park had ceased to have the frisson of adventure.

I hated the Tretyakoff Collection – hated it. The physical

29

preliminaries to a Russian gallery (or restaurant or concert hall) are dispiriting, for you must first pass through chilly regions, caves of ice, where a vast space has been set aside for the storage of the coats and wraps and headgear and overshoes made necessary by the winter climate. Altogether there is too much space: beyond the foyer's emptiness the gallery itself is far too big, and in it there are far too many pictures – and, I'm afraid, for my taste Isaac knew far too much about them. His knowledge was to me as daunting as entries in an encyclopaedia read in a poor light. On every painter and every picture he had information to disburse, facts leaked out with painful care as if disentangled from the workings of a mind occupied with toothache. He neither gave me his opinion of the works nor asked mine; he told me what was the received view of the picture in front of us. Because so few of these Popkovs and Mashkovs and Arkipovs and Pimenovs were known to me I found myself in the Europe-centred trap of seeing in their paintings only echoes and pastiches, not to say travesties, of European painters already familiar to me. Consequently I saw nothing original, nothing interesting, and after an hour or two began to gasp with that airless museum-boredom which threatens suffocation – suffering compared with which even sermon-boredom is a trifle. Still room led out of room. Such kindness as Isaac's nearly killed me, and a sense of my ingratitude added painfully to my burden.

At last the ordeal was over, and we were crossing the park amongst cracked fountains towards a bus stop. Here a broad-smiling woman of thirty greeted us, and I met Isaac's wife Lena. There was a warmth and liveliness and glow of the blood about Lena which instantly raised my spirits. I noticed the evening sun brightening the pale trees and the spring air, noticed the crowds, the bustle of the bus stop, as something cheerful. Hoping to repay kindness I said I'd like to offer them dinner in any restaurant they chose. This caused them to look doubtfully at one another, and to discuss together rapidly in Russian, but a plan formed between them and the three of us caught a handy trolleybus.

So began a long hunt which took us till dark and beyond.

On foot, by bus, by metro, we searched central Moscow for a restaurant which would give us a table. At entrance after entrance a doorman would half listen to Isaac's supplications before contemptuously, and without a word, shutting the door in his face. Some of the places hardly looked like even a Russian restaurant, just a curtained door on the street, but all rebuffed us, and most with scorn. Still, the evening was warm, the trolleybus rides round the Inner Ring were new ground to me, and to have shown impatience would have appeared critical. We didn't discuss the difficulty, simply caught another trolley or metro after each rebuff, and as we rode I answered Lena's questions, Isaac exclaiming to himself as he strap-hung, until we debouched at another inhospitable door.

When at last, having toured central Moscow, we settled down in a queue outside a glass door in Gorki Street – it was almost in sight of the National Hotel – only then did I cautiously wonder aloud at the difficulty of finding somewhere to eat. It is after all a conundrum unique to Russia. Well, said Lena, it was due to shortages. Shortages attracted mafiosi. Mafiosi? It was the first time I had heard the word in Russia, and I asked her if she meant by it a branch of the international criminal organisation. She shrugged: what did it matter? Whatever their origins or connexions, they were criminals who had moved in upon Russian life at all levels as the concomitant of glasnost and shortages. Hadn't I been harassed by their henchmen to change dollars?

Mafia! The application of the word to the various criminal activities I'd brushed against myself gave them a sinister coherence; these were not stray filaments my wings had touched, but the architecture of a web. Did she think Moscow's crime was interlinked, I asked, the money changers with drug trading, the underpass riff-raff with the *blouson noirs* round the National door – was there a spider at the centre of the web?

Lena nodded towards the restaurant just above the street where we waited. At the head of the queue of a dozen or so people, at the top of a couple of steps, its glass door was closed. Mooning behind the glass like pallid fish in an aquarium lounged two or three youths in zippers and jeans. They are all

31

the same, she said in a tired voice. She went on to talk of the miserable shortages of everything necessary, of the time wasted in queues, of the demeaning hunger for any little extra trifle. Listening to her, I thought of a piece I had read in the *New Yorker*, quoting a Leningrad designer as saying, "When there is such a prolonged dearth of basic commodities, the problem of dressing takes on ridiculous, monumental proportions. It's tragic that it drains us of so much energy that should be directed towards more important issues." Poor Lena, her intelligence making it the more irksome to be oppressed in this way, made to covet trinkets and trivia. And it was upon this weakness, for the Western trivia of jeans and records and Marlboro cigarettes, that the new criminals, the mafiosi, had battened their ugly mouths. I looked at the pasty youths behind the glass door who sneered out at our humble queue, and wished them in a Siberian jail. Darkness came on. Isaac waited silently, doggedly shifting his weight, whilst light from the glass door lit his grey-speckled hair and sensitive but sorrowful features.

Now and then, from behind us, a couple of people or so would present themselves to haggle at the glass door. Once or twice it had opened to them. Since we were still at the back of the queue and looked like staying there I asked Lena what "Open Sesame" they might have used.

"They pay in dollars," she said.

"So can we if you like," I said.

"No, it is not good. It is not necessary," she replied. But I had applied the spur. She left us and walked abruptly up the steps. Rapping on the door, which was opened to her, she shouldered her way through the abashed mafiosi and disappeared. Isaac, watching, muttered and groaned. I thought of masterful Russian women everywhere on the attack, guards, floor ladies, gardeners, every mamoushka in the land speaking her mind, and I wondered if Isaac was voicing sympathy for whatever victim his wife was knouting with her tongue.

In a minute or two Lena's robust figure appeared at the door and beckoned us in. We climbed the steps. We passed between the loathsome youths salivating their contraband gum in our faces and proceeded to wait in an inner space, a hall, the half-empty dining room visible through a curtain-swagged arch. At least we had progressed, if not succeeded. What Lena had said to the guards at the door I did not know, but they now ignored us, posturing as before for the benefit of the queue in outer darkness. Though pimply and uncertain, more like school bullies than criminals, that group of youths – and the other so-called mafiosi I'd seen too – gave off a kind of foot-loose, predatory sensation, like the sensation of lawlessness to be found amongst a group of desperadoes knocking in tent pegs round a travelling circus in central Europe. It was uncomfortable to have them thriving like cockroaches within every fabric one touched.

Time passed. It was perhaps three hours since I had suggested dinner. Terrifically loud music beat in our ears. At last Lena managed to arrest a man rushing past in a fury who roared out what sounded like curses at us and jammed us into a table before stamping away like the bad-tempered waiter in a farce. Why was he so angry? I asked Lena.

She looked round the room and shrugged. "It is the restaurant. He is maître d'hôtel. It makes him angry."

The impatience, if not the downright anger, of everyone connected with a restaurant in the Soviet Union is probably not a Russian trait, but the characteristic of a trade which is in a position of power by virtue of dealing out a commodity in very short supply. The menu, and every subsequent mouthful, is supplied grudgingly. The customer is always wrong. The same was true, if I remember, of a British restaurant in rationed post-war England: how the waitress loved to refuse your request, for a piece of bread perhaps, by shouting out, "You've had your quota!" as she marched away.

In a little while a glass of very sweet cherryade was brought to each of us, which Isaac guessed was a complimentary preliminary to our meal, sent to satisfy our thirst whilst the champagne which I had ordered was chilled. I began to enjoy myself. The music, the flock wallpaper, the paisley tablecloths and the cherryade – if the food and champagne turned out to be reasonably good, we had fallen on our feet in these surroundings. To offset Isaac's taciturnity and low spirits, Lena had a merriness which made her company good fun, the twinkle in her blue eyes and the healthy colour in her cheeks both reflecting the good humour and cheerfulness within. Round us in the heavily furnished room sat parties straight off the pavement, street clothes and shopping bags making no concession to being out on a spree. I asked how such customers would pay in hard currency for their meals, if that was the way they had scrounged themselves tables.

Lena shrugged. Though she didn't like the subject, it had become central to Moscow life. Anything, everything, could be bought in Russia's capital with foreign money. That was what affronted her. The fact had created an élite, an aristocracy, out of every twopenny-halfpenny tourist who condescended to visit Russia. In a Beriozka shop a foreign nobody could buy anything – caviare, furs, silks, any Russian-produced luxury as well as foreign goods – and through this power could dispense patronage, and control officials, and set aside laws, with a capriciousness which hadn't been seen since the domination of Russia by its Frenchified aristocracy and its German military caste in tsarist days. She was indignant. Russia was selling out its principles to whatever worthless tourist or native criminal would buy them in dollars. Her outrage wasn't strident; very decided, though, and earnest. The food we had eaten was good, but as yet nothing else had been brought us to drink, so I asked Isaac to enquire after our Georgian champagne. It turned out that we had already drunk it, taking it for cherryade.

IV

Dinner finished, the two of them walked with me towards my hotel. We passed through pleasant lamplit streets sloping down from the Chekhov Theatre towards Red Square, amongst ochre-coloured façades from pre-Communist days which I admired to Lena. "Never come here on your own," she responded immediately. It seemed impossible to forget their fears and apprehensions for a moment; indeed they expected Russia to break apart into chaos at any time, and Lena's last words to me, when we parted across the street from the National (they evidently wanted to keep clear of the malignant circle of activity around its doors) were to urge me to give up the idea of going to Central Asia at all.

Despite the doomsday talk I had been much interested and amused by the evening, by my whole day indeed (except the Tretyakoff), and I entered the hotel with a buoyant step through the ragtag group clustered at its door, and passed between the usual two security men inside and ran upstairs. I would not start jumping at shadows in Moscow, or it might indeed be foolish to go to Central Asia. At the desk at the head of the stairway, a sort of guardpost from which your floor lady hands out your key with an admonitory frown, I found the seasoned but glamorous occupant absent from her bunker. I took my key from its hook. The corridors of the National, as I've said, would be fine places for hide-and-seek, dim carpeted distances between walls full of recesses and shadowed door-ways and portly mahogany chests. In my room the heat was stupendous. The central heating was full on, the window shut. I threw open both casements onto the inner courtyard and, hoping for a draught to disperse the suffocating air, I left open too the door onto the passage.

I was seated at the writing table in the window a few minutes later, writing a telex to send to Tashkent next morning, when I heard a footstep behind me. I turned. In the unlit lobby which took up a yard or two of space between the passage and my room stood a figure. He was tallish, in the skimpy grey suit of a respectable Russian, about thirty. He seemed to have a key in his hand, and he seemed to be smiling. I thought he was a drunk who had staggered in at an open door, and stood up to set him to rights. I hadn't undressed, but had taken off my change coat. Under my shirt was a moneybelt which held about $3,000 and £250 in cash as well as another $4,500 in travellers' cheques; in my hip pocket was about 1,000 roubles: I was a mobile bank. I went up to my visitor and told him firmly to go, at the same time pushing him towards the door.

He raised his hand at me, and in its grasp I saw the glint not of a key but of a knife.

He immediately rushed me backwards by force and surprise across the room. I was hurled onto my back on the bed. His left hand pinned me to the mattress and the knife in his right hand rose above me. I seized his knife hand by the wrist and struck back at his jabbing head with the other hand. We struggled fiercely. I felt anger, no pain. When the knife stabbed down I couldn't stop it, but I turned the blade from my face. He drove it down into the bed, lifted it again. Still I held his wrist. Now his other hand came dragging onto my face. I smelled ether. I felt a rough cotton pad on my cheek, on my nose, and compelled myself not to breathe until I'd writhed my head aside and wrenched back the coarse-tasting cotton from my mouth. So we fought. I fought this creature for my life. Again the knife stabbed down and I turned it, again the stinking cotton nearly covered my mouth. Knocked against the wall my head was gushing blood, my face was torn by his nails, my left hand cut on his knife. He freed a hand to strike me a couple of violent blows on my breastbone which knocked the breath out of me. I knew then I couldn't last. I didn't expect to survive. But I fought as you play a match you know you're going to lose, thinking not of the end but of the game itself from one desperate second to the next.

Then he was gone. First I was free of his weight, then I heard the clatter of his dropped knife, flying feet, the rattle of the door, and I was alone in the bloody sheets and the wreck of the room. There was no breath in my body. I gasped for air, sobbed for breath. Then on my feet at the telephone – didn't know the number to call – dropped the receiver and dashed after him. Passages, doorways, recesses, all empty and silent. I ran for the main stairs. Still no occupant of the floor lady's desk. Down the stairs I dashed. On the stone steps in the lobby I stopped, blood splashing from face and hands, and shouted at the security guards that the man who had tried to kill me was loose in the hotel. I was furious, tense, expecting action.

There was consternation, little else. A milling about, a want of orders, of plan or direction: no authority, now it was needed, where before every trumpery official in the place had been a little Caesar. Young men started in all directions with the terrified indecision of rabbits when a hunting stoat glares through the hedge at them. A very junior soldier with large scared eyes came in from the street and kept his automatic rifle dithering this way and that in trembling hands.

Incompetence made it a farce. As in a farce, I called for the manager, instinctive resource of the hotel guest with a problem. The manager is off duty. Send me his deputy. There is no such official. Send me anyone in authority, anyone who will grasp what has happened, anyone at all who will make some attempt to catch the creature who has tried to kill me in Moscow's best-known hotel! No one comes. Nothing is done. I stand with the anger going out of me, blood dripping more slowly onto the stone steps, whilst a state of exasperation with Russia, familiar to all who have travelled there, gradually occludes all other feelings.

Through the doors now trooped under the weight of cameras and sound equipment an English television crew who had hoped to film a rally of Russians in Red Square demonstrating against the Jews, perhaps even (if things went well) harassing a Jew or two in front of the camera. But the anti-Semites had spoiled it by not showing up. Disappointed, the team filed indoors for an early night, showing no curiosity as to the angry bloodstained fellow countryman in their way on the steps, though their producer, friendly enough, contributed a few ironical remarks whilst he hung about watching me wasting my energy in trying to galvanise the hotel staff into action.

When he had tired of his amusement and gone upstairs there came next through the street door, like the good Samaritan after his precursors, a resourceful half-Russian writer, an American national. She at once took charge, questioned the staff, gave orders, confirmed to me the hotel's incompetence and inanition. She was unsurprised. With a plainclothes police major who seemed to be attached to the hotel we went upstairs. I had locked my room door so that neither my attacker returning, nor anyone else interested in tampering with

37

evidence, should remove the knife and ether pad he had dropped on the floor. There they lay when we entered the room, and I showed them to the major, pointing out also two or three unusual decorated buttons evidently torn from my attacker's shirt in the fight. Any interest he felt in these clues was carefully concealed. He put them in his pocket and questioned me in a world-weary style through the kind American writer whilst his clerk wrote down my answers.

I felt extremely tired. My head and face were torn and bleeding, my chest aching painfully from the blows to my breastbone, my shins kicked raw. In my left hand was a deep knife-cut. But I had been lucky. In a desperate struggle against a man with a knife, whether or not he intends killing you, you are likely to be severely hurt. The mattress had been deeply punctured with stabs. The knife had nicked the skin of my neck so that drops of blood laced my throat. An inch this way or that, a slip of his hand or mine, and the blade would have been in my throat or my liver if not through my heart. I was exhausted, but profoundly grateful to providence.

Nothing had as yet been done for my injuries: a medical team, summoned from some hospital, had gone immediately to the wrong hotel and were still blundering about the town in search of the right one. Now, in a break in the major's interrogation, the good Samaritan writer fetched her husband's aftershave from their room which she splashed onto my cuts and scrapes. Though the sting was keen, it cauterised damage to mind as well as to body: the fight was over, my attacker fled, the incident closed. Don't be aggrieved: don't repine. The major's clerk, putting away his notepad, took the opportunity of his boss's turned back to open his coat enough to show me privily the automatic weapon in his shoulder holster, grunting out as he did so (two fingers stabbing the air) the warlike words "Poot! Poot!"

Just as my room was about to clear, everyone on their feet, the medical team burst in. At the head of the column came a doctor in grimy white, inspection lamp strapped to his brow, box of implements swinging from his hand, the loping stride giving an impression of Groucho Marx which was reinforced by the nurse mincing behind him, all peroxide and lipstick, her overalls splashed with blood as well as dirt. He seized my head in a painful grasp. Nurse delved in the supplies. A bottle of iodine was produced, a roll of sticking-plaster and a pair of scissors the size of garden shears. Having applied these simple remedies – and refused to let me keep the sticking-plaster – they were gone into the night.

With their withdrawal the events of the evening ended. In a few moments I was alone again in my room, the window still open onto the courtyard, furniture set straight, telex to Tashkent still half-written on the table. All was quiet. I sat down and finished the telex, saying that I would reach Tashkent in a couple of days' time, and then, having reversed the sheets so that most of the bloodstains would be at my feet, I went to bed and put out the light.

I couldn't help wondering, when I woke up on my knife-punctured mattress next morning, how a hotel of similar rank in London or Paris would have treated the guest whom a cutthroat had tried to kill in a first-floor bedroom. A larger room, flowers, champagne, even an apology? Clean sheets at least, surely, and a question mark over the security officer's future . . . but I recognised also, of course, that if I wanted the European reaction to the event, then I should have stayed in Europe. Having travelled to Moscow by train especially to establish to myself at how very many leagues from Europe the Russian capital lies, I shouldn't complain at the otherness – the Russianness – of the National's response to what had happened. The want of concern tallied with every expectation. How perfectly Russian was the anxiety to avoid any involvement in a matter which could only bring trouble to those whom it touched. Listen to de Lagny analysing this response and its causes in the Russia of the 1850s:

> The laws are less to be feared than the police, which inspires such terror that everyone shrinks, as he would from a pestilence, from receiving or assisting anyone who is ill or wounded or struck with apoplexy. All the people in the

neighbourhood shut their doors; the place around the dying wretch is deserted, and the surgeons take to flight. No one dares to run for help or to assist the unhappy being; the law expressly forbids such a thing before the agents of justice have come and drawn up their official report. You stretch out your walking-stick, your umbrella, and save your drowning friend: henceforth you belong to the police-agents, and you will be exposed to every kind of vexation and moral torture.*

Russia's police have the same reputation still. I determined to be wary. De Lagny's warning – and that of "A German Noble" writing about the same date, who says that a Russian would as soon ask His Satanic Majesty into his house as invite a police officer – was germane to my case, for I had the prospect of a further appointment with last night's police major fixed for nine this morning. By no means now expecting the fireworks of detection and arrest which I'd hoped for in hot blood last night, my concern was to avoid my own enmeshment in the Russian legal system. I rang up Lena, as I had promised to do, and told her what had happened; but (thinking again of de Lagny) I told her to stay out of the matter, though she had offered at once to come and interpret for me.

For interpreter a kind anxious woman from Intourist was found, who came up to the major's room with me at nine, turning her eyes up to heaven in the lift and murmuring of assassins and robbers in every street of the capital. She lived in fear behind a chained and bolted door. And I had sat writing in a hotel room with the door onto the corridor open? This would be possible in England? She raised her hands in disbelief.

The major's was a small and stuffy room, curtained with blackout material so that a feeble bulb was needed to drizzle its rays onto plywood furnishings and dingy paint. The tele-

---

* The author of *Sketches of Russian Life* relates the story of his wife going unwisely to the police when a diamond ring had been stolen from her, and of how he had only been able to avoid six months waiting at Moscow, without the least chance of recovering the ring, by distributing roubles lavishly in the police office to encourage them to forget the case.

vision was on, and the major politely turned the volume a shade lower as we sat down. I repeated the tale I had told him last night whilst a clerk wrote it down in translation. In the middle of this process I heard the door open behind me. I was told to turn round.

"Is that the man who attacked you?"

A plainclothes man stood holding up a sorry looking creature of twenty or so by his lapel. His scared eyes met mine. "No," I said, turning away, anxious only for him to be freed.

He was removed. The interpreter said, "He is deaf and dumb."

Was I being tested? Was my story doubted? The warnings of de Lagny and of all others who have written of the Russian police were in my mind. My attacker had grunted out one or two syllables as we fought, and had uttered what might have been a dumb man's curse as he fled. Could that wretch in the policeman's clutches have been the man?

I was by now concerned only with extricating myself from a quagmire of uncertainties. Before I would sign my statement I asked to ring the British Consulate so as to discover whether such a document would empower the Moscow police to hold me for weeks, for months, whilst enquiries went forward and suspects needed to be identified. The man I spoke to at the Consulate was cheery: "I'll give our legal chaps a buzz to okay it," he said. Whilst we waited for him to ring back the major surreptitiously turned up the volume of his television, anxious not to miss the Coca Cola ad being at that moment beamed into the wastes of Russia.

What did they think was the truth of my story of being attacked in my room, I wondered as I watched the major and my interpreter mesmerised by the screen. Clearly the idea that I had left open my room door – left it open innocently, for the draught – strained belief. First, a Russian cannot understand that a room may be overheated; second, he cannot imagine a state of mind – of innocence – which does not lock itself in. So did they think that I had left my door open to entice in a passer-by? That the man with the knife had come by appointment? That I had brought him upstairs with me, and a quarrel over payment had caused a fight? Many explanations would occur to a policeman's mind, and if I was a Russian I would probably have been detained in prison by now.

And what indeed had been my attacker's plan or motive? I hadn't thought about that. Stalking the hotel armed with knife and ether pad, did he intend lurking in the shadows to spring out on some person alone in hopes of frightening money out of him? Or to pounce on a single woman as she unlocked her door? Perhaps finding my door open, and seeing me alone at my writing, had seemed such luck it had confused him: uncertain whether ether or knife would serve best, he had hesitated with both in his hand and bungled his chance. Never in a position to utter the famous phrase "Your money or your life" – always supposing he was not deaf and dumb – the size of the jackpot, if he had, would have surprised him.

Or perhaps he knew quite well how much money I was carrying. I had, after all, filled in a form at the Russian frontier declaring precisely what sum was in my possession. A Russian mafia would offer cash for copies of such declarations, so as to winnow worthwhile targets from the chaff. A hit-man told off to follow me, the doorman sweetened, the floor lady persuaded to leave her desk for an hour . . . he would have rapped on my door if he hadn't found it open, and knifed or chloroformed me as I opened it. Thank heaven for Russian incompetence.

At last the telephone rang in the major's bunker. It was the Consulate: yes, I could sign the statement, confident that it would be pigeonholed and forgotten. Encumbering me with no further offers of help (apart from the advice to refuse a blood transfusion if offered), the breezy official rang off. And now, reluctantly except for myself, the major's TV party broke up.

In the course of waiting in the major's room I had taken another telephone call, from a functionary at the Moscow bureau of VAAP (the Soviet copyright agency) named Kirill Ukraintsev. He had heard from London that I was in Moscow, and now kindly came at once to the National. He was a rumpled cheerful fellow, sporting the mane of hair which signals a connexion with the arts in Russia, and he had in his friendly manner something happy-go-lucky, even a shade scampish, which I fell for immediately. It was a relief to relinquish the tense and serious focus which a police office gives to things, and to return to a world less starved of lightheartedness. I told Kirill what had happened, and to him it was a perfectly recognisable incident. Dreadful of course – terrible – but come, this is Russia you are in. Now, is there perhaps a can of Budweiser in your icebox there? Thank you, thank you. And Marlboro cigarettes? You are kind.

Whilst we sat sipping our Budweisers, and I listened to Kirill's account of the consumer goods with which he had pampered himself on a business trip to New York, there came a rap at my door. I opened it expecting the police. But in ran two unhappy washerwomen, squeaking nervously, the soap-suds bubbling on hands which held out a slimy wad of roubles.

"Count them," they begged, "count them!"

I took them. I remembered. In the hip pocket of the blood-stained trousers I'd given the floor lady to launder I must have left the roubles I'd cashed yesterday at the Rossiya – one hundred ten-rouble notes – and here they were back from the wash. I took the money with many apologies whilst the girls backed out still twittering with distress. As Kirill and I papered the floor with the notes, hoping to dry them, I noticed that his tone of voice, in telling me that one of those girls would take eight months of work to put together a thousand roubles, hadn't any note of political rhetoric in it, or any of Isaac's sense of grievance; it was neutral; he commented on a fact of Russian life, and dabbed away at the money with his handkerchief. In this way he was a comfortable companion for a European in Russia.

He said that he would come with me to the Pushkin Museum, and promised a side door entrance if the front hall proved overcrowded. On our way downstairs I asked where we could buy sticking-plaster, for the cut on my hand was leaking blood under the scrap of plaster stuck on it by the medical team last night. "We cannot buy it except here," he said, directing me towards the hard currency shop off the foyer and adding, cheerfully enough, "Here am I, a Russian in Russia's capital with Russian money in my pocket, but only you, a foreigner with your foreign money, can buy some sticking-plaster. Come!"

Even I could not buy a roll of plaster, only negotiate for a further scrap to cover the wound, and pay absurdly in dollars. Then we set out walking together.

Kirill was decidedly not a victim. How different from walking through these same streets beside Isaac yesterday! He was not a victim of Russia – I doubt if any social system could have victimised him for long – instead, he was a survivor. He got out of no one's way on the Moscow sidewalk: with perfect good humour he walked straight ahead. He talked of the chambermaids' wages – the attack on me – the sticking-plaster shortage – the crowd at the Pushkin – as drawbacks to life in Russia to be offset not by radical means, not by social or political revolution, but by protecting oneself with privileges. Go in the side door. He hadn't the injured pride in how Russia might appear to a foreigner which Lena's patriotism afflicted her with. Pragmatic self-interest had set him free from many of the sufferings of more sensitive people and, as we walked through the streets together – his voice ringing with confidence, his hair curling on to his shoulders – I experienced the relief of lower standards. Within limits which were perfectly obvious from the outset you could count on him to help.

A side door into the Pushkin wasn't needed, for the place was pleasantly airy and uncrowded, and I was left to myself by Kirill, who evidently felt no schoolmasterish urge to set me on the correct line. I was glad to go downstairs amongst the calm ideas of antiquity reposing in their cases. Many I recognised. It was not an adventure, it was a rest: an hour or so out of Russia amongst my origins, at home. I know a bronze helm in an English library, Greek work of the fifth century before Christ from southern Italy, leaf-thin, which a sunshaft lights for a moment or two each bright day in December and

January, the low midwinter rays striking it through south-facing windows, and whenever I see the casque so lighted, its fragile green metal sun-warmed as though by a living head inside it, I seem to look, in the eye-holes' shadow, into the eyes of the sole begetter of European civilisation. All is immanent there in the darkness of that headpiece already. Nothing that follows – no sculptures or ivories or books or pictures in that English library – contradicts the promise of that helm glinting in the wintry sun. So in the Pushkin, from the stern grave principles and faces of the Greeks, through the humanism of the early Italians to Poussin and Claude and later ages, it was a walk among the images and ideas which already line the corridors of the European mind. Here are ideas clothed in paint which European books clothe in words. See the face of a worldly cleric caught in the background of a Sittow of the procession to Calvary: it might have served Millais for a portrait of Archdeacon Grantley. I looked into a grand dim painting of Rembrandt's, into the faces of its subjects glowing with possibilities in the chiaroscuro, and seemed to recognise the characters out of a novel of Flaubert's. It is all of a piece, and all descended from the Greek progenitor.

Russia is outside this line of descent. The characters in Russian novels, even in the works of the Europeanised aristocracy, Tolstoy or Turgenieff, only resemble Europeans outwardly, Tartars crushed into European clothes. The characters depicted in Gorki, or Gogol, or Dostoievsky – even in Aksakoff – will not be found in European paintings. They are grotesquely fascinating to a European, their motivation and behaviour and whole cast of mind only comprehensible if their Asiatic roots – their Tartar ancestry – is taken account of. The attitude of Tolstoy (born 1828) towards his serfs as a young man had more in it of the behaviour of a baron of the middle ages towards his villeins than that of a contemporary European landlord towards his tenants, and his novels should be come at through Russian history, and read within a Russian chronology. Says de Lagny of these nobles of the mid-nineteenth century, they were "still the Tartars of Tamburlane, whitewashed over with a coating of civilisation, which is rubbed off

45

every moment".* In an excellent book of Russian sketches, put together from the experiences of an Englishman long resident in the country, an encounter is described between a Russian "baron" cudgelling the peasants out of the road of his travelling carriage, and the English narrator, of whom this brute enquires, "What do you think of that, eh?" "My countrymen [replies the Englishman] would box you to a jelly, or give you over to a JP." "Ha! I'd soon buy up a JP!" "Your whole estate, sir [is the European's response in this clash of eras] would not buy an English magistrate."

Kirill and I were finishing our lunch at the National – a leisurely and talkative meal which I enjoyed – when word was brought that someone was waiting for me below. I went downstairs.

It was Isaac. He groaned aloud when he saw the scars on my face and head, with the pain both of sympathy and shame. I introduced him to Kirill, who had followed me downstairs from the dining room; it was plain at once that they were chalk and cheese, the corrupt air of the National, which Kirill seemed to breathe with delight, so offensive to Isaac that he insisted on waiting for me outside the hotel in the street. Whilst I went upstairs to my room Kirill ambled off into the crowd, a carton of Marlboro under his arm, having promised that the Tashkent office of VAAP would be told to expect me next day.

Evidently prepared to be kept waiting a long time, Isaac had settled himself with his tote bag into a niche between some stone pillars by the hotel door when I came down. With the underdog's low expectations went the ability to curl up in a corner. Aware that we were following a general plan laid down

---

* English versions of a text, like illustrations, can sometimes convey a false picture of the original by over-translation: by translating not words only, but a whole concept – of, say, "a peasant family" – into its English equivalent. Thus we have "the village policeman and tipsy farm workers" given as equivalents (by the translator of a story of Tolstoy's) for the *stanvarog* police agent and drunken serfs of the original, and, in the illustrations to my edition of de Lagny, Russian peasant women are given the rosebud mouth and dancing shoes of a Victorian miss from Barsetshire.

46

by Lena, but not aware of its details, I set out with him for the metro.

Travelling by bus or metro in a strange city is always more interesting than travelling by taxi because it offers the visitor just what is hardest to come by, a glimpse of what it would be like to go to work in the crowds. Share the rush hour with a nation, and you have shared an experience central to their lives. In a Russian crowd, too, with its variety of races and mixtures of blood within the Soviet Union, you have the advantage that there are really no obvious "foreigners"; you may look like a Finn or a Chinaman, and yet be a good Russian, so that no one is stared at for an outsider in the Moscow underground: even my scarred face didn't attract from fellow straphangers the curious attention which isolates the stranger. I suppose it is the hint of spy in the traveller's blood which is gratified by the deception of anonymity, of passing for a native. A New York cop who saw me standing by a parked taxi once so delighted me by yelling out, "Move your cab, fella" that I made the mistake of smiling at him . . . Isaac though, I must say, did his best to draw attention to me as a man from Mars. Afraid I'd tumble over every time the train braked, he kept reaching out his hand to hold me upright, as if I knew as little about keeping my feet in the subway as I'd known about Russian painting in the Tretyakoff. Thus literally in Isaac's hands I travelled, until he led me off the shining train at a remote station.

On the platform waited Lena, her two large shopping bags adding to the impression which her maternal figure gave, that of universal provider, Russian mother. The three of us took another train onward. Our destination and plan was now made clear in Lena's faultless English as we sped towards Moscow's outer suburbs.

After a long ride we surfaced into wan sunlight. Amongst tower-blocks over the streets there came into view painted turrets and domes against the sky, and the crenellated wall of a monastery rose ahead of us, which we entered under the gatehouse with the crowd.

As one of a Russian crowd you have a palpable sense of

47

being looked after: a sense, partly reassuring and partly irksome, that your welfare is the concern of authority. Added to this was Lena and Isaac's solicitude. I was very aware of it, after my morning in Kirill's company: nanny, in however benevolent a mood, is still a relation of Big Brother's. Kirill had been kind, of course, but he had been detached; amused but hardly concerned by the scrape I had got into. With him I was not aware of myself as a liability. He had let me go round the Pushkin on my own. His detachment allowed me a reciprocal freedom towards himself, which I had liked; and I rather hoped the dragoman waiting for me in Tashkent would take an unstifling and carefree view of his duties. For one thing, a half-mocking attitude towards misfortune helps its victim recover his balance, and Kirill's attitude towards last night's attack on me had helped put it in the background.

Lena's sympathy wouldn't allow this. We walked into the monastery garden, a small continental park in appearance, gravel walks and box hedges, pistachio and lemon façades of barracks and dormitories glinting through thin trees, the bulbous-domed churches rising in the midst of all. On a bench Lena put down her bags and, fishing out packages and flasks, unfolded her plan. She was too kind hearted not to worry about me. As well as their own flat, where they lived with their small daughter, she and Isaac seemed to possess another flat, into which she had arranged for me to move. Of course another night at the National was out of the question. From her bag came napkins, cups, a knife; I was established under her wing on the bench with my picnic, a delicious salami sandwich wrapped in foil, a cup of tea; all I might have wished for if I'd wished myself out of Russia altogether and home to Dorset in time for a good tea. Her arrangements for my move had all been made: I had only to pack my bags at the hotel. And at the weekend, if I decided – as she advised me – when I decided not to go to Central Asia, she and Isaac would take me with them to their family dacha, a walk through the woods from Abramtsevo (the country house associated with Aksakoff which she knew I wanted to see). A secure future alternative to my own plans stretched ahead. Like Isaac's steadying hand in the metro, she proposed holding me upright in face of Russian life. I temporised. Wolfing their provisions, I tried to show my gratitude whilst tiptoeing surreptitiously backwards before hoofing it for Central Asia.

Picnic ended, we toured church and museum, and considered the many gravestones raised to "noblemen" which stand rather disconsolately beside paths overhung by the Russian lilac whose blanched pallor, like the pallor of grass when the snow melts off it, seems to typify the grudging Moscow spring. This little space of park round the monastic buildings was full of a crowd gravely stepping along, faces blinking in the sunlight and ashen as the lilac, hats and coats over arms, cautiously welcoming the end of winter. As at the Tretyakoff, Isaac's guardianship took an educational form. He was informative about everything. My back began to hurt. From my morning in the Pushkin – from the metro ride – from this snail-slow walk about the monastery grounds – it was soon hurting in the way which makes standing an ordeal and listening a pretence.

We found a seat outdoors when the tour was over. "Well, have you decided what you will do?" asked Lena.

Sitting stiffly on account of the pain I tried to express my gratitude and tried to unhook, gently, the leading-strings they offered. Without making light of their fears, or of their kindness, I made it clear that I'd never thought of giving up Central Asia, or the National Hotel, on account of a fight. For I hadn't lost the fight. And a single unsuccessful attack on you doesn't make you into a member of a persecuted race, or fill your imagination with all the fears of the Jew in Russia. An example of the state of mind natural and inevitable to a Jew in Russia came up as we talked. They thanked me for having refused the offer Lena had made that morning to come and interpret for me with the police enquiries. "You see," she said, "the police might think we had heard you say you had money in your pocket, then they would believe we had winked to the mafiosi at the hotel door and so . . ." Such is the guilt and fear put into a nation's mind by its police system. Police of the level of demons (says the author of *The Russians at Home*) degrade citizens to the level of beasts.

I don't know whether or not Lena understood my reasons for not changing my plans. It is always the case with someone who speaks English perfectly, that you attribute to them a fuller grasp of English attitudes and ideas than they necessarily possess. Lena showed that she accepted my decision, anyway, by opening her bags again and drawing out the presents she had brought for my family, evidence of her kindness, evidence too (I thought) that she had come prepared for me not to go home with them that night, or she wouldn't have brought with her the things she now put into my hands, the painted wooden spoon, the mamoushka doll for one of my children, whose presence very close to my heart is easily discovered by any mother I talk to.

In the enclave of monastic buildings within the perimeter of walls was one "working church" to which the crowds flocked up a wide flight of wooden stairs. Brought by faith or curiosity we congregated towards the mutter of singing and the source of light. In a long vaulted nave glittering with lamps and candles, the air they breathed loaded with incense and plain-chant, was a restlessly moving crowd of fifty or so. On stage, cynosure of lights and eyes, "popes" as black as crows sang their parts. Railed into a sanctuary glistened the bright faces of a girls' choir uplifted in singing. Pyramids of votive candles twinkled and smoked round the walls, attended by active old women whom I noticed extinguishing with finger and thumb many tapers not a quarter consumed.* Not, for once, the usual public face of Soviet womanhood which mans guichets all over Russia, these old creatures resembled the widows and spinsters to be found busying themselves in the church's penumbra in all Christian lands, and their sisterhood made up

---

* Lord Mayo, in Russia in 1845, noticed that the priests "justly argu-ing that one or two candles are sufficient for the few wants of his or her holiness, put away the remainder of the votive tapers, and they are pres-ently worked up into fresh candles, to suit the pious needs of the next comer".

perhaps a quarter of the numbers of the crowd. The rest were both young and old, couples strolling about or coming and going from the stairs, their activity giving a sense of agitation to the place. It was an audience rather than a congregation, a performance more than a service. There was a decided want of the piety and humility of a place of prayer, I thought. But then I was surprised, standing in the crowd, to receive a scolding from an old dame for whispering to Lena, and I noticed that despite the impiety, to me, of the strolling insouciant play-goers, no one except myself was talking. I shut up. Isaac had left us, and Lena was looking out for his return. Soon he appeared, and put into my hands a present. It was a little gilt and green crucifix he had bought, in thanksgiving for my preservation, from the shop in the church's antechamber. His worn tired face was full of kindness as he gave it to me. We could not speak: I could have found no words anyway: Lena smiled. The choir's voices, the candles, the dim and smoky air thrilling with the curious restless religiosity of the Russian crowd – all this entered my heart with their gift, as it lay in my hand and grew warm.

V

The three of us took another metro and emerged after a longish ride in further regions of high-rise and flyovers and urban waste spaces with here and there a pool of stagnant water reflecting the declining sun. Whilst Isaac took a different route towards the concert hall which was our destination, Lena and I crossed these wastes through which other groups, and single figures, were converging like ourselves over a desert of cement towards the distant oasis of a park. The rich light of the setting sun – the mild air and blue sky – the tranquil emptiness of the scene, if not its beauty, made me enjoy the walk.

The converging figures formed a crowd at the park's entrance, and the shared eagerness of the crowd put a spring in everyone's step as we headed for the humped roofs of our venue, a vast spread of a building amongst the tulips of its garden. Not built as a concert hall – it is a covered athletics stadium – the place had been chosen for its capacity because here, tonight, Luciano Pavarotti was to sing in a concert for the relief of the Armenian earthquake's victims.

Since we were early Lena and I queued for the buffet. You begin to think that for Russians standing in line becomes, like smoking, in the end a habit for passing the time. Our wait produced a beaker each of Fanta for ourselves and a slab of orange fish stretched on bread for a sister of Lena's whom she expected to be late and hungry. The cost of these things was a reasonable thirty kopecks; but pinned to the wall behind the bar were two or three plastic bags printed with one word, Camel, and priced at five roubles. "It is crazy," Lena agreed, "crazy price. But one year ago there were no plastic bags in Russia at any price." Even today there are no Camels.

The vast hall, its tiered seats mounting to the roof on three sides of a cleared central floor, was filling up under the lights as we entered, an auditorium larger than any I was ever in which resounded with the hubbub of thousands upon thousands of eager people finding their places. Remotely, at the end of the empty oblong of floor, rose a stage set with its grand piano and its expectant music stands. The crowd was of Russian vastness, ten or twelve thousand I was told; whether the seats were expensive or hard to come by I don't know, for Lena had said "We have a spare ticket", a conventional untruth which I judged it better to accept without fuss. The stadium lights in the roof dimmed and went out, leaving the stage an island of brilliance. Silence quietened excitement. A storm of cheering and the clatter of handclaps greeted Pavarotti's entrance, his figure made tiny by distance, a shock of light on his shirtfront and the white handkerchief drifting from his hands. At the heart of the applause his voice began to sing, stilled the cheers, rose through the darkness, filled the air.

How he enjoyed himself! The swagger, the flinging about of arms, the floating tail coat and broad white expanse of his chest – it was wonderful theatre. He threw back his black-bearded head and sang, till the rich voice had freighted every atom of air in that space with music as a sunbeam steeps dust-motes in light.

I go to few concerts. But powerful music, live music, discovers an annexe to my everyday self which seems only to come into existence under stress of such attack. Perhaps it is a soul, this annexe. Painting doesn't break down its door. Poetry doesn't. Painting and poetry, objets d'art too, affect me indeed, but affect parts of myself which I know to exist in common life: heart, mind, feeling, touch, memory. I am moved by these arts in the conventional way. But music is different. Only in a concert hall am I aware of a daemonic force. Is it because I know so little about music, and don't play an instrument? My response to paintings and poems and objets d'art is perhaps too complex – too neutered by the brain – to leave room for the soul's function. That peculiar appendix isn't needed where the digestive juices of knowledge are waiting to dissolve whatever the connoisseur nibbles. And music is something else. *La musique souvent me prend comme une mer. . .* Baudelaire knew the distinction I feel between *volupté* and *connaissance*, between the frenzy of the maenad and the connoisseurship of the museum curator. *Je sens vibrer en moi toutes les passions d'un vaisseau qui souffre.* Baudelaire expresses the hammering of music on the door to the soul.

Of course it doesn't last at such a pitch for the whole concert. Rapture is exhausting. The interval came, and with it a returning interest in finding myself here, next to Lena but amongst (she said) Isaac's family, whom I would now meet. But those in our row filed out without once looking at me – not an easy feat as they stumbled over my legs – and left us alone. Was it because they hadn't been introduced? – why did Lena not introduce me to them? I was mystified. However, Lena's sister, the hungry one in search of her fish sandwich, soon came over to us from another part of the hall (where Isaac must have been sitting amongst Lena's family) and talked to me through Lena for a few minutes, an eager, warm-hearted woman of the same comfortable build as her sister, who was very anxious to urge on me the rashness of going to Central Asia whilst Tadzhiks and Uzbegs fought each other over their borders. Residents imploring the traveller to venture no further are a regular feature of the early chapters of travel books, so I had been expecting this, and set it aside. The reason that the traveller records such warnings, I believe, is that he hears them all very clearly. Whether or not he attends to them, he takes them in. Lena's warnings, and her sister's, made me wonder what I would find in Central Asia once I got there.

When the concert resumed (between Pavarotti's appearances other singers and instrumentalists performed) I wondered at the kindness and protectiveness of these people. I hadn't in the least earned it. In fact it depended, I felt sure, on a moral approval of myself which was misplaced. It was assumed, because of the source which had given Lena my name, that I was on the side of the angels. This was risky. What if I offended them with an opinion or an action which they found reprehensible? Perhaps I had already without knowing it offended Isaac's family, that they had trooped both ways over my feet without a glance or a smile. Accepting kindness, you accept the donor's standards with the gift, and so you can find yourself standing on false ground. Ah, what kind of friend is more comfortable, Isaac or Kirill Ukraintsev?

The concert audience was composed, so far as I could make out, of people of similar stamp to Isaac's and Lena's families. It was a restrained and orderly crowd, decently dressed, which had listened raptly to the music. But they were people of a settled social position and educated appearance which is not found amongst the crowd in a Russian street. Suits, spectacles, keen clever faces, a sense of earnest spirits pressing towards the fount of music to refresh themselves; looking round me I felt what I never felt in Russia before, or indeed anywhere in Eastern Europe, that I was in a crowd of the middle-class intelligentsia. No set of people has been so persecuted, but here they were, if I wasn't mistaken, all round me in the darkness in their thousands. It was a heartening realisation.

Excitement meanwhile was stirring. Slowly the crowd's reserve broke down. There had been early, sharp, bitten-off shouts of "Bravo!" out of the dark: now the single shouts multiplied, and mingled with cheers, until the applause was a storm which rolled about in the spaces of the roof and burst and broke over the bright stage and the star's brilliant figure, almost extinguishing his voice, drenching him in multitudinous cheering. Near to us parties that had been sedate climbed up on benches to cling to each other and shout out their "Bravos!" with passionate gusto. Fragments of the crowd below began to break loose, to lose restraint, to cheer even in the arias, surge towards the stage, flock this way and that in the space of open floor. It was a glimpse into the emotions of the race. This gathering, of what is left of a decimated class, was surging towards the source from which Pavarotti poured out his song, people who had forgotten themselves were running towards it, their rushing ardent enthusiasm thirsty for music, throwing flowers in coloured heaps at the stage, pressing mouths to the fountain – talk of the frenzy induced by music – talk of the maenads – all restraint was gone from these people, and all the rapture and emotion of Russian delight swirled about the singer on his lighted stage as he sang encore after encore amongst the heaped flowers with the same magnificent fullness of voice with which he had sung the first note of the recital. Even to the end, when the music was hard to hear in the storm of cheers – still the genial broad figure stood with the crowd clustering in its swarm at his feet, and from the brimming tub within himself he ladled out honey to the famished bees. Exhaustion – the crowd's exhausted withdrawal as much as the singer's retreat – at last ended the performance.

In the park road outside afterwards the sense of having experienced together a significant hour linked the crowd together in spirit as a congregation leaving its church is linked. In their thousands tired happy people walked under the streetlamps and the warm stars, the sound of their feet loud because there were no cars, towards the nearest metro half a mile away. Now you could see that most were sober-minded folk who fill concert-halls the world over; after showing the frenzy of their feelings, thoroughly Slav, they had resumed again the tidy habits of the bourgeoisie. Shaky as is the history of this class in Russia – with almost no power under the tsars they had suffered near extinction under Stalin – such people must be her best hope of recovery and stability in the present crisis. I was glad to have shared such an evening with them.

And it was a pleasure to be part of this crowd walking quietly and companionably through the moonlit avenues of suburban Moscow. Evidently the concert-goers were not owners of cars – perhaps an example of their clean hands and clear consciences – for a knot of limousines with diplomatic plates parked waiting for the *pezzi grossi* were the only vehicles near the stadium. I gauged my feelings as we walked past the shining vehicles and their chauffeurs. Though once my own idea of the stylish life, to be thus cordoned off with the Corps Diplomatique, I found that I was glad to be with Isaac and Lena amongst the walking crowd. There was trust and fellow-feeling. Happy, seeing the large mellow moon as calm as a lamp in a window lighting the road we walked down towards the metro, I remembered that I had seen that moon's first quarter gleaming through the branches of garden trees at home, and that I had wondered then if this at last would be the moon to put right a hopeful young poet's untruth. For, long ago, a teenager steeped in Ernest Dowson, I wrote these lines:

> From the perfum'd wreath of Pleasure
> I have pluck'd the palest flowers;
> In the flame-lick'd caves of Suffering
> I have linger'd fevered hours:
> Through the reveries of Poets
> I have glimps'd th'enchaunted Land,
> And seen the Moon's pale fingers
> On the towers of Samarcand.

This present Russian moon above the Moscow street, of the good many hundreds that had unavailingly waxed and waned in the interval, stood the best chance of rectifying the license of the final couplet by lighting my path to Samarcand at last.

CHAPTER III

Tashkent

I

ONE OF THE MOST unwelcome surprises of my trip to the Caucasus had been to find intensely heavy traffic on ill-made roads in a country where I had expected few private cars; and it is unexpected, too, that every airport and railway station is swamped by such very large crowds in a country where so many restrictions limit the freedom to travel. Coming back from Tbilisi I had strayed out of Intourist's cordon sanitaire and paid the penalty: entering the Moscow airport by a wrong door I had been immersed immediately in a limbo of peasants crouched amongst sacks and bundles in a half-lit hall under the jangling commands of the tannoy. It is the migrant horde which moves slowly and patiently about Russia and Eastern Europe with its awkwardly shaped possessions and sleeping babies. I remember the same sense of chaos amongst a desperately rushing crowd of Romanians swarming upon a slowly creeping shabby train at Cluj: a sense of losing my footing and being swept pell-mell out of my depth. All very well to walk away from a concert with an orderly Moscow crowd, and not to envy the chauffeur-driven cars, but travelling through Russia alone makes you cling to Intourist like a child to mother's hand. Segregation and privilege seem to be essential needs in Communist states as they are not in democracies. Brought by car the thirty or forty miles to an airport south of Moscow I was there put into the care of Intourist and shepherded to the Tashkent plane. We took off over the Russian forest.

In the packed plane I kept my window seat by repeating, with a granite smile, that I could not understand the meaning of the angry folk waving their tickets at me. I was disappointed to be in the air at all, instead of travelling overland from Moscow to Turkestan, and I was determined to see the country from the plane at least. I sat tight and smiled and hoped that the moist clouds of spring would disperse.

Kirill Ukraintsev had laughed when I had asked him to buy me a rail ticket and a berth on the train to Tashkent (Intourist had already refused the commission). "I get you a ticket, sure, but I think you won't like it," he said. I spoke a few stern words about sustaining a little discomfort for the sake of a rail journey which would unfold to me day by day the Russian landscape between Moscow and Central Asia. He shrugged. "It is possible to go, but how long it will take I cannot tell you. Five days, a week? Your train must wait for all freight trains to pass. No food I think maybe. I buy you the ticket, but someone take your berth even so. Also the track is bad, it rocks so people are sick. But if you want it is possible to try." Direct opposition from Isaac or Lena might not have stopped me. Kirill's sardonic indifference did. I bought an air ticket.

But I couldn't help rather regretting that I wasn't winding across Russia in a train when I looked down on patches of forest or plain seen through drifting holes in the vaporous cloud. The regret you feel at having dodged an ordeal, if you suspect in your heart that it would have been worthwhile, long outlasts the sufferings of the ordeal; and in the landscape of retrospect it is the ordeals which are the conquered peaks. Besides this, the railroads laid into Central Asia in the second half of the nineteenth century had been a major factor in binding new acquisitions into the tsar's empire.* Charles Marvin, a Russian-educated English journalist ever anxious to alarm British opinion with Russian threats towards India, spoke of the line from the Caspian to Kyzil Arvat as having "abolished Central Asia", so easy did a railway make it for Russia to supply a military expedition against India. And Marvin did

---

* "In those days [wrote Count Pahlen of the year 1908] it was possible to travel to Central Asia in the ease and comfort of a first-class carriage in an express train straight from St Petersburg for a ridiculously small sum, the journey . . . taking six and a half days."

prod British strategists awake, with the realisation that a part of
the globe which was now connected to the European railway
system – cities you could buy a ticket to from Charing Cross –
could hardly be the unnavigable wilderness of steppe affording
its eternal protection to British India's north-western
approaches. England – the "masterly inactivity" party at least –
was startled. It happened so rapidly. In 1887 an officer travelling
to India, Colonel le Mesurier, arrived by train at Merv and
booked into the Grand Hotel – at Merv, where the Irish journalist Edmund O'Donovan had been held captive in the kibitkas of
its savage Tekke chieftains five or six years before. At Stavropol
on his way back from rough work on the Persian border Valentine Baker was able to abandon Russian winter sledging when
"a wild thrill of delight passed through us" at the sight of a train
which would carry him on uninterrupted rails to Calais.

That "wild thrill of delight" is a pleasingly unaffected
response to the spread of progress. Hard for the Western visitor
to feel it now at the spread of his own concrete and glass urbanis-
ation into remote lands; though if ever I feel inclined to sniff at
Hilton-oriented travel I remember my own feelings, a "wild
thrill of delight" indeed, at the sight of the concrete and glass
tower of Poona's Blue Diamond Hotel glittering above the
dusty palms of the road from the railway station. If it was "spoil-
ing the view" I didn't take offence. I urged my rickshaw driver
to pedal faster. I dreaded finding it full, my heart was in my
mouth as the desk clerk's languid finger ran down the register.
The chill of air conditioning caressed me, marble gleamed,
through a courtyard entrance the swimming pool winked.
Thank heavens they had a room! Outside the temperature was
above 100°, and I had been travelling three days by train from
Mysore, with one of the nights passed on the waiting-room table
of a junction in the jungle, its platform lined with sleeping lepers
. . . but all this was behind me as I mounted to my room in the
Blue Diamond's lift amongst obsequious bearers. Once alone I
rang room service, ordered an omelette and Coca Cola, and took
a shower. Arrival in the modern world was exquisite: so delectable
an experience that I repeated it – another shower, another omelette,
more Coke – before falling into a delicious sleep.

But, in a small way, I had earned myself the Blue Diamond, as Valentine Baker had earned himself the "rails to Calais" from Stavropol in winter. The plane droning south-east over Russia was unearned, and dull. Poor modern slaves and simpletons (I thought), who let themselves be dragged like felled timber over the countries they imagine themselves visiting. The taunt has always suited best the latest invention; and was no doubt thought a keen thrust against any who first made use of the wheel. I read my Ruskin, and duelled with my elbows against the elbows of the large Russian next to me. Water was served to us in ceramic bowls. I had thought at the airport that I'd buy something to eat, but whilst I was queuing at the glass counter, and selecting which of the dryish-looking buns I would choose when my turn came, a mouse poked up its head amongst the pastries and set about washing its whiskers. Ahead of me there was an outcry: a woman who had been chatting in Russian with friends gasped out when she saw the mouse, "Aw Gahd! Will you look at that?" in deepest Brooklyn. All of them switched into American to complain about the mouse. With dual nationality you can dissociate yourself from whichever ancestry you want to scold; but they kept enough of the Slav about them to know there was no use complaining in Russian to the formidable woman dealing out the pastries. Like me, they left the queue to those who had not spotted the mouse.

After an hour or two the clouds below began to dissolve. Between drifts of mist appeared the dark shadow of Russia; then there gleamed out patches of sunlight colouring the varying greens of forest or grass or grain. Soon a clearing desert sky opened a vast extent of landscape below, only a few white clouds and their shadows floating above the sepia-coloured steppe. By good luck we flew along the northern coast of the Aral Sea. Its long white shoreline, more than a mile wide, glittered with salt where the waters had withdrawn, and sandbanks heaved up their shapes in the pale blue-green of its shallows. Though trumpeted nowadays as an "eco disaster" to be blamed on Russian policy, the drying-up of the Aral has in fact puzzled observers for two centuries. An exact, and almost painfully detailed commentator, Eugene Schuyler, who was attached to the American embassy at Moscow in the 1870s and made a thorough journey through the region, says of the Aral, "If we may judge from tradition, and the reports of previous travellers, it seems to be gradually drying up . . . a large inlet at its southern end has recently become a dry bed." This shallow sea, in few places more than one hundred feet deep, has always been mysterious. How can the level of a lake without an outlet fall, which receives the waters of two of Asia's mighty rivers, the Oxus and the Jaxartes? Schuyler noted that the Aral's surface was about 250 feet higher than that of the Caspian, making possible the notion of an underground river draining the first into the second – an idea recorded by Alexander Burnes, too, when he had stood about forty years previous to Schuyler's travels on a spot between the two seas at which his servants heard, or said they heard, water rushing under the sands. (With the lively turn of phrase which explains why his book, *Travels into Bokhara*, made him fêted and famous, Burnes characterises his followers' over-keen hearing as an example of "the clock strikes what the fool thinks".) As we flew on I saw below me the mouth of the Jaxartes (the Syr Darya) opening its enormous brown breadth of water into the sandy wastes of dune.* I put down my book to look out in earnest, for now all the ground below, steppe as it chiefly is, interested me very much.

From the erection of Fort Mangyschlack, founded on the north-east shore of the Caspian in 1833 to protect the Emba fishermen from attack by Turkoman pirates, Russia's conquest of Central Asia – a military advance only halted in Afghanistan in 1989 – may be dated. By 1847 another fort, Aralsk, seemed to be needed to "protect" tribesmen who had suddenly become "our Kirghiz subjects", their safety (from other tribesmen) now said by the Russians to depend upon Russia fortifying a

---

* The cause of the notable muddiness of the great rivers of Turkestan is (according to Count Pahlen) that their waters are a suspension of "the yellowish-grey marl, or loess, formed by the disintegration of porphyry rock; carried by the wind off the surrounding mountains in the form of very fine dust, it gradually settled and built up the Central Asian plateau".

secure frontier along the Jaxartes. It was an enviable region: the valley of the Jaxartes was reputed to be so thickly populated that "a nightingale could fly from tree to tree from Kashgar to the Aral shore, and a cat walk from garden wall to garden wall". The Russians were drawn on, enticed by their search for "a secure frontier", that will-o'-the-wisp which is allowed to dominate policy in which the military have too strong a voice. Under the usual colonialist cover – to perform, that is, his "most sacred duty of preserving the tranquillity and security of our subjects" – General Peroffski laid siege in 1853 to the Jaxartes fort of Ak Mechet, accusing its Kokandese defenders of "oppressing our Kirghiz subjects" and announcing with much circumlocutionary bombast that Russia had come "to stay for ever". He allowed the Kokandese fifteen days to remove themselves; but stormed the fort next day anyway, and renamed it Fort Peroffski. Already the military were out of control. Already these fire-eating Russian local commanders were taking St Petersburg policy into their own hands to advance their own military careers by easy victories.*

If this expansion of Russia into Central Asia ever had a First Cause, it might be found in Peter the Great's spurious Will, which exhorted Russia's rulers ever to keep before them two objectives, the conquest of Constantinople and the conquest of India. "Though the Kirghiz horde† is a wild and giddy people [he wrote], this horde alone is the key and gate to all Asiatic countries." Hence (said British alarmists of the "forward policy" school) Russia's sinister befriending of the Khirgiz along the Jaxartes.

* It was M. A. Terentieff, that venomously anglophobic historian, who identified in 1876 (in his book *Russia and England in the Struggle for Markets in Central Asia*) the fatal *ignis fatuus* which directed Russian policy in Turkestan and would eventually entice the Soviet Empire to self-destruction in Afghanistan a century later: "the hopeless search after a secure frontier; and such a position she will never find until her territories are coterminous with those of a nation which respects treaties".

† "During the tsarist regime the word Kirgiz, or sometimes Kaisak-Kirgiz, was habitually used to refer to the Kazaks, the real Kirgiz being called Kara-Kirgiz." Editor's note to *Mission to Turkestan* by Count Pahlen.

"The key to all Asiatic countries"! – it was this other habit of the military mind, the habit of designating every tribe or stronghold as "the key and gate" to somewhere else, which was to confuse the map of Central Asia until hardly a village would be left out of these strategical cat's cradles. Herat, it was widely said, was the "key to India" – hence British alarm over Persia's Russian-backed siege of Herat in 1838, which one stray English officer in his twenties, Eldred Pottinger, was supposed to have frustrated – but then Merv, an oasis in the Kara Kum desert, was the key to Herat; and Merv had two keys, Khiva and Kyzil Arvat. So it was that a mere two hundred miles of railway from the Caspian to Kyzil Arvat, itself hardly notice-able in the vastness of the region, could be said by Charles Marvin to have "abolished Central Asia". Any movement at all by the Russians east of the Caspian could be construed by some military expert or another, in London if not in Calcutta, as an attempt to pocket one of these keys to India. Very early on in the pamphlet campaign, in 1828, it seemed to Colonel de Lacy Evans perfectly obvious that Tsar Nicholas I was executing Peter the Great's Will, and that a route by way of the Aral and "the Tartarian frontier" was "the best and only convenient line to assail India". The new-built forts of Aralsk and Petroffski were to bear out his warning, and give weight to his further prediction, a highly alarmist projection of the probable outcome of war between Russia and England, a scen-ario in which Russia occupies Spain as well as Turkey, and America occupies Ireland, until between the Bear and the Eagle the Lion goes all to smash. This turmoil would begin with a Russian attack via Turkestan on India. The trouble was, the colonel admitted, Central Asia was "a region of the world which we have left most unexplored, and with which we have the least communication". He was ready to believe in the nightingales, and the cats on the garden walls, making of Tur-kestan a larger Hampstead; he was ready to believe, with Sir William Ouseley (who hadn't been there either), that "there is not a more flourishing or delightful country than this, especi-ally the district of Bokhara, etc.": others, anxious to be com-forted by Lord William Bentinck's "masterly inactivity" in the matter, dismissed the whole region as a howling wilderness which would swallow up every Russian army that tried to enter it, just as the steppes to east or west of Khiva had destroyed Peroffski's expedition of 1839 and Peter the Great's own expedition against that city in 1717.* Nobody knew what "Tartary" was like. The truth was, very few Englishmen had ever been to look.

Of those who had crossed Turkestan's borders, James Baillie Fraser had been captured and all but murdered by the Turcomans in 1822,† and William Moorcroft, after travelling as far

---

* It was Lord Palmerston's opinion (in 1860) that "many generations must yet come and go ere Russia succeed in demolishing the Tartar barrier or approaching the country between Bokhara and India". Palmerston, like the Russian foreign minister Nesselrode – a German by birth and education who controlled Russian foreign policy from 1816 to 1856 – was a European-minded politician to whom Central Asia was at a very great distance from the centre of things.

† Possibly because he wrote a number of melodramatic novels of Eastern life, Fraser's description of his capture is stirring stuff: "I knew but too well the character of these Talish highlanders who live by blood and plunder, and had often heard Mohammed Khan, into whose hands I had unhappily fallen, spoken of as the most cruel and treacherous of all their chiefs. I knew that by all calculations my life was not worth an hour's purchase in their hands . . . one of them, drawing his Gheelanee knife, exclaimed with an oath, that kill me he would . . . I fully expected death; my thoughts glanced rapidly homewards, and to all that I had left; and then with something of a shudder to the great change before me, and the awful presence I was about to enter; such, however, was the powerful excitement of my mind at the time, that the horror I felt was, in fact, much less than, in reflecting upon it since, I could have thought possible. A short prayer was on my lips . . ." Fraser's punctuation seems a system of tripwires to delay the narrative, and his "horror" is surely what would nowadays be called "fear", but the whole passage from which this is taken leaves the reader with a very real sense of darkness and terror in the cold mountains, and the imminence of death. One service my attacker in Moscow had done me was to let me see how it is to fight for your life – to face death by the knife as Fraser and many another traveller did – and I too had been rather reassured to find on reflection that fear – Fraser's "horror" – had been a negligible part of the experience. I could hope that the same had been true of those who had not avoided the thrust of their murderer's weapon.

as Bokhara in search of horses to improve the Indian army's bloodstock, had died (possibly of poison) together with his companions Trebeck and Guthrie on the borders of Afghanistan in 1825. And then, in 1830, "Bokhara" Burnes, with his rather odious ebullience and self-satisfaction, answered everyone's questions about Central Asia, and most other topics too, as the lion of a London season following upon his tremendous journey. "I have measured the mountains, examined the roads, sounded the rivers," he announced to the Shah of Persia at Teheran: and Central Asia allowed him another five years' play in what he called "the boldest game man ever dared" before a mob of Afghans tore him in pieces in the garden of his house in Kabul. Evidently Central Asia was both dangerous and mysterious; as the "key to India" its geography was significant, too, and a reputation could certainly be made by an adventurous journey through the region. Burnes called it "the boldest game" but Arthur Conolly, that good-natured Christian whose book, *A Journey to the North of India*, was eclipsed by the success of Burnes' *Travels into Bokhara*, called it by the name which came to be attached to the whole episode: "the Great Game".

These men, their motives and their characters, Russians as well as Englishmen, have intrigued me for a good many years, their personalities and the details of their journeys interesting me more than the politics of the "Great Game" – itself a bit of a damp squib, since no military confrontation between England and Russia ever came about – so that I looked down eagerly as the wrinkled sand ridges of the Kyzil Kum gave way to the green haze of cultivated land, and the plane dipped towards Tashkent, Russia's headquarters in Central Asia since it was stormed by General Cherniayeff in 1865.

Something optimistic in my nature makes me forget the lessons I have had about losing myself in Russian airports, and urges me to hurry into the first building by the nearest door. At Tashkent I did it again. Perhaps it is the disorientation of air travel. I need the orderly infrastructure of flying – the luggage carousels, funnelled exits, crowd management – which pushes the simplest passenger through the right slot; and I find, in Russia, the imbroglio of a port or a railway station, where it is a matter of *sauve qui peut*. It took an age of wandering to extricate myself. At last, free of the pandemonium of the main concourse, I walked towards an elegant ochre building in an older Russian colonial style, grown over with a vine, where I understood that a foreigner might find his luggage. Acacias lined the path, and it was marvellously warm; clearly the evening of a hot day. My spirits rose: summer was here, with its greeting of swifts diving with fairground screams through the rich blue air. At home in Dorset I had left the first swallows just arrived, but in Moscow I had seen neither swallow nor swift. Here was the promise of summer sweetening the air again.

Walking towards me under the acacias came two men. One was a burly open-faced Russian with a rather gone-to-seed athlete's figure expanding over the waistband of his grey trousers, his jacket over his arm: the other was a slight, dark, neat-stepping Asiatic encased in a suit and dark glasses. By their exasperated air, as of two golfers looking for a lost ball, I knew as soon as I saw them that they had come to the airport to meet me. I stopped.

The Russian stepped forward like one protecting a superior, shielding the Asiatic, and enquired if I was Mr Glazebrook. He was definitely a "minder"; I'd left the rôle of the companion I'd asked for vague in my head, whether "courier", "interpreter", "dragoman" or whatnot: and here he was in the flesh at last, a minder indeed, a large sportsman feeling the heat, dabbing perspiration from his forehead and his pale hair, introducing the impassive Uzbeg as Mr Eshtaev and himself as Alexander Issaev. We shook hands. Mr Eshtaev gestured with a stiff bow, his face expressionless, towards the ochre pavilion. Side by side we set out, exchanging greetings: Issaev meanwhile had managed to slip on his jacket so as to interpret our exchange with maximum formality.

We reached the courtyard of the little building, which crowned a rise with the elegance of a piece of stage scenery, perhaps a guard-post in an operetta set in provincial Russia,

and there under a heaven filled with the swifts' glorious aero-
batics we waited. I made clear my appreciation of the fact of
the president himself of Tashkent's VAAP meeting my plane,
for in my days at an embassy I had learned to judge our degree
of cordiality by the rank of the person despatched to meet
the visitor, and to accept the huffish frowns of the MP or
government official who found himself met only by myself
and a driver. Still we waited. No baggage appeared from
within the guard-post. Nothing happened. I spoke of the
mutual friend in London whose tireless telexing had produced
my invitation. They smiled. I congratulated them on the
weather. Again Mr Issaev interpreted, again Mr Eshtaev
bowed. Knowing that Tashkent was half-encircled by the Tien
Shan Mountains, of which I saw no sign though the air
appeared clear, I asked why this might be. They smiled a
collusive smile, evidently not yet ready to let me into disgraceful secrets. Curbing my tongue from further foolish remarks
to fill the silence, I recalled what I knew of Asiatic protocol –
that Mr Eshtaev wasn't obliged to talk to me simply because
he had troubled to come and meet my plane – and of Asiatic
custom, which does not view silence as the socially destructive
force so feared in Europe. I remembered being present at a
large birthday dinner in rather a grand setting in the Punjab
where the silence of every tongue (except my own) had surprised me until I had realised that the précédence of the place-
ment had been so delicately contrived that no one at the table
was upon a sufficiently equal footing with his neighbour to
start a conversation. Silence is a discipline to be learned by the
European in Asia, and I think Mr Issaev, the Russian, had
learned it, for he said little, without appearing awkward.

Alexander Issaev, a Ukrainian in fact, indeed showed himself
to be a good-humoured fellow in the way he was at ease in
these long minutes of waiting. He took off his jacket again and
slung it from his shoulder, comfortable in himself with the
confidence and directness of physical strength as he stood and
waited in the sinking golden light. I saw that I would like him,
which heartened me for the weeks ahead. A hint of mockery,
disillusion, seemed to be a welcome trait in his manner, for a

month or more in an earnest Slav's company is rather to be dreaded.

At last my two bags appeared and were carried out to me. They were slung into the back of a chauffeured car – my car, as it turned out, and my driver, provided by Intourist, though it was soon clear that Mr Eshtaev was used to taking command of any car he stepped into – and together we took the road towards the city's glittering white rampart of high-rise concrete.

Is there an approach now to any city on earth where expectations are not dashed by the drive from the airport? You know it can't be what you hope for – I knew that Tashkent had been virtually rebuilt since the 1966 earthquake – but still you faintly hope. Only the heavily planted green trees shading streets and squares, the welcome lustrous leaves of evergreens in a hot city, gave a pleasant atmosphere to the place. I knew from Caucasian towns what to expect of an Intourist hotel, so that the shimmer of glass rising to thirty storeys from its desolate plinth didn't surprise me. The tsars built military fortresses; modern imperialism builds these hotels for troops of businessmen and tourists armed with hard currency. My room, a cell high up in the honeycomb, was darkened by a concrete overhang and gave a view only of other concrete towers which pierced the canopy of leaves shading Tashkent's streets and older buildings from the light of the setting sun.

When I came downstairs I was shown directly into the dim extent of a dining hall close-packed with tables. The hotel's manager was with my two hosts, perched at their table rather than seated, his presence no doubt depositing his tribute at Mr Eshtaev's fastidious feet after a calculation of Mr Eshtaev's power. A Soviet hotel dining room is a plant for processing groups of tourists. In it the individual (as I'd discovered at the cost of near starvation in the Caucasus) is ignored and unfed. At least the presence of these three natives of Tashkent at my table meant that the table itself was well spread with an array of salads and raw vegetables amongst bowls of soup and curds and meaty stews, whilst poking up through the assortment of victuals were the colourless shoulders and tinfoil caps of three

vodka bottles. I had never seen so much good food on a Russian table, and my spirits rose. We plunged in. Issaev ripped
the cap from a vodka bottle with his thumb and splashed our
glasses full to the brim. Helping me to two or three large
tomatoes, which he said were the symbol of Uzbeg hospitality,
he made ready to translate into my ear the speech of welcome
which Mr Eshtaev now began to deliver. I watched him, his
eyes and impassive face giving away no more than the dark
glasses he had worn earlier. The speech, not a long one, culminated in a toast, all three of us tossing back our glasses and
setting them down empty together. Clearly my reply was
expected. I thought carefully. It is so easy in the first few hours
of a relationship of this kind to present a false sketch of oneself
to a kind host; for the rôle of agreeable guest is an irksome
one, soon cramping the hand that is obliged to hold such a
mask in place. I didn't want them thinking that I was a jolly,
likeable fellow, fond of vodka and overeating, who would
be the best of company on a tour of Turkestan. I intended
doing pretty well as I liked in Central Asia, certainly turning
over no new leaf as far as grumpiness was concerned. I stood
up, turning in my hand the glass which Issaev had already
refilled.

I was friendly, uttering ornate phrases in reply to Mr Eshtaev's welcome, adding that, whatever the Uzbeg custom, I
hoped that they would call me by my Christian name and
allow me to use theirs – here Mr Eshtaev touched his jacket
murmuring "Ulugbeg" whilst Issaev smote his chest and
grunted out "Alex" – and concluding this first of many
speeches by telling them that the tomato of hospitality which
I had eaten, though converting me instantly into a lover of
Uzbekistan, had not converted me into liking tomatoes, and,
be the consequences what they might, I intended leaving the
others on my plate. They would be appalled and disappointed,
I promised them, at how little I would eat and drink over the
next weeks. Then I dashed off my full glass "To Uzbekistan!"
and set it down empty with theirs again, even the chilly eyes
of Mr Eshtaev almost warming as he reached out his hand to
take mine, uttering my name – "Phleep, Phleep!" – with his

feline smile when the translation of my words had reached him.

So far I'd said not a word in explanation of the bloody welts and scars of my attacker's nails across my face. With a good deal of the meal gone, and the second bottle of vodka opened, I told Alex Issaev the tale of the Moscow attack. It is noticeable that a man of action, such as Alex Issaev appeared to be, will usually show amusement, even scorn, for the victim of some physical upset, so that I expected from him none of Isaac's groaning or Lena's concern. He chewed a match between nicotine-stained teeth and listened intently. Then he translated the story to Mr Eshtaev, whose hard dark eyes rested on mine as he also listened. They conferred together in Russian. Alex clapped me on the shoulder with the half-sympathetic, half-congratulatory gesture of a fighter's second urging his man back into the ring. "Be sure, it would not happen here," he said with warmth. I looked at Mr Eshtaev, and a hint of something like warmth passed again through his eyes too. I had the curious feeling that I had somehow shown solidarity with the Uzbeg cause by placing myself under a Muscovite knife. Approval, if that's what it was, took the form of a third toast, this time from Alex, in a glass of vodka tossed off to health and safety. When we finally left the table I was glad that I had only to travel by lift to reach my room.

Though Alex had been full of plans and bustle for the next day, I had told him that I would spend the morning looking about on my own. I wanted it clear with him from the start that I would do as I pleased. I would lunch alone, too, I said, and meet him at two o'clock to fall in with whatever he might arrange. It was true that I wanted time to stroll about on my own, for now that I was arrived in the place I needed leisure to think about my plans and intentions, and to consider, in situ at last and with the means at hand, how best to achieve my aim. Hitherto it hadn't been feasible to make any plan beyond the one of getting myself to Turkestan.

Cloud overcast next morning's sky. It had rained in the night enough to damp dust and darken pavements, and to bring to my ears on my balcony the rustle and drip of so much foliage as lay below my window. A rift in the misty cloud showed me, for a very few moments, a glimpse of the rock and snow of the Tien Shan in a curious fierce light, then cloud again dropped over the distant scene, and there was only the bluish haze hanging above Tashkent's dripping trees, and deeper mist beyond. It was warm.

From Scotland to the Himalayas I have learned not to expect mountains to appear to order. In the Caucasus I scarcely saw the snow summits of the range, though at moments a wall of ice, rock-fangs, one mighty peak, would shake its shoulders free of cloud and show itself for a few moments above the forested lower ranges. The existence of mountains rimming a landscape, said Edward Fitzgerald, "projects an image of futurity", and I'm aware of a sense of dispossession, of a short-ened prospect, when cloud blots them out . . . it had been the chinese-white line of its snow peaks as they appear remotely across the Black Sea from Trebizond which had made an abid-ing image drawing me to the Caucasus, so that to be for weeks in their shadow and see so little of their magnificence at close quarters was disappointing. But I had not come to Central Asia for the sake of its mountains: I turned my back on the clouded view and went down to a breakfast of cheese and curds and Russian tea.

It was India I found myself thinking about as I walked out into Tashkent's streets and squares. The sharp light and the trees, the heavy green foliage, and something half-finished and reach-me-down about pavements and shop fronts and raw con-crete – a sense of a grandiose superstructure resting on shabby underpinnings – reminded me of north Indian towns. I remembered how the jungle trees in that hot heavy light had seemed to be alive, I mean the very leaves alive, with the sharp metallic squawks of birds chattering within their crowns. Here it was the same, the trees cackling like tin-plate toys overhead. Instead of the brilliant long-tailed parakeets of India, out of Tashkent's trees fluttered magpies. Swifts and magpies: their presence here fixed the geography of Turkestan for me, an extension southward of the northern hemisphere, where

Amritsar or Umballa or Chandigarh are northward extensions of the torrid south. Between the two, as between England's Indian Empire and "the emperor of the North" advancing towards it in the Great Game, rises the geographical division of the Himalayas.

There was not the pervasive hot scent of India which charges every breath you take of its air. Streets and walks under the trees smelled freshly of rain. Strolling about, in a central square like a small park, as close-planted and shady as a wood, I came under the scrutiny of an angry, bushy-bearded bust of Karl Marx commanding an intersection of allées from a plinth engraved in four languages with his admonition to the world's workers. Curious how much crosser Marx looks since Communism started going astray for his followers, that knotted scowl which we once took for concentration now revealed as sheer bad temper. The effect upon the observer of Lenin's favourite pose, too, has been altered by events: in place of a mighty thinker striding into the future we now see a trickster making for the door with what pretence of dignity he can muster. Their days dominating Soviet squares must be limited, that look of uncertainty in their stone eyes a sure prelude to dethronement.

Here and there on the streets stand relics of earlier Russian overlords, the architecture of the tsarist forces which stormed the city in 1865. If an entire quarter of this "Russian colonial" architecture ever stood in Tashkent (as it does still in Tbilisi and Kutaisi) it was destroyed by the earthquake of 1966, so that isolated examples only remain, pleasant cool buildings on a neo-classical plan, a portico of white Ionic columns flanked by wings colour-washed in yellow ochre, its dentil frieze, and its window cases, and broken pediment, each adding the interest of patterned shade to the façade. Of course their elegant street fronts have been chipped and defaced for the light-fittings and metal signs and telephone wires jammed into them with the uncouthness of the peasant who nails his barbed wire to any tree that's handy; but what remains, though faint, is a relic like the mammoth's footprint from which the palaeolithic landscape may be inferred. Quite certainly the Tashkent of

Great Game days was as remote as that palaeolithic era from what I saw on my morning's walk, but I came home feeling my feet firmly on the ground of Turkestan at last. I was able to outline reasonable ambitions, and to decide on what help I must negotiate for from Alex and the deep Mr Eshtaev behind him.

II

At two o'clock Alex stamped into the hotel on his policeman's feet in a state of agitation. Mr Eshtaev was ill. Chest pains: a fluttering heart: doctors were grouped round his bed. He had moaned out a message to Alex to carry to me his regrets that he couldn't entertain me. I wrinkled my brow in sympathy and looked Alex keenly in the eye. I wasn't altogether surprised that Mr Eshtaev's heart (what I had divined of its workings) hadn't stood up to a second day spent in accompanying an Englishman who could do little to make the outlay of time worthwhile, for he had struck me as a man who disposed of all his resources, including his heart, carefully and shrewdly. No flicker of Alex's pale blue eyes connived at my assessment. All the same I gave to him the bottle of whisky I'd intended for Mr Eshtaev, saying that it would be an unthinkably cruel present for an invalid with an unreliable heart.

Then we set out. First we walked through the streets at Alex's rapid pace to the offices of the main newspaper where, so he claimed, the editor himself was impatient to discuss my plans with me. Up and down in lifts we rode, and tramped the length of many corridors. Unsmiling women's faces at frosted guichets directed us with surly gestures further into the maze. At last in the editor's outer office we found a woman sitting with her smug hands laid out flat as fish on the desk in front of her, who delivered herself of a sentence in Russian with sour satisfaction. Alex was taken aback, then sulky. He swept me out of the room with him and explained as we clashed along the corridors that the editor had flown to Frunze an hour earlier leaving behind him a message of regret.

No doubt the gamesmanship between VAAP and the newspaper was complex, its stratagems deep: I felt like a trumped card as we emerged from the building with time on our hands before the next of these meetings which Alex or his masters had arranged for me. It could be a tiresome concomitant of VAAP's patronage. But I put it out of my mind, and commented to Alex on the fifty-yard waterspray gushing up from a long pool fronting the newspaper's offices.

"It's to cool the air-conditioning water," he replied shortly, still irritable.

"You mean it wasn't designed as a fountain?"

He shrugged, not understanding my question. "The water has to be cooled. This way the air cools it."

I was interested by the waterspray – just jets squirting from pierced iron pipes laid in the pool – and by his attitude to it. Here was a utilitarian scheme which no aesthetic influence had been allowed to improve or beautify, an exemplary instance of why Soviet cities are so rough and ready. A little care would have transformed that gush of water into a fountain, but the care hadn't been taken, and Alex didn't know what I meant by suggesting it. It is the very opposite to Victorian engineering, in which every practical invention was almost swamped by the embellishments of an aesthetic consciousness, so that manufactures and power stations were disguised as mediaeval castles so thoroughly that their function might be hampered.

"You want to see fountains?" Alex asked. "In Tashkent are many fountains, many."

He didn't understand what I meant; nor, then or thereafter, did he ever have any idea of what might interest me. He didn't care. He had the want of curiosity of the professional "minder" – or, indeed, of the professional assassin. The visiting card which he had given me described him as "Deputy Head of the Uzbek Department of the USSR Copyright Agency", and his fortunes seemed linked to Mr Eshtaev; but he was not quite the man even to deputise for the head of a literary concern. He asked me no personal questions, and would answer none, except with a dismissive nasal laugh. As I say, he was without curiosity. I liked him already.

When the hour which might have been spent with the editor had instead been passed walking in the streets and visiting shops – better supplied than those in Moscow – we entered one of the pleasant old butter-coloured buildings of tsarist Russia which housed the Tashkent headquarters of the Writers' Union. From the moment of crossing the threshold it was clear we were on enemy ground. I was subjected at once to a hostile barrage from a stocky Uzbeg into whose sights I was led in a downstairs office. Rumpled and disgruntled, his room in book-ish disorder, he had evidently been told that I was interested in Turkestan's past, for he scolded me (Alex translating) for not caring about the Uzbegs' present and future. I looked humble, and was glad to be taken upstairs into a formal room where three or four mild-mannered men sat stirring sugar into tea-glasses whilst they silently regarded me. A pretty girl, very much made up, introduced me round the room, tripping about on her high heels and then leaning her weight against Alex, as she sat on the arm of his chair, in a way which disturbed him. The tinkling of the spoons in the tea glasses emphasised our want of conversation. Then one of the watchers, a small neat Uzbeg, leaned forward on his velvet sofa to enquire what libraries in Turkestan I should like to do my research in, what professors of history I intended meeting, what facilities I should require? I was aware that Alex too, having translated the question to me, watched me for an answer with more interest than was usual in his eyes.

What did I want of Turkestan? Not libraries and professors, certainly. What, then? It was the question I'd spent the morn-ing considering, as I had walked alone about Tashkent.

I had answered the question with a metaphor. Aged ten or so, and passionately fond of cricket, I had looked back at the cricketers of the pre-war world, especially Englishmen and Australians, as heroically lit figures at large in a romantic land-scape. I read their books with awe – *Cricket My Destiny* by Walter Hammond was a favourite – and gazed with almost painful nostalgia at the snapshots of these men in action on

sunlit pitches across the gulf of time. I could get no closer to
them than their photographs and memoirs allowed me. I
wanted more. Had it been possible for me to have walked in
the arenas where those legendary innings were played – to
have seen with my own eyes the wicket at Melbourne where
Hammond made his famous 32 in 1937, or the bumping pitch
at Brisbane where Bradman scored 76 against Larwood's body-
line attack – I would have grabbed the chance. It might not
have worked. I wouldn't have seen the matches or men of the
past again, of course, but if I could have crossed the boundary
rope and walked out onto the turf of those celebrated grounds,
where the heat of the sun would have struck me from the same
blue sky my heroes had played beneath, the experience might
have slaked a thirst I felt in my soul.

Now, my admiration for the heroes of the Great Game isn't
quite hero-worship – inevitably, now that I'm middle-aged,
these characters' flaws interest me as much as their heroic attributes – but I had worked myself as close to them as reading
and reflexion in England could bring me. To visit Central Asia,
and walk in the arena where the Great Game was played,
became my objective. Despite obvious physical changes – new
stands altering the horizon at Lord's – the walk across hostile
ground to the wicket remains what it was to Bradman or
Hammond, and the same charged atmosphere exists at the
centre. "A bumping pitch and a blinding light"; the pitch
where the Great Game was played: that, in a nutshell, was
what I had come to see.

Little use hoping to explain myself to a sofa-full of Uzbegs
in terms of cricket. Stirring tea, they waited. If I wasn't a
scholar, what was I, and what did I want? I cast about for a
means of encapsulating my interest in Central Asia and the
men who had played the Great Game here.

I told them the story of Colonel Stoddart, Captain Conolly
and the Reverend Joseph Wolff's entanglement in the web of
the emir Nasrullah of Bokhara in the years between 1839 and
1842. Stoddart was sent on an embassy to Bokhara: the emir
held him captive, sometimes in prison, sometimes not,
depending upon how Britain's prestige stood (it was the time

of the first Afghan War): the noble-minded Arthur Conolly, having travelled to Bokhara to try for Stoddart's release, was himself imprisoned: both were at length executed, but so doubtful were reports of their death, and such was private English feeling (the Foreign Office did nothing) that an eccentric Jewish clergyman of the Church of England, Dr Wolff, travelled at great risk to Bokhara merely to learn the truth of the matter on behalf of a Captain Grover's Committee for the Relief of the Bokhara Victims.*

These characters and their history contain the core of the appeal to me of the subject of the Great Game and its personalities in the Central Asian setting. Stoddart, sent to Bokhara to forestall Russian influence there, was a touchy, fiery soldier with an exaggerated sense of what was due to an Englishman's honour: "a man less adapted to the purpose [wrote Captain Grover] could scarcely be imagined". He got into difficulties, of course. The Foreign Office disowned him. Conolly, by all accounts (and the fact is clear in his own delightful writings) a brave and eager young soldier, who had been disappointed in love for a grandee's daughter, was suffered by the Foreign Secretary to make his own roundabout way to Bokhara as a "private traveller" to try to get Stoddart out. When he had failed, and both men's throats had been cut with a sheep-butcher's knife in the maidan below Bokhara's citadel, Dr Wolff made the journey which almost met the same end. Through Alex Issaev I told this story to the three men and a girl from the Writers' Union – told it in outline, just, without elaborating all the circumstances of character and incident which make it so intriguing to me, and said that ever since I'd first read of this episode I had wanted to walk about the streets of Bokhara. I did not say that there indeed, in the narrow and fear-haunted lanes of Bokhara, was "the bumping pitch and the blinding light" where the game was played, but still I could not tell what they made of the story. Probably the names, and a version of the incident – the English officers cast as cowardly

* See Appendix for an account of the Bokhara Victims and Captain Grover's Committee.

spies (as they appear in M. A. Terentieff's account of it) and Nasrullah as a patriot fighting off British imperialism – was known to them. They watched me, and listened to Alex's translation, and drank tea.

Perhaps to change the subject, an elderly man with skin as milky-brown as a north Indian's, and exceedingly white hair curled on his pate like fine wool, shifted on the sofa and said that he had been recommended a short while ago by a visiting American, a lady, to read a book of travels, written by an Englishman, which she had left with him. Did I know of it? When the book turned out to be *Journey to Kars* I was able to claim to have written it, which, though less good for my prestige than proving myself a scholar, was better than nothing. Writers do not seem to be placed very high in the literary hierarchy in the USSR: they are the workhorses providing a literary establishment with its living. An author here, I was told in the discussion which followed, is lucky to see fifteen per cent of his earnings after VAAP and the Writers' Union have taken their share; and I must say that I had rather the feeling, as I sat in the velvet-upholstered room upstairs drinking tea whilst they conferred, that they were devising how best to pluck amongst themselves this chicken which had fallen from England into their laps. It was not that I myself should be deprived of feathers, just that my presence in Uzbekistan was a factor from which all might benefit, if they could only see their way to it.

My first day in Tashkent was by no means over. Driving away from the Writers' Union into the evening rush hour beside the brightly painted girl from the meeting I wondered what would happen next. Because of Alex's rapid speech and slack articulation, very often from the front seat of a car in which I had a back seat – as happened now – I only grasped the meaning of about half what he said, and had no idea where we were going.

First, at a busy crossing, we dropped the girl (who had given me a card which described her as "Senior Consultant" to VAAP) and watched her trip away through the crowd of workers like the star of a musical comedy making her exit

through the ranks of the chorus. Next we got lost. The outskirts of the city are extraordinary; blocks of city architecture
dropped haphazard into rustic squalor, skyscrapers built in
fields and reflected in the puddles of muddy lanes. In one of
these lanes we went astray, lost, and Alex and the driver (perhaps another deputy director of VAAP) sprang angrily out into
the nettles. There was no one to ask. Whilst the driver sped
away in search of a telephone, Alex and I waited amongst the
puddles by a brambly hedge. It was a strange and stricken
landscape. Gardens and allotments, a variety of mud-brick huts
and sheds, cluster round the bases of the tower-blocks, then
over the hedge a straggle of field leads to the next settlement.
The obverse of the Western suburban dream of *rus in urbe*, this
was squalid *urbs* dumped in a peasant *rus*. Sweat and apologies
poured off Alex. Irritated and crestfallen, he was no doubt
adding this derailment to the newspaper editor's strategy in
trumping Mr Eshtaev's heart that afternoon.

I could not have explained myself to him, but I was more
interested by these bizarre surroundings than I had been by
central Tashkent. The chance of finding yourself on your feet
somewhere unusual quickens interest immediately. Over the
hedge was a mud wall, and in the wall a timber door, and
through a gap in the door's starved planking I could see a
chicken yard fronting a poor low hovel thatched with reed, its
stick ribs staring through their plaster. This downtrodden rural
dwelling, its sagging thatch overshadowed by skyscrapers,
gave a vivid idea of Tashkent's rapid expansion, of city bosses
striding out into the country, careless of what their feet
crushed.

To soothe Alex, who had darted off to question a distant
passer-by but was now returned – and was looking askance at
me peering through the broken door into the hen yard -- I
withdrew my eye from the peephole and asked him a few
questions about Tashkent's expansion. He told me that it had
been agreed after the 1966 earthquake that nothing above four
storeys high should be built in the city, and that for a good
many years the planners had stuck to it. Then, under "pres-
sures", the rule had been "relaxed". I looked at him. He looked

away. We both looked at the tower-blocks rising out of the wrecked landscape. Sounder methods of construction had now been developed, he said. Like the methods used in constructing the tower-blocks in Armenia? He threw away the butt of one of the cigarettes which he smoked restlessly and continuously whenever out of doors. In Armenia there had been "problems", he said. I wondered if a little relaxation of his official persona would in time humanise our relationship.

At last a sturdy blunt-headed figure could be seen marching towards us across country, striding over thick and thin like a beagler, and hallooing in stentorian tones across the runner beans as he passed rapidly amongst gardens and allotments in our direction. When he drew up, still booming out instructions, I was introduced to Eugeny Berezikov, a painter and writer well-known in Uzbekistan, who had invited us to supper in this suburb. A robust, bull-necked man in his fifties, friendliness radiated from him at once, and a bone-crushing handclasp and a greeting like a loudspeaker announcement welcomed us into his company. We started for his tower-block as if it was a grandee's castle and he had come out to the lodge-gate to greet us.

We rode up crushed together in the lift. At close quarters he acted rather with the panache of a celebrity at a fête, or a gym instructor amongst fourth-formers, with a self-regarding confidence of manner which flattens all other egos in its vicinity. But his hospitality was eager. From the raw rough walls of the landing he flung open a door; and I never stepped through a doorway into a scene so contrasted with what lay without. Under a blaze of sparkling light one room succeeded another packed to the walls with objects, tables, chairs, statues; and on the walls themselves of this enfilade of crowded rooms the pictures, framed or unframed, crowded together cheek by jowl. When I had washed my hands – new soap, fresh towels, pictures packed tight on the cloakroom walls – we visited his museum room by room. He led the way with his attractive blustering enthusiasm for it all. It was the accumulation of objects amassed by a man with the collector's fever in a country where it is next to impossible to find anything to collect. Here lay a pair of black elm doors from Khiva, carved as delicately as lace, obtained God knows how; here were fossils, there on a table a stone carving, in a pottery dish fragments of jewelry, everywhere bookshelves crammed with books in many languages he didn't speak. On the floor against chairlegs leaned more pictures, rugs were folded into corners, glass glinted down from the top of bookcases. In that defeated landscape we had ascended the dead tree of this tower-block and found ourselves in a magpie's nest. I examined everything, looked into all his own violently coloured paintings. Our tour passed several times through a dining room, or dining space crushed between furniture, where a table loaded with brilliant salads and glasses and bottles gleamed silently in waiting, and, when at last every cabinet had been emptied, every drawer opened, and I had scraped the crevices of my imagination for a last comment on the final picture, I was shown back into the dining room which, as if by magic, now contained Mrs Berezikov and a son and daughter neatly dressed under the glass-drop light. All were smiling at the floor, hands twisted together in front of them. We sat down at the table.

Berezikov's massive personality filled the space as his possessions filled the house, so that his wife's slightness, and her fair faint diffident face, and the teenage daughter peeping out of a haze of tulle, seemed crushed for room. He thundered with talk and laughter. He forked gargantuan helpings of salads and meats and potatoes and sauces onto my plate, being sure to refill it – to drop a colossal onion onto it – just as I had worked my way through to daylight. Vodka too was gushed into my glass the moment a toast had emptied it; for conversation, again, took the form of speeches (three of his to one of mine) rounded off by toasts. It was hard work. If only I could have felt like a great man, as he so evidently did, we could have sat complacently in this way, like gods on adjacent clouds, exchanging egocentric bolts of lightning for our Mercury, Alex, to translate. But I hadn't even any book of mine to sign for him in return for the book of his, execrably printed and bound, like a parish magazine of twenty years ago, with which he presented me. Nor could I match the albums of pasted-in comments by local critics upon the paintings he had once exhibited at Delhi. As a visiting writer I was not what he wished me to be.

To talk to children, or to someone as shy as Mrs Berezikov, through an interpreter is as cumbersome as shouting small talk at the deaf, so I had to be satisfied with listening to translations of my host's rumblings as he strode about heaping me with objects to admire, whilst his family once more withdrew into recesses out of sight. I nodded and smiled on the sofa, growing sleepy, turning the pages of the albums he had piled onto my knee.

Though it hadn't been quite the ordinary sociable pleasure of dining out (I thought to myself as Alex and our host and I swung along through the darkness at a late hour towards the metro station nearest to his suburb), the evening had opened a door and shown me a curious interior and its residents. No one making a journey can hope for more. Street lights glittered among the trees of silent roadways empty of people as we tramped along, Berezikov still talking stridently, an island of éclat in the deserted streets. For some reason he supported me with a hand under my elbow, as if I was drunk, or his prisoner. Perhaps it was a mark of honour, like the hand which the great men of Turkestan used to place under the stirrup of a visitor whom they condescended to honour when he mounted to ride away from their gate.

III

The next day was, as I had always known it would be, a Russian holiday on which I couldn't expect my plans to move forward. I told Alex, who had disclosed under questioning that he had a wife and two children, to stay at home and pass the holiday with his family: his last sight of them for some time if my plan to leave next day for Samarcand remained in place.

I was perfectly content to stroll about, in intervals of heavy rain which, falling straight and steamy from amber-tinted clouds, veiled the Tien Shan Mountains as if with the drifting smoke of fires. An idle day in a city far from home is a quiet pleasure: hours passing slowly, walks making the town familiar: it is this idly stretched-out time, leisure to walk about with the holiday crowd, and make your observations and little discoveries – of a pleasant seat in the corner of a square, of a street where families saunter among charcoal grills smoulder-ing on the pavement – that planned travel doesn't leave room for. I'd rather feared that my own itinerary, if left to VAAP, wouldn't leave me this room in the towns of Central Asia. Far rather the gentle boredom of a day too many than the squeeze and rush of a day too few.

Whilst I walked about Tashkent, and watched little girls in flouncy orange taffeta sitting for their portraits to artists who set up their free enterprise easels in the very centre of Karl Marx Street, I thought about the city's past. The description of the place I had in mind was Eugene Schuyler's, who was here in 1873 and found it already Russianised, for it was Tash-kent which had become, in 1867, the seat of the governor-general, Kaufmann, through whom the tsar ruled his newly conquered provinces in Turkestan.

It was the Peace of Paris in 1856 which allowed Russia, whose armies had been tied up in the Crimea, to begin once again to expand into Central Asia.* Defeat of the mountain-eers of the Caucasus, too, secured the Caspian route into

* In consequence of the 1813 Treaty of Gulistan between Teheran and St Petersburg, which had chased the Persians out of the Caucasus, the region between the Black Sea and the Caspian had become an entirely Russian sphere of influence; but during the Crimean War the Allies, who had always underestimated the importance of the Caucasus to Russia, allowed only the dilatory and belated Omer Pasha expedition into Caucasia (a campaign vividly reported by the likeable egotist Laurence Oliphant). According to the historian Popowski it was admitted in Russia that if Omer Pasha's force had landed in the spring of 1855 instead of in the autumn, and had been more vigorously commanded – it crept ahead only a few miles at a snail's pace before becoming bogged down in autumn rains – the Turkish citadel of Kars might never have fallen, and the Russian conquest of the mountain tribes of Caucasia might have been

Turkestan (indeed Bariatinski, commander of the army of the Caucasus, put plans before the emperor for an attack upon India by that road). Advances were made, territory taken to secure frontiers. "No one should understand better than the English [wrote a St Petersburg newspaper] how the conquest of Asia may come about as much by inevitable progress of forces as by aggressive policy." In 1861 General Bezak submitted a plan for taking Tashkent which used just the same cover – "protecting our own Kirghiz" – as Peroffski's first steps east of the Aral forty years earlier. It wouldn't frighten the English (he said) as much as a southward move against Khiva or the Oxus would – "besides, the English are making themselves at home in China, and have no right to hinder us from protecting our own Kirghiz and rectifying our frontiers".*

So the tsar's forces tiptoed towards India, chiding the British for their waspishness but nervous, all the same, of poking

---

long prevented. A Briton who was an admiral in the Turkish navy (Slade Pasha) wrote that if Omer Pasha's campaign had succeeded, "the Emir of Bokhara would long tell his beads in peace". But to the British Foreign Office, as to Strabo and the ancients, the Caucasus was "the gate at the end of the world", and such Eurocentric statesmen as Palmerston could not conceive of the region as a bridgehead for Russia's further expansion into the desert wastes which they presumed to lie beyond. The Eastern Question was a matter of "how to accommodate the collapse of the Ottoman Empire without upsetting the balance of power in Europe", and to that end the Crimean War had been undertaken so as to prevent Russia grabbing Constantinople. Russia's Asiatic ambitions – the other prong of Peter the Great's Will – were left as a separate issue in the charge of the East India Company. Within seven years of the end of the Crimean War the Caucasian mountain tribes were finally defeated and their leader Shamyl was in Russian hands. From that secure base Russia could establish an arsenal and a military headquarters across the Caspian at Krasnovodsk, and initiate the railroad which would supply a Russian advance into Turkestan from the west during the same years that Kaufmann was advancing into it from Tashkent in the east. Peaceful bead-telling at Bokhara was up.

* Bezak's aggrieved tone is echoed in Alexander Herzen's complaint that "Western nations talk of our duplicity and cunning; they believe we want to deceive them, when we are only trying to make a creditable appearance and pass muster".

awake the British lion. "It is generally known [a historian of an earlier Khiva campaign had written] that the English have from remote times diligently watched over the events of the whole world, and that they are always troubled and dissatisfied if fate allows any other nation to have influence over the fate of mankind."* The English democratic system, too, of alternate governments reversing each other's policies, baffled the citizens of an autocracy ruled by decree: first the Liberals with their "masterly inactivity" blew cold, then came in the Tories with their "forward policy" breathing fire; and besides that confusion was the further one of Central Asia falling within the sphere of the governments both of London and Calcutta, the home government and the East India Company. To allay the suspicions and quiet the threats of British statesmen the Russian foreign minister Prince Gortchakoff circulated a Note assuring the world that Russia planned no expansion, but meant merely to reach a secure frontier and spread "Russian civilisation" within it. "Of late years [the prince smoothly began] people have been pleased to assign to Russia the mission of civilising the countries which are her neighbours in Asia." The idea that the Russian despotism of corruption, vodka and the knout might give lessons in civilisation to the most barbarous Khan of Tartary was outrageous to most Englishmen, but Lord Clarendon's reply to Gortchakoff's Note made a different

---

* Arthur Conolly gives this mischievous account of a Persian grandee describing English society at Ludhiana: "The feringhees are by no means a pleasant people to be among, for they have nothing to say for themselves and, considering that they are unbelievers, they have more pride than enough. I saw a great little man, who was very civil, but as dry as a stick [who] gave me tea, which they make deliciously; asked me questions, but when I answered 'Bulli' said only 'Ha!' . . . First came in one Captain, and then another; they looked at me and at each other, and every now and then delivered themselves of a syllable or two; while one man was pacing up and down as though he were possessed . . . formerly a small tribe of merchants, servants to the kings of Ind, but now they have it all their own way. The secret of their rule is this: they have information of everything that passes everywhere, and they make the most of their news. If two men quarrel about a country, they step in to adjust the dispute, and turn both out . . . Soldiers the Inglis are not."

point: the British, he said, "fear not the designs of your Government but the undue zeal and excessive ardour of your generals in search of glory, paying no regard to the views of the Russian government".

This fear expressed by Clarendon was instantly justified by events. Gortchakoff had released his Note in 1864. Against orders from St Petersburg, in 1865 General Cherniayeff took Tashkent by a *coup de main*. He also took Kokand in 1865; Samarcand fell in 1868, Khiva in 1873 and Merv, the last stronghold of the Tekke Turcomans of the desert steppes, in 1882. The truth was that despite the tsar's autocracy and his minister's protestations, it was indeed "generals in search of glory" – the local commanders in Turkestan – who followed their own militaristic policy outside St Petersburg's control. And these local commanders lusting for medals certainly had their eyes on India. "Our presence in Afghanistan," wrote General Kruleff in 1855, "will promote the rising of the Indians against the hated English rule." The Sepoy Mutiny of 1857 encouraged this confidence, and an Indian officer, Colonel Malleson, records the impression of Russian power felt in the north Indian bazaars at the fall of Samarcand. In the view of General Skoboleff, the rather appalling archetype of tsarist soldier-heroes, "Everyone who has concerned himself with the question of a Russian invasion of India would declare that it is only necessary to penetrate a single point of the Indian frontier to bring about a general rising . . . the overthrow of India might produce social revolution in England . . . in a word, the downfall of British supremacy in India would be the beginning of the downfall of England." So much for Prince Gortchakoff's mealy mouthed assurances!

But, though the British government (Gladstone's Liberals from 1868 to 1874) huffed and complained and issued ultimata galore, they made no overt military response to the Russian advances. The quartermaster general in India might "solemnly assert my belief that there can never be a real settlement of the Russo-Indic question till Russia is driven out of the Caucasus and Turkistan": numerous British officers travelling privately might report what they found throughout Central Asia of

Russian influence and Russian intentions; but the British government, Liberal or Tory, had control of its servants, so that British military men, unlike the Russian officers, did as they were told.

"This remind you of England?"

"No!" Surprised out of me, it sounded rude. "Not much," I said less abruptly. The shrivelled elderly American who had asked the question had just moved across the bus aisle from his wife's side to mine. I had been let on board by their tour leader to take an hour's run with them through Tashkent's landmarks, and I had so far sat like a new pupil on the school bus, outside their raucous badinage, as we sped along the boulevards. The stressed-concrete and tree-lined streets didn't remind me of England, no.

"My, this Tashkent!" he exclaimed at the passing scene, "this Tashkent is just beautiful."

I looked again. I looked at the concrete, the grandiloquent steps leading nowhere, the wide desolate spaces where water showered upward from pierced iron pipes. Beautiful? The individual among those Babylonian blocks and spaces is like an ant. Even a crowd huddles nervously together. Since the days of Nineveh this has been the architecture of dictatorship and persecution. Beautiful? I thought of Greece, and the architecture of democracy. Even tsarist Russia built on a human scale.

Nine years after it first came into existence as a garrison town, in 1873, the American Eugene Schuyler gave this description of Tashkent: "I could scarcely believe I was in Central Asia, but seemed rather to be in one of the quiet little towns of Central New York. The broad dusty streets, shaded by double rows of trees, the sound of rippling water in every direction, the small white houses set a little back from the street. . . ." It is hard to be pleased anywhere with what you find, when such a picture has been formed in your mind's eye. Here and there in the Caucasus I'd walked into that handsome fading aquatint of Schuyler's, but here in Tashkent there was no remnant of it. At Pyatigorsk, a spa in the Caucasus, I had seen tall blocks built on Mount Mashuk not to set off or adorn the magnificent prospect of mountain and plain – not to enhance the spa's nineteenth-century reputation for elegance – but to defy all that, with ugly fingers of concrete poked in nature's face. Two buildings stand side by side on Rustaveli Avenue in Tbilisi. One is the tsar's governor-general's residence, a pleasant vanilla-coloured affair of columns and porticoes and shaded loggias, its doors no larger than a man needs to walk indoors with dignity, its windows of a comfortable height to give a view of the garden: next to it stands the swollen monster of the Communist Party headquarters in triumphalist concrete, mighty steps, yawning portals, a pattern of dim arches interlocking far overhead to produce the effect of gloom and apprehension to be found in the *carceri* engravings of Piranesi. It is a building to instil terror.* As a weapon in absolutism's armoury of repression, architecture was not used in Russia so long as Peter the Great's Europeanising influence (which produced St Petersburg's chilly classicism) was uppermost; with the abandonment of Leningrad for Moscow the Soviet government returned to Russia's true Asiatic heritage, and to the soul-crushing monumentalism of Asiatic tyrannies such as those of Nineveh or Babylon.

Next to me the American who thought Tashkent was beautiful moved his head wearily from side to side, on a neck as sun-wrinkled as a tortoise's, to take in the sights. He told me the group was fresh in from Moscow, Leningrad and Samarcand yesterday, and was off to Irkutz, Hong Kong and China tomorrow. He lived in Arizona, which we talked about until the tour leader chivvied us all out of the cocoon of air conditioning and gossip to visit the market.

This was better. Though barely more than a barn roof raised over an area of concrete, it recovered a human scale after the Brobdingnagian oppressiveness of what we had seen: the clamour of voices, urgent transactions, the bustle of trade, made the architecture of the place subservient to human needs. I

* In 1991 this building was gutted and burnt by the forces opposed to the former President Gamsakhurdia.

walked about in the crowd for a while and didn't rejoin the bus. Finding my way home through the town, too, was a pleasant relief after the dreary regions and grim monuments visited by the tour. So tight a canopy does the trees' foliage make that you can scarcely see the tall buildings – the statues' heads, too, are mercifully hidden in the leaves – whilst the quieter streets I walked through rang with footsteps and talk that evening, and smelt of shashlick broiling on smoky fires.

In the crowd of well-to-do families eating and strolling in these streets there was a marked predominance of Russians over Asiatics (in the market my shoulders had brushed the hurrying robes of every race in Central Asia). Here little neat Russian children were carrying balloons, or eating ices, or sitting wriggling on camp stools whilst their portraits were drawn. I came across a merry-go-round, too, and watched a Russian boy of about eight or nine lock his arm tightly for safety across a five-year-old brother's seat, and then, when the machine began to turn, I stayed to watch every child's eye widen with alarm, every child's mouth open with delighted horror, at the gathering pace of the revolving wheel.

This uniformity of children's responses shows the stranger a reassuringly constant factor in the humanity of a foreign nation, especially when the adult population appears bafflingly unfamiliar, and I found as I walked back to my hotel that my idle day with its small incidents had served to make me feel pretty much at home in Tashkent. I found that Alex had telephoned, and later he rang again, to announce our departure tomorrow for Samarcand.

"But Alex, wait – we haven't agreed where we'll go, how long we'll be gone, what it'll cost – anything. We must talk first."

"No problem. I call you tomorrow, okay?"

The Russians, especially in Central Asia, are poor planners-ahead. To rely on an overnight plan would be over-sanguine. I didn't pack.

IV

At about ten o'clock next day I heard heavy footsteps in the corridor and an urgent hammering on my door. Alex rushed in, gleaming with perspiration. Impossible to leave today! The car must be serviced, errands run, documents prepared, telephone calls awaited – to leave before tomorrow was impossible. I saw Alex watching me closely, even nervously, as he poured out his hundred best reasons for delay. I listened, remembering that I had never read of a journey made through this part of the world which had begun on time . . . "I had already disposed of my possessions amongst my saddle-bags, and taken leave of the *mirza*, when one of my people came to me with a long face and a longer tale of how chopped straw for our horses would not be obtainable in the market until a late hour, and, in short, of how, for a thousand reasons with which he would not trouble so fine a gentleman as myself, departure was impossible. Of his own dilatory ways, and fondness for vodky, he did not speak." A sentence along these lines occurs regularly in books of Asiatic travel, so I wasn't surprised, and told Alex I didn't mind a bit, so long as the hotel could put me up for another night. But what (I asked him) was our bargain to be, for making the tour to Samarcand, Bokhara and Khiva with himself and a driver?

"We discuss. Soon! Next time!" He was backing towards the door.

"Why not now? Look Alex – this hotel costs practically a hundred dollars a night, and I can't stay here forever at that rate, nor can I pay that rate in dollars for three people all through the other places we're going."

His hand was on the door knob. "I telephone at six tonight, okay?"

"You give me an all-in figure for the trip, and I'll see if I can afford it."

"Okay, okay – no problems." He was gone.

And I had another leisurely day in Tashkent ahead of me.

One of the many advantages of being alone where arrangements are chancy is that no justification or apology is needed

when plans go astray. Resentment simmers where blame must
be apportioned. "I knew we should have fixed it yesterday."
"Well, if you knew, why didn't you do something about it?"
"Because I thought you were dealing with Alex." "Anyway
it doesn't matter." "Except we've got another day stuck in
bloody Tashkent." "I don't know why you came." Alone, if
such painful dialogues do ever occur deep in the heart, they
are too swiftly passed to leave scars. The day was fine, the
mountains hazy, and I soon walked out into the warm green
town again.

The loss of its Great Bazaar – of something similar to,
say, Aleppo's stone-arched bazaar of winding covered lanes
with a separate quarter for each variety of merchandise –
has impoverished Tashkent as a city where a curious Westerner may amuse idle hours. Eugene Schuyler recorded the
details of the old Tashkent markets with a meticulous eye.
I liked to picture him, in his "usual grey tweed suit", hands
behind his back, learning the three ways of tanning leather,
or the five methods in use of forging sword blades, and
writing everything down with such amplitude – he spins
out even the uneventful by saying, "Our journey was, in
many respects, greatly lacking in incident" – that his *Turkistan* takes up two weighty volumes.

Schuyler was an acute and incorruptible observer of the rule
of the tsar's governor-general, the odious Kaufmann. This
little bald-headed German martinet, extraordinarily vain, kept
up in Tashkent an emperor's state in the 1860s and '70s, permit-
ting no one to sit in his presence and no one to meet him
unless in full-dress uniform, even ordering the erection of a
fresh triumphal arch to greet his every return to the town.*
Schuyler – unlike another American, the journalist MacGahan,

---

* "The army is overrun with greedy German officers and doctors: too
commonly men who, while poor, will submit to any degradation; but
who, when they get up in the world a little, are fastidious and proud. The
Russians hate them with good cause, because they are cruel, extortionate,
tyrannical and practically useless" – *Sketches of Russian Life*. "All these
Germans form the principle prop of despotism" – Gurowski.

whose eulogistic account of Kaufmann's Khiva campaign is evidently influenced by Kaufmann's favour towards himself – coldly condemns such pomp. Indeed, though he seems rather to enjoy himself in their company, Schuyler condemns Russian society in their new Asiatic provinces, particularly for their want of knowledge or interest in the place and its people. "It seemed to many [of these Russians]," he wrote, "difficult to understand how I could be interested in a country, and come so far to see it, which for them was the epitome of everything disagreeable."

The truth was, that Tashkent society was made up of exiles from St Petersburg who had disgraced themselves, or bankrupted themselves, and had come into this wilderness, as they regarded it, in desperate hope of recouping favour and fortune by some bold stroke of commercial or military adventurism. Hence the officers' impatience to attack everything, every city and every khan, but most fervently of all to attack the world's richest prize, British India.

Typical of such desperadoes with nothing to lose, who played the Great Game wearing Russian colours, was Captain Vitkevich. Born a Lithuanian count, he was exiled at seventeen to Orenburg for his part in the Black Hand Polish Plot of 1824, and drafted as a private soldier into the army (a common tsarist punishment for turbulent nobles). Exploits against the Kirghiz, and expertise in local affairs, brought him promotion under General Peroffski until, made a captain in 1837, he was sent from Teheran to Kabul on a secret mission whose object was to separate the Afghan ruler, Dost Mohammed, from his allegiance to the British. Alexander Burnes greeted him in Kabul (the British had learned of Russia's mission by a chance interception of Vitkevich in the Khorassan desert*) and asked him to Christmas dinner. Very different was the official recog-

---

* Lieutenant Henry Rawlinson, whose career as scholar-soldier-diplomatist was to be amongst the most distinguished of all Englishmen in the East, met Vitkevich in the desert, guessed his direction and its significance, and rode 700 miles in 150 hours to alert the British legation at Teheran.

nition accorded these two men by their respective governments. Carving the turkey was Burnes, brimming with
bounce, knighted by his Queen, at thirty-two an established
figure whose knowledge of Central Asia was much valued by
his superiors: but Vitkevich, though successful in his Kabul
intrigues, found no support or even recognition on his return
to St Petersburg, the foreign minister declaring that he knew
no one of that name "except an adventurer . . . lately engaged
in some unauthorised intrigues at Cabul". And so, like the
Lermontov hero ("If I die, I die: my carriage has come –
goodnight"), Vitkevich drove to his lodgings and shot
himself.

Certainly there were bankrupts and soldiers of fortune
amongst the British in India, men trying as best they could
to shake the pagoda tree – certainly too the Indian Army
was looked down upon by British regiments – but India
was upon the whole run by a core of men who were
knowledgeable about the country and much interested in it.
This was never true of Russian Turkestan, for the Russian
who was not at St Petersburg or Moscow felt himself an
exile from all that counted in life, and regarded Central
Asia (just as a Turkish pasha regarded his pashalik, or an
Englishman, later, was to regard Hong Kong or Shanghai)
as a Godforsaken posting amongst a savage people, to be
exploited for the mending of the exile's fortunes as rapidly
as possible. There were few ideals or scruples amongst the
Russians in Turkestan.

And yet, adds Schuyler in a somewhat resigned tone,
despite the place attracting "the scum of military society",
and suffering an administration wanting in "the high moral
qualities which should have caused Russia's civilising mission", more harm would be done to Central Asia by Russia's
withdrawal than by her continued presence. "Having once
taken possession of the country it would be almost impossible
for the Russians with any fairness to the natives to withdraw
from it." They had interfered with the structure, and were
now committed to propping it up. But he reckoned that the
government of Turkestan had cost the Russian treasury a

deficit of nineteen million roubles between 1868 and 1872, and concludes, "had Russia known fifteen years ago as much about the countries of Central Asia as she knows now, there can be hardly a doubt that she would not have moved in that direction". That of course was the argument of the British russophobe: Central Asia of itself was no use to the tsar, who had "conquered it merely for the prospects its acquisition opened in respect of India".* For whatever reasons, by Schuyler's day the Russians' rule looked permanent.

Today, the Russianisation of Central Asia is so long established a fact that I doubt if a native of the khanates which existed before Russian conquest would know quite what to eliminate in order to return to a pure pre-colonial state of things. I was thinking about this as I walked behind a watercart spraying the Tashkent streets. Would Uzbegs, left to themselves, think it an important priority, to splash water about the streets with so prodigal a hand? Not only are streets washed, and swept by women with twig besoms, there are no pi-dogs in these wide well-planted avenues either, and no beggars or packs of dirty children. Vultures do not load the rooftops watching for carrion and offal to be dumped in alleys, and no lepers lean against heaps of rubbish. In short, Tashkent doesn't really resemble an Asiatic city at all. But is this state of things how the Uzbegs themselves like to find their cities? – or is it the hated sanitisation of colonialism, which will be allowed to lapse, as soon as Uzbekistan is free of Moscow, until Tashkent again resembles the truly Asiatic cities of Afghanistan and Pakistan?

My question was partly answered when I came upon a gang of workmen dealing with an emergency – and dealing with it in such a reach-me-down style that I could see in their efforts the compromise between Russia and Asia. A branch had fallen across the pavement into the roadway. The weight of foliage

* General Skoboleff wrote that Russia must perforce invade India "otherwise the hide is not worth the tanning, and all the money sunk in Turkestan is lost".

in these acacias and planes seems to be enough to crack off branches, which lie about the squares with wilting leaves; but in this case the limb, still attached to the trunk, had fallen amidst the traffic and must be attended to. A team had arrived. In the West, possibly even in European Russia, the road would have been coned off, vehicles with winking lights and hoists would have congregated, a frontliner in hard hat and ear-defenders would have ascended by hoist with a chainsaw to sever branch from trunk, and a good deal of tea would have been drunk at the heart of a major traffic jam. The method I watched now was Asiatic, and simpler. After many duff shots a rope was flung over the branch overhead. To this rope, twisted so that it gripped the branch, the team of five or six Uzbegs attached themselves and, rushing into the traffic in a half circle first one way and then the other, like maypole dancers getting up steam, they endeavoured to generate a violent enough swing on the bough to break it free of the trunk. With the cars and buses tearing past they took their chance. A crack! – the branch broke and fell – down tumbled the team in a heap in the road – the job was done. I felt encouraged: there would surely still be odd corners of pre-Russian Turkestan left, if only I could find a way into them, whether helped or hindered by Alex.

V

At about eight o'clock that evening I found myself seated under a vine arbour at a supper table in a quiet and leafy mud-walled garden, half an acre of fruit trees and melon beds, which was the property of the low dwelling behind me. Through the vine soft stars shone, and the sweet sound of fountain water lapsing into its runnel rose and fell behind the Russian and Turki conversation at the table. It was the flight of a magic carpet from the Uzbekistan Hotel's dining room.

We were eating much-spiced tomato soup, into which all

dipped fragments of the flat heavy bread torn up in heaps amid the dishes of scraped carrots and spring onions and quartered tomatoes which covered the table. The mud floor underfoot was tamped hard, the mud garden walls whitened. Light from the dwelling rayed out towards the table, lighting the fruit trees as the night grew darker, lighting the faces of those opposite me at the table. It was warm and, like the others, I had hung the jacket of my suit (together with my MCC tie) in a tree by the fountain, to sit and eat at the friendly table in shirt sleeves.

Besides myself there were six men round the table. Next to me sat the now familiar bulk of Alex, across the table was last night's host, Berezikov, no less ebullient or stentorian, and beside him was a dark, humorous-looking little Uzbeg with a thick head of black hair growing low on his wrinkled brow, and a pair of bright, sharp eyes. At the table's head sat the sly figure of Mr Eshtaev, fingers toying with bread, his heart happily allowing this reappearance; though it was hard to tell whether the impression he gave of aloofness resulted from concern with his health or concern vis-à-vis the two rather gloomy Russians also seated at our table.

Alex, as he had promised, had telephoned me about six o'clock with a proposition for the tour. In return for an all-in sum paid in dollars VAAP undertook to fund the outing completely, hotels, petrol, fees of all kinds: I would be driven to Samarcand, Bokhara and Khiva, staying as long as suited me in each, and, on returning to Tashkent, would have my hotel and flight to Moscow also paid. I thought about it, calculator in hand.

"If you convert the dollars you're asking at the black market rate you get a huge sum," I said.

"But you pay Intourist, you pay in dollars not roubles," he reminded me, "and you would pay much more dollars than we ask."

It was true. My dollars were only worth a theoretical sixteen roubles each: if I paid my own way in Intourist hotels they cost, like this one in Tashkent, ninety-six dollars a night. VAAP could turn my theoretical sixteen-rouble dollars into reality for themselves, and feed me back about half the benefit. We each would profit.

"And VAAP –" I began.

"No more VAAP!" His voice was urgent, swatting the copyright agency into oblivion. "VAAP is finish. Now is TURON. No more VAAP!"

What did he mean? Bewildered, I agreed to the deal. If I was to be plucked, I was confident that they would pluck me gently, and leave me enough feathers for myself.

Alex had thumped on my door himself a short time after we had talked – for reasons I never fathomed he always came up to my room rather than ringing from reception – and together we descended to the car park. In that waste of concrete two cars waited, their doors open, one a Lada, the other a rather superior dark blue Moscva whose windscreen the agile little Uzbeg with the mane of black hair was polishing. This was Anatoly, whose firm hand and keen glance I liked at once. Introduced to him and the others, all the men who were to dine together, I was put into the back of the Moscva next to Berezikov, who gripped my arm in a grasp like a mastiff's bite, and we darted out into the traffic behind Anatoly crouched at his steering wheel as if aiming a projectile through the streets. Leaving the Tashkent I knew from my strolls we sped on into outer rings of high-rise, the tall pale fingers of concrete catching the late light, until suburbs and building sites ended abruptly in a low landscape of mud walls and orchards all powdered over with dust. Lanes intersected these walled orchards, and Anatoly, after bumping along a good many such lanes, drew rein at a pair of plank doors in a mud wall. It was within them that we found the supper table laid under the vine arbour.

I wondered about the presence of the two Russians at the table. Self-important Muscovites in nylon shirts, heavy men, they appeared to be envoys connected with the mutation of VAAP, the copyright agency, into TURON which seemed (from what I understood of Alex's whispers in my ear) to

be an organisation for "foreign trade". Mr Eshtaev had been
"deputy head" of VAAP: of TURON he was designated
"president". I watched him at the head of the table. A tapping
finger, impassive indifference, gave him the look of contained
energy you see in a cat whose only impatience is a twitching
tail. I felt sure that TURON had been selected or created with
caution and forethought as his vehicle for self-advancement,
and that the men from Moscow, whom he now rose to toast
in a careful speech, were emissaries of a central power bringing
him a treaty which satisfied his ambition – for the moment at
least.

These toasts!* Alex whispered to me a translation of Mr
Eshtaev's low phrases of welcome, and of the Muscovites'
replies. By now the porcelain tea bowls which served for
glasses had been twice emptied of vodka. Both Muscovites
leaned gravely towards me and exclaimed "Mr Phleep!"
before dashing off a third bowl; Berezikov too, in his
peroration to a lengthy speech on the need for solidarity
amongst writers the world over, spoke of me as an old
friend. Bottle upon bottle of vodka was emptied into our
bowls. I felt old friends with them all. The stars shone more
brilliantly through the arbour: indeed the moon may well
have joined them, so cheerfully did the faces glow around
the cloth.

A mound of rice and a basin of meat and gravy was now
reached into the middle of our company by the hand of a
dark unnoticed creature who flitted to and fro in the shadows
between ourselves and the dwelling's lighted doorway, serving
us, or rinsing plates and cutlery at the fountain. Into these
common dishes of meat and rice each man dipped not his hand
but the spoon he ate with. I felt extraordinarily content, and

* "The hospitality they extend to the wandering Briton is a thing to
be remembered all one's life . . . The only fault I had to find was the fact
that I was expected to drink a pint of brandy with each meal, moreover
if I tried to get off with less my host appeared greatly hurt" – Ralph
Cobbold in 1900 (who noted that the price of Guinness in Turkestan at
that period stood at eight shillings the pint).

as satisfied to be amongst them as if I'd come to Turkestan for no other purpose. Not the setting of the feast only, or the dishes, or the manners, or the varied intriguing faces around me – not just the vodka in my blood – but an outflow from the heart in our common humanity, in our lives' intersection in this walled garden under the Central Asian stars, made me feel like embracing the whole company.

It was this sense of community which the driver Anatoly emphasised when he rose in his place to speak. I did not then know what a large part this man was to have in my life for the next weeks, but he immediately interested me. Below middle height, compact and strongly made, with a kind of quick decisiveness in all his movements, there burned in his dark eyes the light of an active mind. Before Alex could translate his words I watched him speaking. He took up a round of the flat bread of his native land and, breaking it in his hands, pushed a fragment over the chequered cloth towards each of us. There was real benevolence in the lined face which looked at us in turn, and I didn't need Alex's translation to tell me that Anatoly welcomed the strangers to Uzbekistan, offering us the bread of friendship. As was often to happen on our travels, I knew that when Anatoly's penetrating eye rested on mine he understood me and knew what I wanted, though he never spoke a word of English.

Every one of them had now been upon his legs and addressed the party. An ancient dog, hitherto asleep at the foot of a tree, got to his feet and tottered towards the table, sensing no doubt the meal's end and titbits in store; and a black cat watching from a wall leapt softly down towards us too. I could delay my own speech no longer.

I told them that I was a cautious person, who never cared to compliment my host on a meal until I had eaten it, or my fellow guests on their company until I had shared it, and for that reason I had waited until a late hour to give my opinion. All bent their heads towards me to catch the sound of spoken English, the two Muscovites (who very likely understood it) moving their lips as they listened. Whether or not Alex had told them how I had come by the damage to my face I don't know, but I found myself again aware of the scars when I stood up with all eyes upon me, like the vestiges of a fancy-dress which needs explaining. As Alex translated, my listeners sat back in the darkness in comfortable relief – had they feared an outburst against Russia on account of my injuries? – whilst one or two fingered their vodka bowls, brimful once more of course, in hopes that the toasting phase of my address would soon arrive. It did. I said only the obvious things; but then, I truly felt the obvious things. Gritting my teeth, I swigged off my bowl of vodka "To friendship!" and sat down.

The table soon broke up. It is speeches and toasts rather than conversation which seem to make up the entertainment, and with these done the party is over. I took the chance to look into the dwelling raised a couple of steps above the mud yard. A bare cement room was exposed under cruel lights, a kitchen of sorts at one end and at the other a raised platform draped with rugs for a sleeping-place, this dais dominated by a large but antiquated television. There was no sign of its inhabitant, who had cooked and served our supper. Outside, we recovered jackets from the fruit trees in which we had hung them, re-knotted ties, stood talking for a moment by the fountain with the hut's glare on our faces. The night beyond this garden's walls was extraordinarily quiet: stars, the silver shiver of aspens, silence. Though so close, none of the racket and sodium glitter of Tashkent's suburbs penetrated to us. Daytime walks hadn't shown me an old quarter of the town, but here on its outskirts this evening had happened in an Uzbeg past which the Russians had evidently made part of their present – a commonplace part of it, too, for our supper party had by no means been the carefully resurrected affair of doublets and madrigals which goes with an old-tyme evening in England. Through its timber doors we left the garden, this secret garden to which they have taken care not to lose the key.

Once in the cars we were very soon amongst the over-shadowed deserted streets of a Russian night town. Alex half turned in his seat and said to me,

TASHKENT

"Tomorrow Samarcand, okay?"

"I believe you."

"Is true. Tomorrow at nine or eight o'clock I come."

CHAPTER IV

Samarcand

I

THE FIRST ENTRY in my pocketbook under "Samarcand" makes no mention of "the moon's pale fingers" and shows all the irritability I first felt with the place. "From his dealing with Eastern European package tours [I wrote] the Russian hotelier has acquired the contemptuous and case-hardened attitude towards his guests of a butcher towards sheep." I remember that sentiment, and a crowd of others just as resentful, coming into my head as I stood in my eighth-floor room, the lavatory dribbling miserably onto the tiles behind me, and looked out through curtainless windows over a city of tin roofs glinting amongst a canopy of leaves which was pierced here and there by the grim toadstool of a concrete high-rise shooting upwards into an exhausted sky. A haze of heat and glitter lay upon the view. It was six o'clock in the evening, and I'd been in Samarcand four or five unfruitful hours.

We had arrived about two o'clock, in the heat of the day, and had found with difficulty the government office from which Alex extracted a *chinovnik* who came with us to dignify our arrival at the hotel. Here the manager was found, and a lady with henna'd hair from the Tourist Office, and a gangling Uzbeg youth who had been appointed my guide. Amid this entourage, whistled up to make the sort of group which might surround a minor union official, I stood exchanging remarks through Alex in the hotel entrance. When would I like to visit the library – meet the professor – tour the study centre? At last the company moved into the dining room, where Alex and Anatoly and I were left to eat in peace.

Left to eat –! Here, where we could have done with a little helpful deference, only idleness and rudeness were to be met

with. However, it was Alex's problem. He had summoned up
the absurd suite with which he evidently planned to hamper
all freedom; he could wrestle with the kitchen also, just as
Anatoly could wrestle with the traffic. Freedom I had given
up voluntarily, by my decision not to travel alone. In these
first few hours in Samarcand I felt the miserable resignation of
the escaped prisoner who has surrendered because he'd rather
pick oakum than live by his wits. I wondered if there was in
the end no satisfactory way to travel in Russia.

After a wretched lunch our guide was waiting for us. He
folded himself into the back of the car beside me and began to
insinuate a stream of inaudible information into my ear, gold
teeth winking, the mop of black hair now falling over his
intelligent brow, now tossed back as he pointed out notable
Communist buildings along the streets. Though I know that
we drove first to the Shah-i-Zindeh, a string of mosques and
mausoleums on a hillside burial ground, and then to the observatory of Ulugbeg, and then to the Registan Square, I remember almost nothing of them but their names. Here was the dry
hillside of the Shah-i-Zindeh, the mounting domes, a shady
court round a mulberry. Then rapidly we drove to the shaft
cut deep into the earth for Ulugbeg's sextant, walked round a
glitter of objects in the museum, and were back in the car. All
the time the pliant young guide unreels a string of facts. Used
to dialogue, my mind searches for reactions and responses to
what he says. But he does not want an interlocking relationship. He does not want me to know anything he has not told
me about Central Asia. The effort made to sound interested
by his words succeeds in nothing save annoying him. Alex and
Anatoly wait by the dark blue car, Alex strolling and smoking
like a guard taking his break from duty, his large pale face
glistening, Anatoly washing the windscreen, polishing dust off
the bonnet, tugging a comb through his springy black hair.
As soon as I reappear with the guide they jump aboard and we
dash off into Samarcand's traffic. It is hell. I never saw an
uglier town.

Where possible, a dressing of cruelty and unpleasantness is
added to the eyesores by people's ugliness to one another.

Watch the bus that doesn't stop quite at the bus stop but ten yards off, forcing the fat woman with bags into a bundling run, the bus very likely hissing shut its doors and pulling away just as she reaches it. In a Communist society every vestige of power, even the bus driver's, is abused. The car driver too – Anatoly did it – winds down his window and shouts for directions when he is lost, the passer-by on foot cringing up to the window with his reply, expecting no smile, no thanks, as the window is closed up in his face and the car speeds off. It is probably part of his Tartar heritage that there never was any courtesy between a Russian with a little power and a Russian with none – the *starosta* and the *stanvarog* of a tsarist village between them pretty well skinned and flogged the *moujiks* – so that in Central Asia rudeness between strangers is natural to both races, a grating together of humanity like grit in the air which pollutes every breath you draw.

Now and then, between festoons of wire looped from rusty stanchions, or revealed for a moment among the concrete, I had glimpsed against the sky the shattered eggshell of a huge turquoise dome. To the height of this glimmering dome there rose on its gantry a crane angled like a bird's beak about to strike at the cupola and destroy what was left. Though its destruction (or, worse still, its restoration) made it an urgent matter to go and see it, I knew that my present mood, and company, would give the place a worse pecking than the beak of the crane. I would have to find my way there alone. I hung onto the plan like a means of escape whilst enduring the Registan. Back at the car my guide offered as a last stop either the Gur Emir or the market.

"The Gur Emir is Timur's tomb, isn't it?"

"In Gur Emir mausoleum is buried world-conqueror Tamerlane, living 1335 to 1405 this era."

"Let's see the market."

I had an instinct to save the Gur Emir too from the general wreck of Samarcand. I knew that these places could not seem as wretchedly unsatisfactory on my own – as empty, as wanting in resonance – as they had been in the guide's company. In that one small court of the Shah-i-Zindeh, under the shady mulberry, with its echo of an Italian cloister, I had learned at the beginning of the afternoon what I was missing by not being alone.

But company wouldn't trample the life out of the market. Alex and Anatoly came too, Alex swinging from his wrist the expedition's exchequer and documents in a purse which he never let go, Anatoly quizzing the stalls, running his thumb along a knifeblade, testing a pomegranate's ripeness with a pinch of his fingers. The plainness of the market building – a roof supported on girders above an acre of sloping concrete – was overwhelmed by the variety of races crowding into it, and by the diversity of their stalls and robes and clamour. It wasn't the stone-built labyrinth of the bazaars at the other end of the Silk Road, Kayseri for instance, where sun-shafts fall through stone orifices to patch the crowd with colour, or the shuffling, echoing passages of Stamboul full of footsteps and chatter. There was no embellishment. There was no material link with the past. But the rough and ready structure had been put up to shelter from today's snow or sun a spirit of trade as old as the oldest stones of Samarcand, the genius loci which has survived the destroying hand of every conqueror since Alexander laid waste Maracanda, and which would survive like the sparrows in the rubble, or the ants in the dust, though every shop was a ruin. Behind heaps of apples squat wax-yellow old men with Chinese whiskers and almond eyes: or heavy dark men waddle by kicking their robes: or women in dresses of shimmering colours, worn over loose trousers nipped in at the ankle, count the pomegranates which the shopman drops into their bag: or a Russian woman with blonde hair and blue eyes and a summer dress pauses to quiz the strawberries. These are the property of a wizened countryman in a muslin turban and a robe of glazed blue cotton sitting cross-legged on a piece of sacking. She questions him, tastes a berry: then flips open one of the transparent plastic bags she has bought at the market entrance and shovels into it, with the tin plate provided, an avalanche of musky strawberries. Grown and picked on the collective farm where he lives, and sold in the market as "excess produce", there is a profit for his whole community in the sale, and strawberries she can afford for the Russian housewife. The same story is behind the cherries, apples, nuts which heap the long counters, and behind the stacked cabbages and onions offered for sale. Here, unlike a Soviet shop, the seller hopes to catch the buyer's eye: the carrots and radishes have been tied in bunches and scrubbed till their colours shine. The buyers, choosy and watchful, press along the gangways between the displays, spill out into the sun, finger materials at stalls showing clothes, try on shoes, look at implements. Voices and footsteps make an active hubbub: everyone is intent on business: the atmosphere is charged with the avidity of the bargain-hunter.

At a stall selling farmworkers' tools were stacked spades and mattocks attached to rough staves. From a grindstone where the fellow in charge was sharpening a reaping hook there gushed out sparks which drew a crowd. The hook wasn't shaped like the sickle of the Soviet emblem; it was a short straight blade pushed into its handle of rough-peeled wood, a primitive tool. Just as there was no embellishment to the market place so there was none to these implements: the hook's handle had been branded with a criss-cross of burnt scars, to give grip to a sweating hand, but these scars were haphazard, different on each. What was useful and necessary had been formalised into no pattern by the touch of custom or art. Whoever made them had no aspirations.

I was rather puzzled by this want of a decorative impulse. Nor did I see for sale any of the rich colours, or patterned cloth, which I saw worn by the elderly, the striped loose cotton robe, the indigo or nectarine-coloured muslin of turbans, the soft leather boots. If you wanted clothes, or the material to make them, there was only the utilitarian Russian article, a tide of garish nylon. Perhaps it is surprising that the indigenous colours and materials have lasted so long in face of one hundred and fifty years of Russian imports: the ruler of Merv, last khanate of all to fall to the Russians, returned from his first visit to St Petersburg wearing a frock coat and top hat, an outfit he never after abandoned. On the market stalls I saw only dresses or suits for sale, none of the robes or native outfits

still so widely worn by the crowd, nor even the wide loose
trousers which are called shalwars in both Turkish and Turki.
I told Alex that one of my daughters often wore a pair of
shalwars I'd once bought in the market at Trebizond.

"How old is your daughter?" he asked.

"Fifteen. I've another of six."

"We can find shalwars for the two."

"I wish we could."

I responded warmly so as not to seem frosty towards any
enquiry about my home. His want of interest in it, odd in a
Russian put into close contact with a Westerner, though not
unwelcome to me – rather the opposite – gave his company
the indifference of a bobby doing his stint at a suspect's door.
Anatoly meanwhile was filling a plastic bag with fruit of various kinds from the heaps on show. I watched two little Tajik
children, a boy and a girl, he as black as a Moor with short
curled hair, both of them in filmy fluttery pyjamas, who were
slipping like eels amongst the crowd and swinging their bags
of oozy strawberries: I watched a spry old warrior trudging
along in skull cap and belted robe with a knife in his long soft
boots, and legs as bandy as a jockey's: I could have watched
the crowd for hours. For want of attention our guide had fallen
huffishly silent. The light was fading when we came out of the
market into one of the rubbish-littered roads at its gates. Again,
not far off, I saw the half-cupola bulging up into the dusk
beside the threatening crane.

"What is that dome?" I asked the guide.

"Bibi Hanum. Powerful masterpiece. Is close. Is close for
restoration."

Dread word on a Soviet tongue! In the Caucasus I had
climbed spurs of the mountains to find forts restored entirely
in cement. The crane was poised to strike the Bibi Hanum
dead. In the car Alex turned to ask me: "You want to go to
Gur Emir now?"

"Let's go back to the hotel."

The guide sat back with a smile of triumph. Another tourist
defeated! He had crushed out of me those words of surrender
heard on so many exhausted trippers' lips, "Back to the hotel",

and there was no need to waste ammunition pumping leaden facts into my corpse. When the hotel was reached he shook my hand with a last derisive glint of his gold teeth before stalking off into the ugly cacophony of the town.

So this is Samarcand –! The disappointed and resentful thought filled my head as I stood at my hotel room window eight floors above the city. Then, across the tin roofs below, beyond the suburbs' high-rise, over hazy violet distances – far, far away – there gleamed suddenly a white snowface veined with rock. Mountains! It was a glimpse of mountains like an idea floating into the mind's eye as you fall asleep. It was a chance of sunset light fading as I watched. But it had lifted my spirits. There was more to come, so that "image of futurity" seemed to promise across the vale of Zerafshan – there was more to Samarcand than I had seen.

I had been thinking that morning in the car, as we entered the flat wide landscapes clear of Tashkent, of the Halcyon of causeless happiness which suddenly appears in your mind when you are young, and vibrates its brilliant wings a time or two, and is gone. Once, leaving Rome for the sea in winter, that bird flew through my mind. No doubt the window by which it enters is closed up by middle age; yet now, leaving Tashkent for Samarcand, with Central Asia ahead of the dark blue Moscva, if I couldn't be sure of the shudder of the Halcyon's wings, I was sure of a sudden expansion of the heart with exhilaration, or happiness. We had left behind us the heavy traffic of town driving, the dust and confusion hazing the early sun, and now the road sliced straight into the distance ahead, broad black tarmac so rough that the tyres howled, so pitted that the bumping would have flung you against the roof if you hadn't clamped yourself down. Anatoly clung to the wheel like a helmsman in a squall: Alex fiddled static out of the radio. On either side of the wind-battered car a vast plain stretched to every horizon, its cotton crop as yet scarcely greening the well-harrowed plough. In the plain stood trees in groves, many trees, the silver-trunked poplar, oak and elm, acacias. Trees lined the road, too, mulberry chiefly, and the *chinar*, the oriental plane: so much foliage in the landscape gave to the haze into which horizons faded a tint of green. Here and there, in a strip of uncultivated land beside the road, grew a scrub wilderness of thorn and whin which supported the widow's cow, a camel or two, or a couple of rangy square-headed horses, all the animals hobbled or tethered. It seemed that into these strips of wilderness all the old pre-cotton life of the country was confined, as the gypsies of Europe are confined to patches of roadside grass. Everywhere, cotton was king.

We approached, after thirty or forty miles of these cottonfield landscapes, a cluster of shacks and brick houses on the road where trucks and buses had pulled in anyhow under the shade of dusty trees, and amongst them we too stopped. The sunlight fell hot and heavy on my shoulders as I followed Alex and Anatoly over the road towards a pair of rusted iron gates which stood open amongst the houses and trees. Alex dropped a few kopecks entry-money into the tin plate guarded by a silent ancient in skull cap and spindly beard at the gate whilst Anatoly bought himself a plastic bag. Under the trees' shade was a fish market: we had stopped on the banks of the Jaxartes.

It was the girth and abundance of the gloomy fish exposed for sale here in the innermost heart of a continent, so far from lake or sea, which gave the market its air of plenty, of bountiful nature heaping good things upon the Uzbeg – a bounty absent from those roadside strips of rough ground which seemed to be all that King Cotton had left them of their native steppe. Once amongst the slabs of fish meat, never mind that a factory could be seen a few hundred yards upstream, its chimneys belching oily smoke and its pipes no doubt discharging poisonous waste, for here in the market were fish in any quantity taken from the venerable river, their lineage relating them to the fish of legend, and, besides raw fish, aromatic cauldrons of fish soup to be eaten at tables under the trees where a varied crowd sat scouring their bowls with bread taken hot from the ovens nearby. Such an active market in these wastes of cotton was a friendly thing to find, comforting as to the perpetuation of the country's own life and past, the counterpart of

Tashkent's surviving market, or Samarcand's, in the midst of those urban wastes.

We had soon crossed the broad mud-stained current* and left market and river behind us as we drove into distance after distance. Once we entered some low hills, climbed by zig-zags through the rocks to a brief upland pasture of stony ground greened over with coarse grass, but we were quickly amid further plains under the same blue sky. The road thumped at us through the wheels, the wind hammered at the windows. Once I saw a grim outline in the haze to the south, tall black chimneys and the block-built shapes of factories within a ring of high-rise, and learned from Alex that it was "a new town". Alex rarely spoke. Occasionally he exchanged comments, laconically, with Anatoly as we passed – slowing down for the occasion – one of the police posts beside the road, its boom raised and an idle policeman twirling his baton with a vacant gaze. Road noise and wind noise made it hard to catch any comments chucked over his shoulder to me. But I wasn't bored. The mind speculates and enquires of itself, when the eyes are busy on fresh scenes, in a way that the mind, mine anyway, does not work under a stream of information fed into the ears by a guide.

I thought about General Kaufmann advancing on Samarcand by this route amid the praetorian guard of one hundred Cossacks without which he went nowhere. "He came to Central Asia with no knowledge of the country [Schuyler reported to the American government] and, by holding himself in a very lofty position, has acquired very little knowledge of it during his stay." Seizing as his excuse for conquest on a rumour that the Emir of Bokhara was assembling an army at Samarcand, Kaufmann marched from Tashkent over these plains with a force of 3,500 in April 1868. The emir's army, if it had ever existed, had vanished by the time Kaufmann approached Samarcand, but he entered the city, garrisoned it, and set out

* "Near the bank of the river the uneven ground was thickly covered with high reeds, affording, as I was told, lurking places for numerous tigers" – Schuyler.

to chase a handful of Bokhariots retreating rapidly enough to Bokhara. However, he was soon brought back to Samarcand by news that its citizens, aided by a certain Jura Beg, had taken advantage of his absence to shut up the Russian garrison in the citadel, where its plight was desperate. Indeed the Russians were on the point of blowing up themselves and the citadel when Kaufmann, returned by forced marches, took his revenge on Samarcand. His excuse was the city's "treachery". For firing on the Russian garrison he executed men out of hand, as if for a criminal act. Schuyler says, "It is impossible to consider it in this light": civilians had given up the city to Kaufmann when their protectors (the emir's troops) had abandoned them, but when another friendly liberating army appeared, under Jura Beg, they joined him in attacking the invaders. However, for the soldier who thinks brutality an effective quietus, an excuse for firm action is soon found. What Samarcand suffered was nothing to what Kaufmann was to inflict upon Khiva five years later. Still, the Emir of Bokhara was sufficiently impressed by the brutal German banging about in his kingdom that he signed a treaty which, though preserving Bokhara itself under his own tyranny, made him virtually a vassal of the tsar. Thus the Russian conquest was extended.

The country between the Jaxartes and the village of Dizakh, forty or so miles short of Samarcand, where the road crosses the Zerafshan (the river of both Samarcand and Bokhara), was in those days the desert of sand that it had always been. "It is necessary to look towards some high mountains [wrote an early traveller by this road] and seek for abandoned bones, to know how to recognise the path to be followed." I hadn't expected such desolate scenes as that – I hadn't known what to expect, or where we would first meet with the unchanged desert steppe, which was why I had wanted to drive between the cities instead of flying – but I could not quite school myself, as we drew nearer, to expect nothing wonderful of the approach to Samarcand. "There is no place in Central Asia, the name of which has so impressed the imagination of Europe, as Samarcand. Surrounded by a halo of romance, visited at rare intervals, and preserving the traditions of its magnificence in a mysterious impenetrability, it long piqued the curiosity of the world." Was that pitching it too high? "We saw before us the clay roofs, crowned with large blue domes and lofty towers, and knew that we had reached the famous Samarcand": surely Schuyler's low-key description, at least, would not be disappointed in the event.

We came upon Samarcand past the hill of Ulugbeg's observatory, past a ruined mosque on one hand and the scatter of the Shah-i-Zindeh's tombs and domes on the other, with the city suddenly seen ahead and immediately plunged into, a hot glittering maelstrom of concrete and glass and motorcars which closed over our heads in a moment, before any general view could be registered.

As darkness fell, the gleam of the far mountains gone, I stood looking down at the city below my curtainless window. Well well. I felt disheartened and tired, but, as did Schuyler on his arrival here, I felt I should be out looking about the town I had come so far to see. Like ourselves he had entered by the gate of Shah-i-Zindeh "and found myself on the new boulevard, with its good pavement and shady trees, which the Russians have made". "Assailed at every step by lepers and beggars", knowing no hotels in the town, he had gone for assistance to the Russian governor, General Abramoff, who was permitted to wear a black skull cap on account of a head wound. Once installed in rooms, "I could not resist the temptation of driving about the town and taking a hasty view" of so famous a city. I felt the same restlessness. I went down in the lift. The concrete-flagged area outside the hotel was brightly lit, but the streets were dark. I felt my way almost from house to house uphill over broken paving towards the Registan through this darkness, traffic rushing every way over the unlighted crossings. I reminded myself to keep smiling. I turned round and walked back to the hotel, went upstairs and, smile still in place, lay down to read *Middlemarch* until it was time to eat. "Bitter indeed the disappointment [wrote the Hungarian traveller Vambéry of his arrival here a few years before the Russian conquest] in the case of Samarcand . . . in spite of all my enthusiasm, I burst into a loud fit of laughter."

II

Next morning at an early hour we were again in the Moscva speeding south. I had agreed to an expedition to Shakhrisyabz half out of disappointment with Samarcand, half in hopes that the glint of snowy peaks seen at sunset promised something better. At supper Alex had said, "Tomorrow Shakhrisyabz, okay?"

"Well, I don't –"

"Is fixed. One, two hours by car."

"I'd meant to spend –"

"So, eight o'clock we leave."

I didn't fight it. I'd already wrestled Alex into accepting that I would order, and eat, my food in a manner highly eccentric to him, now that we'd left Tashkent, so I accepted his programme for the next day. I had told him to ask in the kitchen what food was ready, and to order me from this menu a bowl of soup and a piece of chicken, which I ate without touching the side-dishes and salads and raw vegetables with which Alex and Anatoly covered the table. Nor would I drink vodka, obliging Alex to order wine, however bad. I wanted a rest from the punishing regimen of Tashkent's tables.

Clear of Samarcand to the south, we were soon amongst orchards and fruit gardens. Lines of poplars and elms made a framework of shelter which domesticated the landscape, and the varied foliage in the gardens gave a tint and texture very pleasing to the eye. Indeed such gardens "constitute the beauty of all this land". I watched them pass, wondering about the domestic life of the people who worked them, for, at a fuelling station where we had stopped, we had had a glimpse of a curious ménage.

Ahead of us in the queue waiting for petrol in one of the desolate scrapyards selling fuel – you help yourself, sometimes from a parked tanker-truck with its engine running, and hand in your coupons at a guichet – was a grave-looking motorist in skull cap and dressing gown, a knife thrust into the top of his wrinkled boots, impassively fuelling a white Lada. In the back seat of the vehicle crouched three tightly wedged ladies, three bundles of veils and wrappings without a word or a stir of life amongst them. In what setting had this party risen and dressed? A smoky hut, chickens at the door, half-naked children dappled in leaf-shadow, water drawn from the well? That's the background their clothes suggested. But the white Lada, the air of a bourgeois outing: as background to that I saw a tinny, echoing tenth-floor flat in the city's suburbs. In which setting were they at home? For not only the old dress – the boot, armed with a knife, pressing the accelerator – but the old arrangements, a back seatful of veiled and silent women, looked a poor fit in the Lada. The clash of epochs seemed to have left them dispossessed. I recalled a recent book about life in an Iranian village, its mud houses furnished with ice boxes and washing machines, in which an irritable paterfamilias (I could imagine the man with the Lada in the rôle) had shut up the village story-teller with the words, "Lies! All lies! Turn on the television". Perhaps they don't feel the confusion an outsider thinks he sees. Perhaps it only appears confused, dislocated, to the eye of a European, in whose own history the middle ages have not overlapped the invention of the motorcar.

Wherever that party in the Lada had arisen that morning, in flat or hut, it was certain that their first action was to put a kettle of water to boil on electric ring or dung fire so as to brew up tea – the early bowl or glass of black tea without which neither native nor Russian can stir.* In our hotel, though, at eight o'clock there was no tea. Breakfast would begin at nine: until that hour, no tea. In the old hotel which the new one has replaced – in the lodgings an earlier traveller would have found – however filthy and uncomfortable, a samovar would have

---

* "Gigantic Russian tea-kettles, ever on the boil, are held to be the *ne plus ultra* of refinement and fashion" – Vambéry.

been on the boil at all hours for the comfort of tea. But the samovar, with the ostler and the boot-boy, has been consigned to history, and such advances meant that we had had to start for Shakhrisyabz without any tea. Of course there was none to be had at the petrol station. As Alex and I walked about the yard waiting our turn at the tanker I noticed that the far-off snow mountains, until now visible across the plain, had faded and vanished into the same violet haze which had dimmed yesterday's horizons. I remarked on it to Alex. He only smiled. "Is it the weather?" I asked. "Or the time of year? When is it clear?"

He shrugged, smiling still. "Always so." He spiralled a hand upward into the air. "Smoke."

The car fuelled, we drove on towards the vanished range. From my bedroom window in a spa near Kutaisi I used to look out each morning through air of limpid serenity to the wooded Caucasus above – "dark clustered trees fledge the wild-ridged mountains steep by steep" – until, on the stroke of eight, volumes of black smoke began to belch from a set of tall chimneys in my view, the smoke soon rafting into oily layers which would lie sullen and heavy upon the landscape for the rest of the day. I supposed Turkestan was similarly blighted. I knew already that it was no good quizzing Alex; he made his statement, always smiling a superior heartless sort of smile, and clammed up. His attitude towards me was neutral: indifferent, equable. He offered his fact – "smoke" – without a gloss. Take it or leave it. He certainly wasn't going to interpret the smoke into discreditable signals.

We came into the lowest slopes of the mountain range and began to climb through rough rocky hills at the Moscva's best pace. The road followed upwards the cleft of a twisting stream, huge cracked rocks impending above, villages of mud and wattle squeezed into the valley below. Vines threw out their tendrils over the village houses, and apple orchards clung to terraces above the tumbling course of the brook. Sometimes a glide flowed beside level sward, where a donkey or two cropped the turf and switched his tail against flies. I thought of streams I have fished in Wales. To my mind hill country is all cut from the same cloth, shares a likeness, as lowland land-scapes do not. I felt I already knew the twisting stream, thought of one a little like it in the Lycian hills, another in Antrim, another in Transylvania; and so the links went out which the mind is so anxious to forge in order to connect what is new with what is known. The pass through these hills is a low one, its summit of grass and stone above the stream's source soon reached. The view beyond was immense. We stopped.

What first struck the eye in that tremendous prospect over innermost Asia were the lustrous snow peaks of further and more magnificent mountains faint and far off across the plains. These dimly shining walls of ice belong to the outworks of the Pamirs amongst which the Oxus rises, and therefore form northern ribs of the mountain spine of Asia whose southern ribs I had seen many years ago from the Himalayan foothills above Mashobra. Impossible ever to complete your travels into a survey of the globe, when you look at the thinness of the line traced across its surface by each trip: you can't possess yourself of the world in a net formed of those criss-cross lines, as you might take home a melon in a string bag, but it is an allowable illusion, when you stand on a mountain pass and strain your eyes to see beyond what appears, to massage eye-sight into making a grand intersection now and then, so that the world does not seem hopelessly and infinitely large.

Let alone the distances, the plain at our feet was striking enough. Closed by the glimmer of mountains to east and south, and on the north by the range we stood upon, this plain lay open to the west, receding into remote distances of sandy haze far beyond the fertile expanse glittering with cities which lay below us in the heat. That way, to the west, led to Bokhara. At the plain's southern limit flows the Oxus where it forms the frontier of Afghanistan. Balkh, the oldest village on earth, lies not far across the Oxus. This is the heart of Asia.

As the car took us down by speedy zig-zags into that cockpit of the Great Game I thought how clearly our morning's drive had illustrated the difficulties of forming frontiers in Asia. From Samarcand, if you had just conquered it, your eye would rest on the snow peaks to the south and you would say to yourself, "There is my secure frontier". Advance thirty miles to that southern frontier and you find yourself through the range by an easy pass, with a further plain, and further mountains, enticing you again southward. Seize the plain, reach the Oxus (as the Russians did); still it is necessary (as the Russians found) to enter the Afghan mountains in order to subdue tribes sowing disaffection over your frontier. The British had expanded willy nilly in this way up India into Afghanistan from the south. "Englishmen [wrote a St Petersburg newspaper editor in 1875] with their Indian experience to teach them, know how difficult it is to avoid the acquisition of fresh territory in the east, however much they may charge us with the lust of conquest." Though the tsars somehow held back from taking that last disastrous step across the Oxus, leaving to their successors one hundred years later the fatal advance into Afghanistan which was to prove the beginning of the end of the Russian Empire, in the 1870s Russian expansion into Afghanistan from the north looked inevitable.

In 1878, bumptious and aggressive, a Colonel Grodekoff was commissioned by the tsar (and permitted by General Kaufmann) to make a trip from Tashkent into Afghanistan. A grandiose passport issued by Kaufmann for the whole of Central Asia (save only the Merv oasis) showed off the swagger of Russian dominion, and made it seem certain that Grodekoff's ride was a preliminary to an invasion across the Oxus, where the Afghan Uzbegs (despite being beaten with stones into providing food for him) were reported to be pining for Russian occupation: "Are the Russians coming soon? [the colonel quotes them as asking] Would to God the time might be hastened! The English [one of them cannily adds] we do not like at all." Grodekoff, who was another short, bald, irascible soldier, this time glaring at Central Asia through rimless eyeglasses, had little respect and less patience with the natives and their customs along his route, seizing a spade, when he found himself delayed – "I had not brought a single book" – in order to dig a drainage canal across the courtyard of his dwelling, ignorant (or regardless) of how such an activity degraded him

in Asiatic eyes. He wore full uniform all the time. "Any mas-
querade I might have adopted would only have impeded my
movements, on account of my unsatisfactory knowledge of
oriental languages, and my ignorance of the ceremonial obser-
vance which Mussulmans make use of at almost every step."*
If there is a contemptuous tone in these opening remarks, it is
nothing to the colonel's restiveness en route. Having landed at
a marshy spot on the Afghan bank of the Oxus, and fearing
for his health, he refuses to wait even a day whilst permission
to forward him to Mazar-i-Sharif is sent for by the local chief:
"'I am tired of all this nonsense,' I said, raising my voice."
The ride to Mazar did little to calm him, for he is soon screaming out again, "What nonsense you talk! Put an end to this
farce!" and stamping in and out of his tent in a fresh huff at
every happening. "I exploded with anger" – "I lost all control
over my temper" – in the way he indulged his rage with
orientals, Grodekoff could claim to represent a new breed of
traveller in Central Asia.

It is a style which would have got him into deep trouble a
few years earlier. At the root of Colonel Stoddart's fatal difficulties at Bokhara had been his inflexible sense of his own
dignity, which, combined with ignorance of local observances
(customs Burnes had mastered well enough to survive there a
few years before) gave mortal offence. The admirable travellers
of the 1820s and '30s, Moorcroft and Trebeck, Conolly, Pottinger, Richmond Shakespear, Fraser – all these resourceful
men took pains to move quietly without giving offence,
whether or not they kept up a disguise, amongst the tyrants
and autocrats of pre-Russianised Turkestan. Their lives
depended upon it. But by 1878 the grumpy Grodekoff, and

---

* There is a distinction between the European who wore native dress
for the low profile and the comfort of the thing, and one who intended
by his appearance to deceive the men he travelled among. Burnes and
most others were in the first category, Vambéry and the mysterious
Lieutenant Wyburd (murdered at Bokhara) amongst the very few in
the second. Colonel Stewart (*Through Persia in Disguise*) admits that his
intention in disguising himself was to avoid the interference of British
soldiers and diplomatists with his plans.

SAMARCAND

English officers too such as Captain Burnaby or Colonel Valentine Baker, men with a good deal of the bully in their manner, could swagger about Central Asia pretty much as they pleased, secure amongst tribes cowed by Russian fire power (though Grodekoff, his "unsatisfactory knowledge of oriental languages" notwithstanding, makes out that he heard his guards conspiring to murder him every night of his journey).

The sun was at its zenith and the heat terrific when we got out of the car at Shakhrisyabz. Alex's stride carried him up a path between dusty acacias to the hotel – I had only to watch this confident splay-footed tramp of Alex's for it to revive in me the question of whether or not he was a policeman: it didn't matter to me in the least who he worked for, but as a key to his character I could not help wondering who paid his wages. I caught him up. He turned to me from his conversation with the desk clerk.

"Guide in half hour," he said.

"Isn't there a map of the town? A map would do me perfectly well."

He smiled, the indulgent but stony smile of one who understands his charge's gambit and has no intention of falling for it – a policeman's smile, in short. He said nothing. I went on, "I heard someone say in Moscow that maps are to be issued for the whole country soon. Do you think they will be?"

He smiled again. "Maps, maps!" he said, raising his arms and letting them drop. As I followed him out of the hotel, and down the path to the kerb where Anatoly was leaning against the car in his tracksuit, I said with asperity, "A map would save you both getting lost at every crossroad and needing a guide in every town." Water off a duck's back. Maps are such an unknown adjunct to Russian life that there is even no wish for them. Possessing no detailed map of the Caucasus, and hoping to find the ruins of a summer palace of the Georgian kings of the twelfth century, I had been obliged to take a guide one day from Kutaisi: herself mapless, the guide turned for help to the bus station, where she questioned any number of drivers before leading off into the country, from one passer-by to the next, until enquiry at last brought us to the famous ruin amongst its reed-fringed dykes. To this pleasant and anxious woman I had gently suggested the usefulness of maps – I was navigating myself round the Caucasus by means of a tracing which I had luckily taken from *The Times Atlas of the World*, scale 1:2,550,000 – but she had smiled the same policeman's smile as Alex. There are no maps for sale in Russia, just as (in a similar prohibition of curiosity) there are no telephone directories.

The telephone was causing Alex a lot of trouble. Ever since reaching Samarcand he had been trying to ring Bokhara, I suppose to book hotel rooms, and he now explained that the task should be easier from here, a smaller town, and that he and Anatoly would set to work on it if I didn't mind a few minutes alone. Leaving them wedged into a booth I walked off into town.

The muddled-up nature of the traffic thronging the streets, cows and goats and bicycles entangled with hooting cars, as well as the bazaar-like sheds which served as shops, and white-clad figures resting on mattresses under the trees, gave Shakhrisyabz the look and feel and smell of an oriental city, which I had missed in Tashkent and Samarcand. Such a crowd! There seemed no predominant type, but an equal showing of the dark Turkic race – Uzbegs, Tadzhiks, Kirghiz – with the Mongol features of the eastern territory. Most of the younger men wore jeans and shirts, most of the women bright prints; there wasn't the pleasing half-oriental style of dressing which you see in an Indian town, the undercurrent of soft colours and grace which Western habits only overlay. There was a good deal of the tawdriness and shabbiness of Russia. I found a bookshop down a couple of steps off the street.

In the take-it-or-leave-it style of Soviet shops the place was a shed fitted out with trestles on which books had been dumped in heaps: books on grey utility paper, books in ersatz cloth bindings, books in stacks which numbed the mind with the dullness of their appearance: it was like stepping down into a compound where the written word had been imprisoned in convicts' clothing. Books have gone to the wall in Russia. The copy of his novel which Berezikov had given me in Tashkent had rather appalled me: at no time in its history – yet – has the West so degraded the written word. I was too much oppressed by the bookshop to stay in it, and went back into the street.

Walking under the dusty trees I was aware of the need to avoid a constant negative irritation with Russia and its un-European ways which has always affected Europeans, and threatened to put me into the state of huff of a Colonel Grodek-off amongst the Afghans. Why should Russians care how their books are bound? – amongst the forty million liquidated by Stalin were certainly almost all those who were fastidious about bindings. Berezikov was a passionate man who clearly felt and cared strongly on any number of issues; and he was content to see his books in print, however smudged the type-face and coarse the covers. And why should Russians want maps, when they lack all the Westerners' reasons for needing them? – the holiday excursions by way of by-roads, the tramp along footpaths with knapsack on shoulder, the hunt for a "second home" amongst the lanes of Devonshire or the Dor-dogne. Russians have no uses for maps. Along the street ahead of me, as these thoughts went through my head, there tottered a wasted, thin-shanked old man in a turban and a blue robe, his staff (of gnarled wood petrified with age) pecking away at the dust and a plastic shopping bag hooked onto fingers as old as the staff. Only this shopping bag connected him to the world I know. Because I recognised as familiar this one possession in a being otherwise unfathomable, I wanted to use his shopping bag as a way into his head: I wanted to pop a map and a well-bound book into it, just as if, like me, he desired these things: just as if I knew what he was like. I remembered the three railwaymen beside the track outside Moscow, and the mystery (to me), tainted with unease, of what was entrapped in the bag into which they all cautiously peered.

It is this combination – the familiar plastic bag, its unknow-able contents – the jeans and T-shirts of the West covering Asiatic hearts – which has always irked the European visitor to Russia and provided him with his standpoint to deliver a scolding. Perceptive and reasonable men, a Mr Grenville Murray for instance, in *Russians of Today*, examines town and country, rich and poor, army and church, and commends everything about the Russia of the 1870s which resembles or imitates a British blueprint. When he comes to the lack of an English parliamentary democracy in Russia, however, his eye darkens and his temper rises until the book becomes a catalogue of venomous insults. "A German Nobleman" of the 1850s works himself into a similar passion, the Frenchmen de Custine and de Lagny are worse, whilst a Pole, Count Gurowski, calls it Russia's ambition "to extinguish light, engulf civilisation, and stop the onward progress of the European world". Never content to comment upon Russia and its people with the impartial curiosity of so many European travellers in, say, Africa or South America – Mansfield Parkyns amongst the Abyssinians is the model to this day for all travellers to the "third world" – these visitors seem to be roused to their paroxysms of fury and disgust by the hybrid nature of Russian culture, half Asiatic, half European, which they regarded as a deception practised upon themselves. In cities and country houses superficially familiar to a European he felt himself assailed and threatened by a Tartar undertow in all Russian happenings and habits.* In Russia the knout flayed the backs not of black kaffirs but of white Christians resembling himself, and these white Christian peasants were owned as slaves by French-speaking Tartars pretending to be country gentlemen. The European was bewildered and upset, and, as soon as he was safe home, began to scold. The punishment which all foresaw for Russia's wickedness, and bankruptcy, and aggression – the revenge which their outrage wished upon Russia in countless predictions – was the disintegration of the evil empire and the

---

* It was nearly impossible for an Englishman of that day and class to comprehend the Russian view of life on a country estate as a tedious exile from all that counted. Mr Cottrell in discussing the matter writes that "the country gentleman is a race peculiar to England, general civilisation being nowhere else sufficiently advanced to create it"; but that English gentlemen had always thought the provinces of England worth living in was in truth the chief factor that had made them so.

destruction of its corrupt ruling class at the hands of "the most violent and disgusting plebs in the civilised world".

Along the street I followed the trembling relic with his staff and shopping bag, until I watched him climb aboard a bus, which had as usual teased him into a broken run by hissing shut its doors, and which now carried him off into his mapless life. I remembered my father, as he dodged a bus in a Rome street, attributing its bully-boy style of driving to Italy's unpurged Fascism. Here one can blame Communism. I determined not to deliver one of the lectures in favour of parliamentary democracy which come so readily into the Englishman's head when the bus misbehaves, but to look for a shady seat from which to enjoy the spectacle of life in Shakhrisyabz whilst I waited for lunch, or for my guide, or for Alex and Anatoly to give up trying to telephone to Bokhara.

I was rather appalled in bed that night by how little I could remember of my tour of Shakhrisyabz. I remembered the guide's claim that Tamerlane's birthplace there had been dis-covered by a child tumbling into it in 1963. I remembered the great mosque's grassy dome and stone-flagged court, and the shade of its old plane trees, and the guide's voice promising transformation as he waved his arm over the delightful scene: "UNESCO has visited. All is now scheduled for restoration." A few such scraps were all that had stuck in my head. The tour had been a waste of time. Still, I looked forward to tomorrow, certain of better things in store.

By chance – no maps – we had entered Samarcand in the evening through the Zerafshan orchards upon a shaded road, a lane between mud-walled gardens and low dwellings which brought the country almost into the centre of the city. Stopped at a *chai han* in this rural suburb, where trestle tables stood round an elm-shaded pond, Alex refilled his thermos with *kvass* and we all drank tea. By showing us this spot – by letting us reach the centre of town by this sequestered road – Samarcand promised better things. I was hopeful. Besides this, at supper a charming thing had happened: Alex had produced from his bag a bottle of the Shakhrisyabz wine which I had praised at lunch. He filled my glass.

"Thank you, Alex. You are very kind." I drank it gratefully.

"No problem." He looked pleased. "Enough for the journey in the car. For every day."

It was thoughtful as well as kind. For the first time he had done more than was required of him. That spark of warmth cheered me as might the kindling twig in his watchfire have cheered an earlier traveller, token of a generous blaze to come. In responding to it I felt warmth in my own heart for Turkestan. Just before I fell asleep there came into my mind's eye a scene from the day's drive: a wide gravelly river flowing rapidly among sandbanks, a donkey or two on its shores of grass and reed; beyond the riverbed, across a stony plain, I saw the outline of a walled-in dwelling and its reed-thatched sheds, a homestead within the shelter of a grove of poplars ruffled white by the wind; beyond this again rose bare hills speckled with sheep and goats, many of them black; whilst above all and beyond all, nearly beyond imagining, rose the hint of those snow mountains like a line of music scarcely heard. It was a landscape in Central Asia, never to be forgotten. It isn't a wasted day which has engraved even one vignette onto a corner of the map, where it may be found brightening the page whenever in life you care to turn the leaves of the atlas.

III

At worst what is useful about museums is that they make clear to you by means of labelled objects in glass cases what it is that doesn't interest you at all, and can be skipped without further enquiry. In Samarcand I found two or three rooms of one of the Registan medressehs fitted up as a museum, and I looked in. Archaeological remains of the time of Attila, of Timur, and of Babur don't much excite me. I was alone, thank heaven, and so able to walk rapidly amongst cases full of scraps of this and fragments of that, and pretty soon to walk out again into the dazzling courtyard.

Here I sat down in the shade of an awning stretched between trellises over the centre of the yard, and took out my book. Abundant red roses, the marvellous roses seen everywhere in Turkestan, grew in a bed in the flagstones beside me, and a vine climbed the trellis; it was quiet and peaceful and hot, perfect conditions for reading *Middlemarch*, which I did for some time before laying down the book and considering the buildings forming the heart of Samarcand which rose around the courtyard.

The design and construction of Islamic architecture interests my head but does not touch my heart. Round this court glistened the tiled façades, in every façade its tiled arch, in every arch its fantastically carved door, every surface writhing with the violently coloured patterns of Islam which blaze up like flame, vivid and restless, to end in the sudden cut-off of the flat-topped wall. Above float the aquamarine domes, beautiful things, in shape and substance serene in a way that the tilework is not. The domes and cupolas I love: it is the garish walls, the fidgety detail, the over-repeated arch, that makes me admire the restraint of Greece all the more heartily . . . still, sitting in the shade alone amongst the roses of the silent court, I remembered the crowds of the Acropolis, the heat and crush of the Athens museums – where interest obliges me to elbow a way to every object on show – and I couldn't help feeling that it was rather wonderful, whether or not I appreciated my surroundings, to be the only tourist in so celebrated a spot as the centre of Samarcand.

What had most interested me in the Registan museum were a number of photographs taken in Samarcand in the early years of the century. Dirty and ragged, under turbans or tall lambskin hats, gloomy tribesmen bolstered out with robes grasped an arsenal of weapons and loured into the camera. Camels and pack mules, and the strong little horses of the Turcomans, plodded amongst ramshackle markets propped against half-ruined fortresses, and a good many Russian soldiers stood about in their baggy uniforms. This was Turkestan as the

Russians had found it, the Samarcand of Trebeck and Vambéry, the middle ages photographed in the early twentieth century.* These were photographs of "the bumping pitch and the blinding light". I would have given a good deal to have been able to walk into them.

The first Europeans to come upon these cities did not much occupy themselves with architecture or aesthetics. Arminius Vambéry, who reached Samarcand disguised as a dervish in 1863, five years before the Russians took the city, is an incurious and superficial observer, wholly preoccupied with maintaining his alibi and surviving his adventure. He had no mission, as had the British and Russian travellers, to survey the ground or assess the towns' strength and the people's loyalties; a lame Hungarian philologist, the self-set purpose of his journey from Constantinople was to discover the root of the Turkic tongue, and to indulge an "eager pursuit of adventure". It is his self-portrait, drawn in company with the dervishes and pilgrims and beggars he travelled amongst, which makes his book interesting. In contrast to the vagueness of Samarcand's appearance in his pages there is a sharp scene set in the city's Ark in which the Emir of Bokhara interviews him. Vambéry is always at pains to make clear what most travellers – certainly British officers – conceal: the peril of his predicament and his own tremulous state of mind. Quitting the emir's presence (he says), "the servant led me through a number of yards and halls, whilst my mind was at the time cruelly agitated by fears and misgivings as to my fate; my perplexed imagination conjuring up pictures of horror and seeing myself already travelling on the road to the rack and that dreadful death which was ever present in my mind". No time to take architectural notes, evidently – though on this occasion the emir's plan was only to present poor shaking Vambéry with a new suit of clothes.

The reality of the dangers these travellers ran, and the military man's way of conveying his peril and his sang-froid in the

* Vambéry writes of a Registan "filled with booths and ever frequented by buzzing crowds" amid the "ruinous medressehs"

same breath, is an interesting factor in their writings.* How risky was a visit to Samarcand in those days?

Judging from the diversity of accounts, it was as dangerous as suited your character and your readership. The writer's purpose, to construct for himself a heroic alter ego as the bold adventurer, may be perceived behind many a book of travels: I suspect a wide difference, in a great many cases, between the author himself and the redoubtable figure he depicts as his book's narrator. Never, I think, would the reader close a traveller's manuscript journal with the same impression of its author's character as he will receive from the printed book of travels based on that journal. Certainly there is wanting from Edward Lear's Cretan journal, which he never worked up into a book, very much of the patient, humorous philosophising of, say, his Albanian volume of published travels; yet, with perhaps greater interest, we can see that the man who jotted down his vivid, quirky, irritable thoughts each evening in Crete is the same man who wrote *The Book of Nonsense*: the "real" Edward Lear is there, as different from the polished and reflective Victorian gentleman of the Albanian book as a limerick from an Alcaic stanza. Just in the same way did Lear make on the spot his brilliant fugitive sketches of landscape, to be worked up in his studio into the highly finished easel paintings which his public wanted for its walls.

If the taste then was for a finished self-portrait of the traveller as gentleman-hero, what's wanted nowadays is Mr Average in the midst of a humorous calamity: the Lear of the limericks, in fact, not the Lear of easel paintings and lofty reflections. It isn't a matter of the writer consciously altering or falsifying events to please contemporary taste, for the *Zeitgeist* is at work at a deep level within himself, prompting him to tell his tale in modern terms; yet the same event may be made to appear very differently, if it is differently recorded. I cannot tell what opinion the reader will have formed of the attack made on me

---

* "There is an educative and purifying power in danger that is to be found in no other school, and it is worth much to a man to know that he is not 'Clean gone to flesh-pots and effeminacy'" – A. F. Mummery.

in Moscow. I tried to set it down in the first words that occurred to me, and I daresay it comes across very much as an event typical of the 1990s. Had it happened one hundred and fifty years ago it might have appeared in print in other words:

> Whilst at work upon my papers I was alerted by a sound at the door of my chamber, and, thinking it was my fellow with hot water, told him to set it down and be off. Before I could well make out what was "up", however, a big burly scoundrel had darted upon me with a knife, and, catching me for an instant off my guard, had flung me upon my back. Nevertheless, a very few moments of this rough-housing served to teach my cowardly assailant that he had "caught a Tartar", as the saying is, whose knowledge of "the noble art", learned long since in old Eton days against the Brocas bullies, somewhat outshone his own homely aptitude for a scrap; and the ruffian ignominiously took to his heels, with a cry of fear, flinging down, as he made off, an ugly knife, of the Gheelanee pattern, with which he had intended coolly cutting my throat. These, then, are the elasticities of limb required by visitors to "civilised" Russia's second city!

Never a lie in it; my precursor would have written down the incident as honestly as I wrote it down myself, but the self-portrait produced – that confident English gentleman in a tweed suit doubling his fists – will decidedly not match any picture of the present writer which may have formed in the reader's mind.

As I sat in the shade in the Registan's inner court I wished very profoundly that it might have been 1860 or thereabouts for a few minutes, not for the sake of reincarnating the bold English hero in whose company I might have travelled, but so that I might have walked into the Samarcand of those photographs, or of Verestchagin's paintings – Samarcand before UNESCO got at it – Samarcand in its natural Asiatic state of perennial collapse. "What strikes one most of all about the East," was Colonel Stewart's tart comment after crossing Persia in disguise, "is that no one ever repairs anything." Alas, they do now. The Russians do. A taste for ruin and decay, and for the powerful sense of continuity with past times which they evoke, is hard to satisfy where the hand of Russia has either destroyed or restored. But I kept one chance in mind until it was almost dark.

I knew that the shattered turquoise dome threatened by the crane belonged to the mosque of Bibi Hanum, said by the guide to be "closed for restoration". In the evening I walked towards it. A pleasant long-shadowed street led me past the governor's palace and other dignified buildings of the town which the Russians had just begun to construct in Schuyler's time. I took a lane, dusky, silent between windowless walls, which I followed until big timber doors in a mud-brick arch barred my way. They were chained, but not closely. I pulled them enough apart to slip between them and found myself in a quiet open court. The light faded upwards, flushing the tops of walls. One or two gnarled bushes with the seamed trunks of thorn trees grew out of the paving, and there were stone-cutters' tools, and a pulley and hoist, left idle in the dust as though from centuries before. In the court stood the curious worn stones of the lectern, the rahla, as solid a shape as an axiom in Euclid. All was still, with the settled stillness of neglect and peace which comes to ruins with nightfall.

But overhead the dusk was wonderfully alive, twilit air amongst the crumbling towers of masonry shot through and through with the thrilling rush of swallows and swifts, speeding black darts which seemed to gush out shrieks like rockets spilling fire as they winged high and low through the evening light. I stood watching the aerial show. The mud bricks of the mosque's cracked walls, dusty tints patched here and there with the glimmer of tiles, rose like sea-worn cliffs into the dusk, carrying the eye upward to the dome's half-shell hanging with the glow of a moon over the dark courtyard and its ruins. Present by stealth I stayed in the shadows, like an eavesdropper whom chance has put at the right keyhole.

From the shadows I soon found that I wasn't alone. Between the timber doors, where I had entered, slipped a succession of figures, some robed, some in Russian clothes, who hurried lightly through the dusk. The chain on the doors clinked with each arrival. Perhaps it was a short cut. But it seemed to me that a group of men was assembling somewhere amongst the ruins of the mosque.

The light faded from the sky and from the upper works of the ruin, the swallows found their nests, and I was able to leave the courtyard as secretly as I had entered it. I hadn't been there more than half an hour but it was worth all else I had seen as yet in Samarcand. The pleasure of it carried me through supper – a supper improved by another bottle of the Shakhrisyabz vintage – and even carried me through a brief visit afterwards to the *son et lumière* show at the Registan, as vulgar a blaze of noise and dazzle as could well be devised. Almost nobody attended it, ten or a dozen people dotted about the slatted benches amongst fountains and roses, and I soon gave it up to walk home through those strangely dark streets to bed.

CHAPTER V

Bokhara

I

WE PLANNED TO LEAVE Samarcand early next day, and unfortunately had not kept the plan to ourselves. A porter of some kind, perhaps a nightwatchman, hammered on my door at five o'clock; a chambermaid's fist followed his upon the panel at five-thirty; my alarm buzzed at six, and at six-thirty, as agreed, I was downstairs ready to leave, lifting feet and luggage out of the path of women cleaners in white caps who sluiced the floor with long-tailed mops. The idle hour upstairs at my window had shown me the Samarcand dawn which has discovered two thousand years of merchants' and pilgrims' caravans leaving the city's gates. There was a full pale moon in a pearl sky. The mountains we had passed through on our way to Shakhrisyabz showed rocky violet peaks; above them and beyond them, touched alight by a sun which had by no means yet risen at Samarcand, glittered the ice summits of the further range. The clarity of the dawn light was wonderful.

The moon, now grown pale as paper, hung over the land-scape for the early miles of our journey towards Bokhara. Low mauve hills lie at a distance both to the north and south of the Silk Road, but industrialisation has stained and suburbanised the near landscape. Gaunt blackened factories of the steam-power era stand on desolated plots, workers crowding through prison-like gates, trucks loading coke, rusty iron everywhere and the smoke, thin and vicious, sneaking out of the chimneys to cross the moon's face. There are not along this road the gardens and orchards of the Shakhrisyabz direction, nor is there desert; where there are still fruit trees they are neglected, and under a death sentence, like the broken-paned greenhouse in the walled garden condemned to development. Through it all, wide and black as a runway, the road leads straight towards the horizon.

After an hour or so we stopped for breakfast. The sun had risen, hot already, and Anatoly pulled the car into the shade of some roadside elms. A small pond was closely hemmed in by thorn trees; beyond this began an undulating country cultivated for cotton, with mere leftover scraps of rough grass and thorn to vary the dull sweep of dust-coloured plough. From the shade of the poplars round the pool I watched Anatoly set out our breakfast picnic. To everything he did he brought the same deftness and quickness, chopping tomatoes, tearing the flat bread, opening the jar of cream, as if every chore was worth his best effort. Now, having carefully cleaned the large dangerous-looking sheath knife which he used for kitchen work, he made a gesture offering the food spread on a cloth on the car's roof. This he did with his winning, worried smile. Despite the elasticated track suit and the furiously driven Moscva, Anatoly's character and his manners fitted him into an old style of hospitality. Thinking of earlier times I asked what had become of all the caravanserais which used to offer travellers water and shade within safe walls every twenty miles or so along this road.

Alex, if for some reason or other he didn't want to answer a question, would translate it and pass it to Anatoly. This he did now. Anatoly, wolfing down spoonfuls of yoghurt, shrugged without looking at me. I said, "There are still a good many caravanserais left at the other end of the Silk Road, in eastern Turkey. The ruins of them, anyway."

This too Alex translated. There came a brief, bitter reply from Anatoly: "Turkey had no Stalin."

"Turkey had Attaturk," I said.

A contemptuous laugh. "No Stalin."

Stalin (Anatoly told me) had destroyed whatever buildings were peculiar to Mohammedan culture, or necessary for its expression, and had secularised the rest by defilement – making mosques into museums, for instance. So he believed. I thought of Isaac insisting to me in Moscow that Stalin had murdered forty million Russians, the entire middle-class intelligentsia of

132

families resembling Isaac's own. Citizens of Russia as different from one another as Isaac was from Anatoly understood Stalin's acts as a policy directed personally and particularly against themselves, and, because of the scale of Russia and the precedents of Russian history, they counted his victims and his levelled buildings in terms of the crimes of Tamerlane or Ivan the Terrible. Attaturk secularised Turkey – made a museum of Santa Sophia – but instead of active destruction he relied on Turkish indifference and neglect which, added to a few earthquakes, has accomplished the gradual collapse of the sacred framework of Ottoman life.

I walked down the field track beyond the pond thinking of this. In this landscape were none of the graceful old mouldering piles of stone and broken arches, of the turrets of a castle or the lantern of a caravanserai, which mark the routes of trade and conquest across the high steppe of central Turkey. There were two or three old women lugging cows along on strings to snatch a little grazing amongst gravel and thorn, otherwise only the undulations of empty plough and here and there a patch of grain showing green. And there was a railway track: twice during breakfast freight trains had pounded heavily and slowly by. I had walked down to the rusted rails when the second of the two came shuddering and groaning up the incline towards me, four engines drawing seventy-odd coal trucks, and I watched it rumble past shaking the earth. I walked back to the picnic and stood looking into the pond, my irritation with myself for not having come by train to Turkestan revived by something dignified and ponderous in the locomotives' passing. A dimple in the inky water alerted me to the presence of fish in the pond, and I threw in a crumb of the bread I was eating: the rush of fishes, tiny but ravenous, surprised me. Why should such a forsaken puddle as this teem with fish? It is unexpected to a European, that these unpromising land-scapes, and fouled rivers and ponds, are evidently so fertile.

Likewise the mulberry trees beside the highway were full of fruit. All along our road, as we drove on across the plains, these double avenues of mulberries were being pollarded, their branches stacked in swaying loads on to donkeys or three-wheel trucks or the sidecars of motorbikes, on their way to nourish Bokhariot silk worms. The silk of Bokhara is woven still: sent into European Russia, the profit from these roadside mulberries, and from all Uzbekistan's fertility and mineral wealth, is engorged by Moscow. Anatoly had allowed himself a few bitter words on the subject, translated by Alex with his usual neutrality, in light of the freight trains taking Uzbekistan's coal out of his homeland as they took its wool and silk and gold and cotton. I did not ask whether the transformation of VAAP into TURON, under the crafty Mr Eshtaev, had been effected so as to profit from these Uzbeg riches if Moscow's grip on her empire could be loosened.

Probably Moscow would maintain that Uzbekistan cost her money: the balance sheet of an empire is sufficiently complex to prove any claim. Schuyler wrote that the deficit of income over expenditure in the Turkestan government in the five years before 1873 amounted to nineteen million roubles, and supposed that the Russians must regret their expensive involvement in Central Asia. On the other hand, if Russia really had designs upon India, she might have expected an eventual profit on those nineteen million spent approaching the Indian frontier: it was only a bad bargain if she stopped short of the Himalayas. There was no commercial profit in invading Turkestan, and British advocates of the "forward policy" in these regions seem to have forgotten that a trading concern like the East India Company couldn't possibly pour blood and treasure into Central Asia without profits clearly in sight. Russia had captured early what market there was. By 1825, when Moorcroft visited Bokhara, he found its bazaar already stocked with Russian manufactured goods, which, though poor in quality, were difficult for English merchants to oust in lands beyond reach of British ships and British railroads.*

---

* When Moorcroft reached Bokhara in 1825 he was much disappointed to be greeted by the cry "Ooroos! Ooroos!" – indicating to him that the people took him for one of a race already familiar to them, the Russians, and that English manufacturers had therefore been beaten into the Turkestan market. "Enterprise and vigour [he wrote] mark the measures of Russia towards Central Asia, whilst ours are characterised by misplaced squeamishness and an unnecessary timidity."

The Russian railroad, carried two hundred miles east of the Caspian by 1882, put England's "forward" party into convulsions of fright and fury as they watched Russian troops and armaments debouched by the trainload to destroy the Tekke Turcomans at Geok Tepe, hitherto an independent native fortress which lay within a march or two of all those keys to India which Nature had scattered through Central Asia. By 1888 the future viceroy, George Curzon, could travel by rail all the way from the Caspian to Tashkent riding this iron yoke which Russia had laid for military purposes across the conquered steppe. Nowhere in Russia did railways serve primarily the needs of merchants or travellers, as they did in Europe and America. In the 1850s a line was laid from St Petersburg to Moscow which followed a line ruled across the map from one city to the other by the hand of Nicholas I himself, whose intention was not that the railway should benefit trade or suit passengers by passing through intermediate towns – the tsar, like Wellington, believed that railway travel would only increase the common people's restlessness and contumacy – but that it should carry troops as rapidly as possible from his capital to Moscow, where the disaffected nobles gathered to plot against him.

Such at least is the reason for that line's directness offered by the British resident in Russia whose anonymous *Sketches of Russian Life* give a vivid and gossipy idea of the times.* These books by foreign observers, and there are a great many of them, are interesting to me for the picture they paint of Russian life, and for their analysis of the Russian civilisation which was billed to bring such benefits to the conquered peoples of Central Asia. In their lively anecdotal pages we can examine the

---

* He tells how "an old *tavishnik*, or shopkeeper of the peasant class" travelling to Moscow had met a friend from the St Petersburg-bound train in the magnificent refreshment rooms built by the American engineers at Bullagonie, and how both men had returned together to his carriage on the Moscow-bound train. After a good many miles spent exclaiming at the miraculous railroad, the second greybeard said to the first, "Aye, and most wonderful of all is, that I am going to St Petersburg and you to Moscow, and yet we travel in the same train."

features and character of Terentieff's "physician from the north" whose liberating régime was said (by one or two Russians) to be so eagerly awaited by an India suffering under the tyranny of British quacks. The truth is, scarcely one of these writers – French, German, Polish, American or English – has anything but disgust and contempt for the dirt, brutality and corruption of everyday life in Russia. In the provinces there is sluggish barbarism, in the chief cities only glitter and make-believe. Here and there we meet enlightened landlords, and noblemen of real cultivation, but it is the ever-present knout, the police spying, the oppression of serfs by sadistic German bailiffs, as well as the drunken boyars in their dirty linen dancing in Moscow ballrooms, which give all these pictures their sombre and haunting general tone. To visit this country, you understand, is an ordeal. "What has man done to God [asks the Marquis de Custine] that twenty million people are condemned to live in Russia?"

Nor is the picture painted of Russian life by Russian writers – by Gogol, Herzen, Dostoievsky, Aksakoff, Gorki – significantly brighter. All depict a fierce and uncomfortable society suffering under a tyrannous despotism, a semi-civilised organism with few merits and no claim whatsoever to confer benefit on the tribes conquered by its soldiers. Yet again and again we read in official writings – apologists, military historians – that "in the broad spaces of Central Asia, Russian civilisation and power must develop themselves inflexibly and unceasingly". In the Crimea and in the Caucasus (as well as in the convict settlements of Siberia) already existed a model of what conquest by Russian civilisation really meant: whole populations removed from their homeland and decimated by transportation, as had happened to the tribes of Circassia; Russian taxes, passports, secret police and military rule; these benefits imposed by the corrupt bureaucracy of a central government whose political theory was contained in the words of Colonel Fadieieff: "All over Europe humanitarian views are giving way to the idea of the omnipotence of the State." As a poet called Taras Shefchenko warned the mountain tribes after their final defeat, "Now you will be taught how prisons are built, how knouts are knotted, how chains are forged – and how they are endured."

No doubt it is the natural prejudice of an Englishman (unless he belongs to the modern school of historians who like to beat their forefathers' breasts with the cry *Vestra culpa!*) to believe in the benefit to our colonies of British institutions. But our system of rule in India forced even from a Frenchman the reluctant comment that "a sense of justice compels us to admit that Great Britain has not neglected in India any of the duties of a civilised government". By no observer whatever could the same compliment possibly be paid to Russia. "British policy in the East [wrote Grenville Murray] tends to protect the people against the malpractices of their native rulers; the policy of Russia is just the reverse, for it gives carte blanche to the chiefs just so long as they remain loyal to their conquerors." Russia's practice was made possible, as he says, by an autocracy's unlimited secret service budget available to "buy up Asiatic chiefs as fast as it wants them" – chiefs who, for a "red velvet dressing gown" and the "heavenly sherbet" of champagne, will sell their power and their subjects any day of the week. Vambéry, in his *History of Bokhara*, relates how General Per-offski had learnt to "tickle the haughty Nasrullah behind the ear with pompous titles", and certainly there was a good deal that looked suspicious in a subsequent emir's sudden retreat from Samarcand, in face of General Kaufmann's approach, to be left undisturbed as vassal-ruler of his emirate whilst the Russians tramped all over it on their way to attack Khiva. Indeed a titular ruler of Bokhara was to remain on his ancestors' throne, practising their immemorial cruelties and vices (Berezikov's novel contains photographs of a headsman decapitating his victims there) until the last emir decamped to Afghanistan with what treasure he could carry in 1924, and those final "physicians from the north", the Bolsheviks, at last "liberated" the city.

Bokhara, and its cruel king – the far-off glint of sapphire domes across the sand, the threat of cold steel, the fountains and the fruits of Zerafshan – lay at the heart of the spider's web which the word "Turkestan" spun within an Englishman's imagination. Burnes had drawn a clear and clever picture of the city in his widely read *Travels into Bokhara*, and Burnes had a colourful pen, so that a graphic background to the drama was available to the many people whose sympathy was aroused when they heard of Stoddart and Conolly trapped by that malignant spider in his vermin-infested pit. It was a graphic background, like an illustration to a tale in Grimm, or Scheherezade, of a remote and outlandish scene in which the two English officers suffered their ordeal. It caught and held the imagination. I felt the frisson of it myself as I looked ahead into the heat-hazed distances for a glimpse of those sapphire domes.

The trouble is that half-failed Soviet schemes of irrigation, the desert half cultivated, has blurred the clear line which once existed between steppe and oasis, and taken a good deal of the drama of contrasts out of the journey. I knew that the desert of Malik, an extent of sandy steppe between the two cities, had always divided the oasis of Samarcand from that of Bokhara, although the same river Zerafshan, "scatterer of gold", waters both. Was a patch of waste we dashed across, its sand and sky criss-crossed by pylons and cables, was that scrap all that was left of the famous desert? Soon the road again ran between cottonfields, here a gleam of water, there a glimpse of smooth mud walls enclosing poplar groves and flat-roofed dwellings. Had we entered the famous gardens of Bokhara?

Traffic thickened. A contraflow of donkeys came titupping against the rush of trucks and cars, stout owners drowsing on their saddles in robes and skull caps; wide loads of mulberry branches, donkey carts, bikes, furiously driven buses: you could have a collision with every century's transport in Asia's history. Heavy traffic is evidently so recent a fact of Russian roads that no one's habits yet make allowances for it, drivers using whichever side suited them best on the dual carriageway which began on the outskirts of Bokhara.

Just as irrigation has blurred the division between desert and sown, so suburbanisation does a good deal to obliterate under bricks and mortar the natural topography of a famous city's site. Rome's seven hills take careful counting nowadays. No far-off view apprised us of our approach to Bokhara the Holy: we were in the middle of the place before we knew it – lost of course – driving amongst colonies of low houses in stunning heat until we fetched up at journey's end in a builder's yard of unfinished development.

Stunning heat, and, like a liner adrift under a sullen sky, the Hotel Bokhara rose in tiers of decks above its lagoon of concrete. On this lagoon there seemed to float circular flower beds of unspeakable brilliance, like fluorescent life buoys flung down from the crippled ship.

I determined to make use of the guide whom Alex obliged the hotel to produce – a large soft lady with tangerine hair – simply as a map and guide-book lent to me for half a day. I would not allow myself to become interested by her personality any more than if it were the binding of a Baedeker. I would learn from her tour enough of the geography of Bokhara to find my own way about it next day, and trouble or irritate myself with nothing further. I would not let the woman, a Russian, place herself between me and the view, as I had let happen in Samarcand.

Out we started in the Moscva. How hot it was! The lady guide fanned herself amply with her notebook, so that scent-laden air swirled round the car (whose windows Alex kept shut, the temperature outside even higher than within) and we all breathed her slipstream. Would it rain, I asked, glancing at the lead-coloured sky? She smiled. It never rains at Bokhara at this season. There (she leaned across to point it out) there is such-and-such a public building, and there on the other hand is another. Party headquarters, Party offices, government buildings, rose in a cluster of towers from the only patch of ground a little higher than the rest, tiring the eye by their appearance, wearying the mind by the monotony of the interiors which it suggested. In the open space outside Bokhara's walled citadel, the Ark, we left Alex and Anatoly to fan themselves by the car in the shade of a *chinar* whilst the guide and I mounted the ramp which enters the fortified gateway. How very hot it was! The air trapped amongst the walls and little rooms of the fortress touched you like sticky fingers. Warmish myself, I was struck by the fuss this woman, born and brought up in Central Asia, made about the heat, flapping the front of her dress, dabbing her dewy hair line, smudging her lipstick, as though the mercury had never before risen to the 40° at which it stood that afternoon. Perhaps Russians make a point of not acclimatising to the heat, as a means of retaining a superior Russian birthright to air-conditioned Party offices. I don't know: I didn't want to speculate about her character and its possible quirks, and listened as little as possible to her voice until we stood together in front of a cartoon on the wall of one of the crooked, cramped museum rooms within the Ark. In the cartoon a Mephistophelian tsar encloses within his cloak a pyramid made up of the strata of Bokhariot society. Below the tsar's head a bloated Russian governor-general shares a throne with an emir grasping the instruments of slavery and torture: beneath them a crowd of richly robed nobles tramples upon a layer of mullahs, who in turn weigh heavily on a merchant class: the whole structure, and everyone in it, is supported on the crawling broken backs of labourers. The cartoon, I guessed, was a Bolshevik propaganda product of the 1920s, and evidently depicted life in Bokhara during its domination by tsarist Russia. I waited for her comment as we stood side by side looking at the suffering proletariat like so many toads under the harrow.

"You can see," she said, "how the People carried a double burden – at first."

"Which the Bolsheviks freed them from, you mean?"

"That is correct."

"But Moscow still – -"

"In 1924 last Emir of Bokhara –" here she looked at me with the portentously widened eyes of a prophetess revealing Truth – "was so much unkind with his people that all the people sent him away. After, the Soviet bring new order."

"Didn't Enver Pasha and the Nationalists fight the Soviets for national independence in the 1920s?"

Her eyes closed as I spoke, then re-opened: "This is not

correct," she said firmly. She had no difficulty or doubt about history and truth: having been correctly instructed, she wished to instruct me in what's correct. It was like elementary maths: any answer but the one in the book scores zero, or worse. Nor is there a welcome from teacher for any sign that the subject is interesting or familiar to the pupil: there seems to be no expectation of general culture or general knowledge amongst Russians. Perhaps the Soviet Union is too big: an empire composed of too many cultures for general knowledge. An inhabitant of Bokhara, like my present teacher, no more expects any knowledge of Bokhara's history in the Poles or Lithuanians she has been trained to instruct, than she herself knows anything of the history of Moldavia or Kamchatka. Besides, for centuries a Russian has had to be careful as to the orthodoxy of what he knows. History has for so long been invented by successive régimes – tsarist propaganda had the same creative approach to facts as the Soviets, always representing Waterloo, for instance, as a Russian victory – that it is not a subject you can safely know anything about until you have been instructed in it by the powers-that-be.

Certainly a discussion of the 1920s civil war in Turkestan, or of Enver Pasha's quixotic bid for power against the Soviets (a romantic episode matching Turkestan's romantic history which ended in his head being struck off by the scimitar of a traitor as he drank from a fountain) was not on the cards with my lady guide. She now distrusted me, spoke shortly and guardedly as we clattered through the citadel's rooms and passages. My interest had put her on the defensive. She would admit to no knowledge of any of the travellers to nineteenth-century Bokhara, Russian or European, whose tales and sufferings virtually created the place in Europe's imagination. She seemed never to have heard of Khanikov's or Vambéry's histories of the khanate. She was glad to be finished with the Ark.

"We now visit summer palace of emir, workshop of Uzbeg crafts where you may buy, many historical buildings."

Off we went by car through the heat, the clouds ever lower

and darker over the still trees. "It does look awfully like rain," I said.

She smiled, but impatiently. She had already given me the correct information about Bokhara's climate in May, and now pointed out the cotton cleaning plant which we were passing. From the summer palace, which the final emir built for himself in 1914 (his forebears had passed their summers at Samarcand before Russia took it from them), Anatoly was instructed to drive to the Kirov Park for the last leg of my tour. I had made no adverse comment on the palace, anxious to regain the guide's goodwill, if I could, by restricting myself to a low whistle at first seeing it which she was at liberty to take as a show of delighted admiration. It was a preposterous pile. Westernised to the extent that conquered Asiatics imported the ritzy veneer of turn-of-the-century Europe without the Ritz's solid comfort, the palace was oriental in the tawdriness of construction and decoration – a flim-flam palace by a pool of stagnant water. It was awful. My guide consulted her notes before remarking cautiously, "It is a building in two styles." I did not disagree with this.

Alex and Anatoly came with us into the Kirov Park, possibly for the exercise, for they set off down its concrete avenues at the cracking pace of a deputation sent to measure distances with their strides. It was no less hot. The concrete pools were all empty except for rubbish; from loudspeakers fixed to iron posts there drizzled music; marching in step over potholes and broken glass, passing roses pushing up through beds of weeds, we made a rapid circuit of the park, taking in its two tombs, Ismail Samanid's and the prophet Job's. A nod at the gate to the Regional Comedy Theatre, a nod to Lenin frowning at the theatre from his plinth, and we were back in the car, the tour's end in sight. We got out at the hotel. Exercise had so warmed up the guide that she fairly sparkled with sweat, but it was not a bead of sweat which splashed heavily onto her hand as she shook mine in farewell. I knew that it was rain, and so did she, but I made no comment and she did not look upwards, even to shake her fist at a sky which had let her down.

*　　*　　*

Looking out from my room over the glistening trees and wet roads I was glad of the rain. You think of earthquakes in such a stilly heat as this shower had already relieved; besides, to see Bokhara by varied and unusual lights, instead of by its unvarying sun only, is to have your view enlarged. I could not take adverse weather personally, like the thin English rain which seems vindictively directed against your plans, and rather enjoyed watching the shifting grey light over the town in intervals of reading at my window. By evening the sky had cleared.

Alex was always anxious that I should do something positive with my time. I think too that he was anxious to show his readiness to pay for anything I might wish to do; anyway, I had allowed him to book me a place at a Festival of Uzbeg Music which was to take place in the court of one of Bokhara's medressehs that evening. After supper thither I went, aboard a coach taking a tour group from the hotel.

In the courtyard, in the clear evening air, twenty or thirty Europeans settled themselves rather uncomfortably onto the wooden bedsteads which serve well enough as seats if you are happy to squat cross-legged, and faced a stage erected in front of the façade of the medresseh. Through a curtain the musicians came out and twanged their instruments, and songsters came out and sang their songs, the performances amplified through loudspeakers which carried every note to the deaf of distant oases. The artistes were well prepared to produce not only the music of Central Asia, but to accompany it with violent dances.

I watched with my hands over my ears. The turns were excellently done, but it seemed to me as the performers succeeded each other that a mistake had been made, the fundamental mistake of lavishing so much training on the wrong people. No one had ever asked if our players were fitted to their parts physically: perhaps doctrinaire adherence to the principle of equal opportunities prevents the question being raised at a Communist casting-session. These game but dumpy Russian aunts kicking up their heels, and the shoe salesmen bawling out songs beside them, however accurately their feet hit the stage or their voices hit the notes, only suited their parts in the sense that a pantomime dame suits hers. True, in England amateur talent just as unsuitable often takes up Morris dancing or Scotch reels, stamping and jingling twice monthly, but in Britain, where peasants and clansmen are things of the past, there is no alternative to these artificial revivals by aunts and shoe salesmen. Here in Central Asia, on the other hand, the genuine article could easily enough be found, and a show put on in which the music and dance of the country was not the preserve of these bourgeois revivalists but the expression of a current vitality. I don't suppose Muslims would perform in a mosque building, but that too would be an advantage. Where the real thing is available, the counterfeit is inadequate. On an English nature trail you are resigned to the wolf being a stuffed one, but on a nature trail in Russia you may hope, surely, for the real thing.

The uproar on stage, the crescendo of song and dance, ended in an interval. When I withdrew my hands from my ears (having contrived to keep them there as if by an accident of the position in which I squatted on my bedstead) I was at once aware of the swifts speeding and screaming above the roofs. I couldn't help wishing this mosque courtyard was ruined and empty like the Bibi Hanum at Samarcand. My position was a little to one side of the crowd, and my nearest neighbours, three ladies from England, had gone off for refreshments, so I was able to sit quietly and look about. I thought of Arthur Conolly, and wondered if he had seen from his prison window this evening sky criss-crossed by the cruel freedom of swifts and swallows. Or he might have seen them through the grating of the underground pit in which Nasrullah kept him. The sufferings of this gentle soul are almost unbearable to read of.

But back came the three English ladies, stepping lightly with plastic cups of wine, and my attention became wholly absorbed in them. Settling as gaily as they could onto their uncomfortable bedstead, lips puckered by the wine's sourness, they turned shudders into laughs and discussed absent friends. I watched them, and thought about them, and listened to their voices. All day my observations and reflections had been taken up, willy nilly, by people – by Alex and Anatoly, by my hot guide, now by these neighbours – and I thought of something Mark Pattison said, that he had not the power of commanding his attention in the presence of another human being. Nor have I. Once let a link form itself, one little hook of interest snag your mind, and it is fatal to the buoyancy of solitude. I had not come to Bokhara to study these English ladies on the next bedstead, but they stood foursquare between me and the view. Things got worse after the interval. As at a sing-song in a holiday camp there were audience participation numbers in which a crowd of all shapes and ages danced to the music and sang along with the vocalists. I decided to walk home. At least from my guide I had learned the geography of the town, and at least I had tomorrow to myself. In streets that were silent under the stars pleasure soon returned, contentment with being where I was, and I remembered the phrase of the Kashmiri, Mohun Lal, who had travelled with Burnes to this remote and dangerous city: "When the day is closed and the drum is beaten, none dare venture to walk in the streets of Bokhara the Holy."

II

Clouds, slow and sultry, were again moving across the sky next morning when I set out on foot for the old town from the world of concrete surrounding the hotel. It was hot, but not the breathless heat of yesterday before the rain. Soon I was among lanes between half-ruined walls, crossing patches of open ground littered with rubbish, stepping into the sudden shadow and echo of an alley – amongst the evidence of decay which alternates, in a prosperous old Eastern town, with the glimpse through an arch into some verdant court-yard round a dripping fountain, for within a hovel-like exterior may be found the shade and water of the Muslim paradise. These were the streets Colonel Stoddart rode through on his way to his first meeting with Emir Nasrullah in December 1838.

The children stopped playing, a foot on a bicycle pedal, a fist raised to strike a friend, to stare at me out of curious eyes. Smaller sisters with fingers in mouths came to doorways to watch me pass. Stoddart had been in the East, at Teheran and Herat, for three years before he was sent to Bokhara; but he had never been on his own in the hostile East beyond British power. What did he make of the straw-flecked mud walls in these twisting streets, of the tracery of the low carved doors? Against all advice and precedent he was on horseback in a city where infidels were forbidden to ride. Burnes and his party, in Bokhara four years earlier, had all walked, and had all sub-mitted to put on the cap and waist cord of the unbeliever.* Did Stoddart as he rode past mosques and medressehs feel the threat from their stork-capped minarets and turquoise domes? He was (wrote his friend Captain Grover) "a mere soldier, a man of the greatest bravery and determination, with a delicate sense of a soldier's honour; but he was a man of impulse, with no more power of self-control than an infant . . . for a diplomatic mission, requiring coolness and self-command, a man less adapted to the purpose could not readily be met with". How did he come to be chosen for this adventure? Successful at intimidating the Afghans at Herat out of accepting Persian (and with it, Russian) influence, he had been sent by the Minister at Teheran, Sir John MacNeill, to dissuade the Emir Nasrullah from accepting the same Russian influence at Bokhara. He was certainly pleased with himself, under the cloak of humility: to his parson brother in England he wrote of his Herat success, "I cannot tell you how thankful to the Almighty I feel at being the humble means of effecting this

---

* "Our first care on entering Bokhara was to change our garb and conform to the usages prescribed by the laws of the country . . . we knew also that none but a Mohammedan might ride within the walls of the city, and had an inward feeling which told us to be satisfied if we were permitted, at such trifling sacrifices, to continue our abode in the capital" – Alexander Burnes.

change from War to Peace." In keeping with Captain Grover's sketch of his character, and with his own notion of how to browbeat a native ruler, he doubtless felt grimly secure on horseback in these streets thronged with every race in Asia as he drew near the central markets of the city, his horse carrying him above the crowd in a fretting wind off the desert. He would have seen these sandy buildings, heard the doves purring in the recesses of the markets' many domes, ridden through the sunshafts which fall on the many-tinted robes of the crowd. His heart might have beat a little faster when first he caught sight of the tall dust-coloured minar, the Tower of Death, which rises above the medressehs and mosques whose domes and flat roofs make up the skyline of Bokhara. But I imagine him to have been riding in that glassy state of pride which is aware only of self – which takes in nothing of the outside world, being intent wholly on holding up the fabric from within. The streets, the crowd, the colours were a blurred background to the bold personal adventure of a man determined to assert what he believed to be the dignity essential to a British envoy. He saw no more of the background to his ride than a man charging with the Light Brigade saw of the wild flowers in the Balaclava turf.

And like such a brave soldier, he was in that state of nervous excitement which sees an enemy to be sabred in whoever touches him or tries to interfere with his blinkered charge. "Now [says Grover], the Oozbeg etiquette requires that a person on being presented to the Emir should be supported by two attendants on entering the presence-chamber, who place their hands under his armpits." Stoddart wasn't having this. "Not being disposed to submit . . . he shook off these attendants. The master of ceremonies now approached." This dignitary's attempt to frisk the colonel for weapons fared even less well, for "his zeal was rewarded by a blow, which laid him prostrate; and Colonel Stoddart entered alone into the royal presence-chamber".

Can any man in history, about to be received by the autocrat of a remote kingdom – a tyrant who has waded through his brothers' blood to the throne – can anyone ever have behaved with more misguided effrontery? No doubt it was Stoddart's reflex response to the sensation of edginess he must have felt on entering the Ark by its sloping tunnel between bastion towers, like the entry into a fortress of the middle ages, and making his way amid the jingle of armed natives by passages and little courts to the centre of the web. He wished to be back in the saddle, controlling events, not pushed about by "Oozbeg etiquette". In a letter he wrote three years later, still the emir's prisoner, he talks of "topping Death's grizzly fence", the choice of phrase showing this courageous man still defining his ordeal in terms of a foxhunter facing a double-oxer. Nerve was the thing. Nerve and dash would carry you over. He would have betrayed his idea of himself if he had used Burnes' pliability in creeping about unnoticed in a suit of inoffensive mufti. Placed on half pay in 1833, Stoddart does not seem to have had much of a military career behind him; here was his opportunity, as envoy of his Queen – which he certainly believed himself to be, whatever Lord Aberdeen at the Foreign Office was later to write about "private travellers" – here was his chance to show an uncompromising boldness, the best of British characteristics as he understood them, in face of the airs of a petty sovereign. So he rode through the streets, and buffeted the chamberlain aside, and strode into the emir's presence in his flashy full dress, his sword at his hip, quite in the style of one of the knights in Tennyson come from Camelot to search out the wizard in his barbarous haunt.

I walked round the presence-chamber thinking of the scene and of Stoddart's character. It is about the size of a tennis court, open air, with a rough-paved floor and a raised platform a yard wide against two of its mud-brick walls. The tiles and bricks are much broken, and heaps of rubble moulder everywhere. Within the entrance stands the stone screen behind which those granted an audience must retire backwards out of the royal presence when they had learned their fate. This screen is the sole object left from the wreck of Nasrullah's grandeur, but it gave the place, to me at least, something tangible of the scene

I had so often imagined. The emir, strangely, appeared satisfied with Stoddart's visit, though he had seen him on horseback in the Registan before this, and had stared at him coldly and long. Goodness knows what schemes had animated his brain in those moments at the sight of this proud Englishman fallen into his grasp.

England's Indian Empire was a dreadfully confusing factor for a Central Asian strategist trying to assess England's strength. How could it be that an island far away to the west, which some said was merely a dependency of Russia, could yet rule the greatest and richest kingdom on earth, far beyond Kabul to the east, the kingdom of Hind? It was a conundrum. And British policy in Central Asia was indeed confused by being shaped from both London and Calcutta. The Europe-minded Foreign Office of Lord Palmerston and his contemporaries, of either political party, viewed these half-savage khanates as marginal to British interests, concerning itself chiefly with the balance of power in Europe. The East India Company at Calcutta, on the other hand, saw Central Asia close and clear, a great deal nearer than Europe, and expected a Russian invasion of India by way of the suborned kingdoms of Central Asia. Between London's indifference and Calcutta's apprehensions there was plenty of room for confusion and bad faith. Stoddart's mission to Bokhara was part of Calcutta's plan to baulk Russia in two ways: first, by persuading the emir to free all Russians held as slaves in his territory (these creatures were the victims of Turcoman border raids sold into slavery at the Khiva market) so that Russia should thereby lose her excuse for invading Bokhara; and, second, by persuading the emir of the delightful benefits of aligning himself with the all-powerful rulers of India, who were at that moment known to be assembling a fearsome host for the conquest of Afghanistan, his own neighbour across the Oxus. Charged with these commissions by Calcutta, Stoddart considered himself an envoy, and impressed his status upon the emir. But Lord Palmerston and Lord Aberdeen at the Foreign Office in London could not see a thirty-two-year-old captain with the local rank of lieutenent-colonel, who gave himself airs with an Asiatic kinglet, in at all the same limelight as Calcutta saw him, or as he saw himself. The difference in views was fatal to Stoddart.

As I found my way about the passages and courtyards of the Ark I wondered what assessment Stoddart made of the emir's character at that meeting, or indeed if he allowed the matter of character much weight. Mohun Lal starts off by giving Nasrullah rather a good reference, saying that, though severe, he is religious and just; but he is obliged to admit that "ambition" had caused him to murder all his brothers and all the chief nobles to secure the throne to himself. Ambitious, and careful too: his water was brought to him direct from the canal in a sealed container, food in a locked box from the kitchen, both to be tasted in his presence by a servant before he would eat or drink of them. For arousing his displeasure the punishments were various, cudgelling, execution with the knife, confinement in the *sia tchah* pit which crawled with vermin, or an assisted fall from the Tower of Death which overshadows every view of Bokhara. Knowledge of Stoddart's fate perhaps makes a modern visitor over-sensitive to all that was ominous and alarming about Nasrullah and his city. To Stoddart himself, Bokhara probably appeared, as it had done to Burnes, a fascinating and thriving town, its markets and streets full of the bustle of trade, altogether an enthralling spectacle of oriental life only faintly over-shadowed in his eyes (as it was in the eyes of the Bokhara crowd intent on their own affairs) by the presence within the Ark of a tyrannical ruler. Burnes in his enjoyment of the town noticed that even the beggars in Bokhara could afford ice in their water, and remarked on the beauty of its Jewesses, and surprised Mohun Lal by his energy in walking for enjoyment about the streets – "on foot in the hottest days, to feast his eyes, while a gentleman in India never moves a span without calling 'Bara chhata lao!'". Burnes wasn't granted an audience with the emir; perhaps it was as well for his health that those "small eyes, in a visage gaunt and pale" never activated the malevolence of the brain behind them by lighting upon him.

All poor Stoddart's pluck was needed on the fourth evening of his stay. Sent for by the emir's vizier, the *reiss*, he was set upon in the vizier's house by twelve men who seized and bound him. Then appeared the *reiss* himself armed with a long naked knife. "Colonel Stoddart, thinking his last hour had come [wrote Captain Grover] said in Persian 'May God forgive you your sins' and patiently awaited the result." The vizier soon darted off, whilst Stoddart was dragged about the town by the light of torches in the rain – one of his tormentors said that he must be a sorcerer, for "it is impossible that any human being could face death with such calm indifference" – until he was flung down, still bound, on his back on a board in a dark chamber where he lay two hours. Then by the glimmer of candles came a rustling muffled figure, whom Stoddart took to be the emir, to whom he made a dignified request for his liberty; but it was in fact the chief of police, who soon went away, Stoddart himself ending that night in the emir's pit-dungeon, where he was kept two months. "The blood [says Grover] tingles at my fingers' ends whilst I write these horrors."*

For three years Stoddart's life hung in the balance, now in this dungeon, now in that, now temporarily freed to live in the house of a sly servant of the emir, Abdul Sameet Khan. The British government did nothing in the least bit effective. Palmerston, then at the Foreign Office, would neither threaten the emir with force nor would he comply with the emir's request, which was simply that Queen Victoria herself might write to him, as he had written to her, instead of insulting him with letters signed by underlings. Many years later, speaking in the House of Commons in favour of sending an expedition to Abyssinia to force King Theodore to give up his British captives, Sir Henry Rawlinson (Oriental scholar and traveller and Indian administrator of great authority) cited England's loss of prestige in the matter of Stoddart's captivity as a chief

---

* It is hard to see how this account of Stoddart's heroic demeanour and sang froid can have been provided by any pen but his own.

cause of the Afghan rebellion and the Indian Mutiny. "Prestige [he said] may not be of paramount importance in Europe, but in the East, sir, our whole position depends upon it." Whether it was ignorance or wilfulness, the Foreign Office's want of understanding of the Asiatic mind in this matter was to cost Stoddart and Conolly their lives.

No doubt Englishmen in billycocks and tight, high-buttoned suits used to come and stay with the final emir before the Bolshevik Revolution ended his reign. If you were to saunter out of the Ark as the emir's guest, and board one of his motor-cars or landaus at the foot of the ramp (just where Stoddart and Conolly were executed), you would be driven off to the railway station or to the summer palace I had seen yesterday. The road passes along a street of glass-fronted shops, in front of them a raised wooden walkway to keep pedestrians out of dust or mud, and past municipal buildings constructed in the last emir's day out of a vile railway-tunnel brick. The visitor whirled through these up-to-date scenes in the back of the Daimler might well have overlooked (as visitors to Native States in India overlooked) the realities of both past and present in this picturesque little capital – the slaves, vice, corruption, persecution, which underlay what was on show for the emir's guests from Europe or from Russia. The benefits of Russian civilisation? On his return from St Petersburg, which he visited after his submission to General Kaufmann in 1868, the then emir (Nasrullah's son) had a dais and throne installed in his presence-chamber, upon which in future all emirs sat like European rulers instead of squatting like Asiatics. This, though, was the extent of the emir's reforms. Count Pahlen, visiting Bokhara as the tsar's envoy in 1908, records the repulsive condition of the prisons – holes in the ground covered by an iron grating which confined the captives in darkness, filth and hunger – as well as giving an unsavoury picture of the emir himself, "a cunning and acquisitive personality . . . one of the world's richest men", his wealth "amassed after the Russian occupation of Turkestan because of the protection he had gained as a result of our orderly administration".*

I did not take the brick-built street of shops and municipal buildings when I left the Ark, because I had noticed yesterday that the citadel's walls in the opposite direction had not been "restored", and still rose like melted toffee above the roofs of simpler dwellings. Walking that way I was at once in a lane between gardens, little watered enclosures of greenness around the doors of mud cottages, nothing very much, but interesting: a patch of vegetables round a fruit tree, a brood of ducklings scrambling after their mother across the hollows scooped out of the mud for melon beds, a child on a tin tricycle ignoring

---

* Count K. K. Pahlen, a Latvian landowner, was sent in 1908 by Nicholas II's command to make an investigation into the administration of Russian Turkestan, which had become a byword for incompetence and corruption. His own account of his mission, dictated from memory many years later, maintains two conflicting points of view: that of the patriot, asserting that the benefits bestowed on Central Asia by "just government" had made it "something akin to paradise" compared to British India; and the viewpoint of the zealous inspector, uncovering every kind of malpractice by Russian officials wherever he travels, and committing droves of them to trial and prison. The governor-general himself resigned as a result of Pahlen's disclosures. The Caspian fleet he found in rusty ruin; he found extortion and murder commonplace amongst the vices of the District Officers; the history of the attempted reconstruction of the Murghab Dam might stand as a case-book study of peculation and incompetence in colonial government: and yet Pahlen continues to speak of the happy benefit to the region of "European civilisation coming as a blessed and a freshening wind". His Report, published in twenty volumes, was widely discussed – and shelved without action. Turkestan resumed its old ways. "One of Gorbachev's first steps upon assuming power in 1985 [writes Francine du Plessix Gray in her *Soviet Women*] was to purge the Central Committee of Uzbekistan's Communist Party; as exposed by his régime, the network of graft and racketeering which had thrived . . . during the rule of Uzbek Party Chairman Sharaf Rashidov – a lethal gangster worshipped like a mediaeval khan by the Communist Party's local hierarchy – made the Gambino family's scandals look like kindergarten candy sales." (It was Francine du Plessix Gray who, with her husband, walked through the door of the National Hotel in Moscow the night I had been attacked there, and took time and trouble to interpret for me and splash me well with antiseptic.)

153

a tirade of scolding which issued from a dark door. Not much, but authentic. What is "authentic"? An atmosphere that convinces you, before you've had time to analyse it for anachronisms, of its intrinsical aptness to this place and its history. The wire enclosures, the tin tricycle – a hundred details were modern, but they didn't destroy the authenticity of the scene. Lanes threaded their course between these gardens and dwellings which lay higgledy-piggledy amongst vines and fruit trees. Above the leaves shading the low roofs rose the walls of the fortress against the sky, protection as natural as a dune of desert sand, so that the whole quarter of cottages and gardens lay snug in their shelter like a flock of sheep under a hedge. This arrangement – the citadel's protection of humble houses – made me realise that Bokhariots, the poor at least, had cause to be glad of their emir's strong rule in pre-Russian days of independence and warfare. For the subjects of an age-old absolutism must acquiesce in its tyranny; each nation evolves over centuries its own contract between ruler and ruled. In bargaining away their freedom (or the European idea of it) in return for permission to live and trade under those protecting walls in the most thriving market in Central Asia the Bokhariots had made a contract which was tolerable to themselves.

Russia didn't interfere with the emir's tyranny, except to demand the release of Russian-born slaves – a wonderfully progressive *casus belli*, from a nation that itself only abolished slave owning in 1861 – and I do not know of Colonel Stoddart having complained of the emir's rule before he became its victim. But Arthur Conolly brings into the picture a new moral element of regeneration and reform. It is agreed by his contemporaries that Conolly, at thirty-one a year younger than Stoddart, was as winning and warm-hearted a man as ever lived. "If the reader [wrote the historian Sir John Kaye] remembering what I have written about the careers and characters of Alexander Burnes and Henry Martyn [the saintly missionary], can conceive the idea of a man combining in his own person all that was excellent and lovable in both, and devoting his life to the pursuit of objects which each in turn sought to attain, the image of Arthur Conolly will stand in full perfection before

154

him . . . ready to dare everything and suffer everything in a good cause; full of faith and love and boundless charity, he strove without ceasing for the glory of God and for the good of his fellow men." This character that Kaye gives him, and his own purpose in travelling to Turkestan, separate him from Stoddart the soldier and political envoy. By his character and purpose his danger, if anything, was increased.

His father a merchant who had shaken the pagoda tree pretty energetically in eighteenth-century India, and one of six brothers all sent to the subcontinent, Arthur Conolly began his service at sixteen. At twenty-two, after an English leave, he returned to India through Turkey, Persia and Afghanistan, a journey which included being captured by Turcoman slavers during a dash towards Khiva – he was luckily turned loose again – and a journey which fixed in his mind the ambition to visit Kokand and Bokhara. He wrote a delightful account of these travels in which his charm of character shows in every incident, convincing the sceptical reader as the panegyrics of contemporaries never quite can. Listen to him on a night march with a Persian caravan between Herat and Kandahar, alone amongst such a gallimaufry at twenty-two:

> Being well clothed we felt the air bracing rather than unpleasantly cold, and as we had all become intimate, we rode socially along in the bright moonlight, chatting with each other, or joking aloud, whilst occasionally one of the party would shout out a wild Pushtoo song. Syud Moheen Shah and I had become great friends, and our affection for each other was strengthened by our mutual liking for tea: we generally took the first watch and cooked a kettleful which we drank sociably whilst the others were sleeping round us.

It is an enviable picture of an Eastern journey.

Once back in India, at Cawnpore, Conolly made a friend of the most outrageous and weird of all the figures travelling the East in those days, the Anglican missionary Dr Joseph Wolff, who had already been in Bokhara, and had rambled about the whole of Asia, and indeed the wide world, as if it were his

Yorkshire parish, disputing with mullahs, suffering beatings and imprisonments, even losing all his clothes to one set of attackers so that he was obliged to wander naked through the Pamir. This rumbustious clergyman is rather too absurd and far-fetched to seem credible when described, but he emerges from his own writings as a wholly convincing eccentric of strong magnetic charm.* Of his meetings with Conolly at Cawnpore – which were to be the cause of Wolff's narrowest squeak with death – he wrote that they "took sweet counsel and walked in the house of the Lord as friends".

Now occurred the chastening factor in Conolly's life. In India he fell in love with a travelling nobleman's daughter and, following her to England, became betrothed to her. For some reason unknown to me – and Conolly is at pains to blame no one for the wreck of his happiness – the engagement was broken off. Much dejected, as his letters of the time show, he took refuge in conceiving of a grand design, to free the slaves of the Central Asian khanates, and to keep Russian influence out of Turkestan by forming the emirates into a federation of independent states. Here were diplomacy and philanthropy hand in hand. In Constantinople on his way back to India from emotional shipwreck he held talks on the matter with an emissary of the Khan of Kokand who, with the Emirs of Bokhara and of Khiva, shared control of Turkestan. Encouraged by these talks Conolly next persuaded the Governor-General of India to approve a mission of himself and Henry Rawlinson to Khiva. But just then, in 1839, the Russian expedition under General Peroffski against Khiva (ostensibly to free Russian slaves) foundered in disaster in the freezing steppes of the Aral.

Lord Auckland, the governor-general, withdrew his permission. But Conolly stuck to his plan. Indeed it became an obsession, to which he added the further purpose of freeing

---

* I know of no more convincing endorsement of the Anglican Communion than the existence of this zealous figure, born a Jew and educated as a Catholic seminarist, who, after extensive and disputacious enquiry into sects in almost every corner of the world, was content to settle as a clergyman of the Church of England with a curacy in Yorkshire.

Colonel Stoddart from his detention at Bokhara. Peevishness, even jealousy, is detectable in Burnes' comments in a letter: "He is to regenerate Turkestan, free all the slaves, and looks upon our advent as a design of Providence to spread Christianity . . . Conolly having been beaten out of Kokand has chalked out for himself a mission to Bokhara to release Stoddart . . . he will stand a very fair chance of keeping Stoddart company if he goes."

What Arthur Conolly was determined upon was a mission in one direction or another. He directly disclaims that his broken engagement was the spur driving him into Godforsaken regions where he had once already fallen into the hands of the Turcomans; but he does say, writing of his disappointment at Lord Auckland's change of mind, "I felt the blank that a man must feel who has a heavy grief as the first thing to fall back upon." Go he would, somehow. No doubt he remembered the happy times drinking tea with Syud Moheen Shah on his earlier journey, and forgot its fears and hardships, for there is a real exhilaration in his letters to Rawlinson (whose promotion had meant that he could not accompany Conolly) when he is sure at last, in August 1840, that he is really off. In describing the significance of Rawlinson's new work, that of uniting the Afghans (under Shah Soojah and British protection) into a state which was to stabilise the North-West Frontier, Conolly was no doubt thinking of his own work too, the mission of creating a federation of Turkestan's rulers – as well as rescuing Stoddart and releasing other captives and slaves of the khans – when he wrote to Rawlinson: "You've a great game, a noble game, before you . . . we may keep the Russians out of Toorkistan altogether, if the British Government would only play the grand game."

In walking about Bokhara that day, looking into mosques and medressehs, peering into corners between the cracks in plank doors – through one such crack I saw into a sandy yard where four or five of the shaggy little Bactrian camels were reposing – I came back now and again to the central maidan of the old city, the *divan beghi*. Over a large oblong pool lean ancient trees, mulberries and willows, whose leaves dapple a surface of shadow and sungleams. At one end stands the emblazoned façade of a medresseh, pierced by a drop arch and flanked by towers of pale narrow bricks: opposite this formal presence, across the water, sprawls at its leisure all the casual, easy-going entertainment of Asiatic town life of the old sort. Wooden bedsteads with dirty striped covers stand about on the stone flags near the pool. From a ramshackle *chai han* tea may be bought, or bread and fruit, or sherbet. Customers of every race between China and the Black Sea, some in robes, some in suits, some in rags, squat on the bedsteads playing draughts, or talking in screeching tones, or making a ceremony of stirring quantities of sugar into their tea-glasses with tinkling spoons: behind the crowd rises a jungle of green leaves filling a small garden up a flight of steps, its promise of shade completing the tally of comforts needed for peace and rest in a desert life – water, shade, refreshment, and, reflected in the water, the arches and cupolas of the Faith. To be alone in an unregarded corner of such a scene is a pleasant moment, and I sat tailor-fashion on my bedstead stirring my tea, my book in my lap, contented with the spot to which my journey had brought me.

I didn't read: my thoughts still followed Stoddart and Conolly. Indeed I reflected on the two of them all day. The drawing together of the strands of the story – the enticement of the second fly, Conolly, into a web baited with the first – was a perfect tragedy, for the fate of each followed inevitably upon the development of the character of each; and the emir too played out his part wholly in character, so that the catastrophe is no surprise, but the outcome of intertwined destinies. I think it is in the *Phaedra* that the chorus warns in an early scene, "Things are already set in train; there is not much left to do", and the same might be said of the Bokhara victims from the moment MacNeill chose Stoddart as his legate to Nasrullah.

In the summer of 1841, when Arthur Conolly was at last able to set out on his mission to regenerate Turkestan, Colonel Stoddart viewed his own altered situation at Bokhara with self-satisfaction. "Thank God [he wrote] I have fought my way from imprisonment to the highest favour." He was then living at the house of the Russian envoy, and indeed had refused to take advantage of the emir's permission to quit Bokhara under Russian escort to Orenburg, saying that he had not been ordered away from his post by his own government and refused to profit by the intercession of a foreign power – the helping Russian hand no doubt made uncomfortable to his ticklish sense of honour by the fact that his own purpose in Bokhara had been to frustrate Russian designs on the khanate – and adding also, to the emir himself, "No doubt the Russians would treat me well, but when my own government demands me, what will your Highness answer?" At which "noble answer" the emir laid his own cloak of rich sables on the colonel's shoulders and bade him ride where he liked through Bokhara the Holy. Nasrullah must have laughed in his quilted sleeve to see his sables so temporarily laid upon that prison-wasted frame, for Stoddart was caught fast, trapped as much by his own soldierly characteristics of honour and courage as by his captor's orders. That the experiences of three years in the hands of this capricious despot had affected Stoddart's judgement – had brainwashed him into an oriental attitude – may be surmised from his choice of the words "highest favour" to describe an enviable situation. "Highest favour" is the description of a perch attained by a dependent servant fawning his way upward at an oriental court, to be tumbled down to nothing by the frown of caprice. It is not a European term. "Influence" is what the envoy of Great Britain set out to achieve with a native ruler, not "favour". The Colonel Stoddart who had first swaggered into the Ark and knocked out the chamberlain would have sneered at the emir's "highest favour". But living a life dependent on the whims of a tyrant, with periods of favour the only relief from immersions in intolerable dungeons, had brainwashed him until he looked at matters as did the oriental courtiers who were his only company. Under duress he had even repeated the Muslim creed. It was in this altered character, and more or less as a creature of Nasrullah's, that Stoddart sent Conolly an invitation to join him at Bokhara.

Conolly had been travelling in Turkestan for nine or ten months, had visited both Merv and Khiva, and was now, in the autumn of 1841, in the camp of the Khan of Kokand, who was (as usual) at war with Bokhara. So anxious, however, was Nasrullah to catch Conolly too for his menagerie of Englishmen that he promised a slave his freedom if he carried Stoddart's invitation safe through enemy lines. When Conolly accepted it, and came into the emir's camp at Mehram, he was sent under escort to Bokhara. By mid-November Nasrullah had both men in his grasp in one house in his capital.

Quite what the emir wanted, if indeed he wanted anything rational or specific, is as hard to make out as are the intentions of modern hostage-takers in the Middle East. To keep up his prestige with fellow tyrants at Kokand and Khiva he perhaps caught at the Englishmen as a means of showing that he had the power to command the attention of the rulers of India, who had by that time established themselves also as the sovereign power at Kabul. Whether it was British policy deliberately to deny the emir this source of prestige, or whether it was mere muddle and vacillation (as Captain Grover claimed), the rulers of India more or less ignored Nasrullah and his two prisoners.

It isn't easy to make a fair judgement of the London and Calcutta governments' behaviour in the affair. Perhaps Stoddart was an envoy of sorts, but he had only been locally commissioned, by the East India Company's representative at Teheran, and was a person of no standing: perhaps Conolly's journey had been, as Grover claimed, "sanctioned in a private letter from authority", though Lord Auckland's successor as governor-general denied it. Certainly neither man was a diplomatist; both were obscure young Indian officers eager for the adventure which brings fame or death, and in this they were material ready to a government's hand in the equivocal game of testing the water in Turkestan without making that official commitment which would have to be backed with troops in case of failure. Not Conolly's "noble game", quite, but the half-hidden "great game" an Imperial government must play to protect its interests, using for its purpose the noble-minded if need be. In a later age they would have sent spies disguised as salesmen, or as embassy attachés, but there was no organised secret service at that date. So, if one or two of these young adventurers went astray and found himself in hot water, so far as Whitehall and Calcutta were concerned he immediately became the "private gentleman" and "innocent traveller" of the mild rebukes which the governor-general despatched to the emir.

Neither the governor-general's mild rebukes nor the letter which Lord Palmerston wrote him, in English – it was a reply to the letter he had himself addressed to Queen Victoria assuring her of his friendship as a fellow sovereign – were at all what Nasrullah had hoped for. There was no prestige to be had from a letter from a government servant; and another letter which the post brought, one which the British had persuaded the Sultan of Turkey to write him about his prisoners, so provoked him that he threw it away exclaiming, "This man is half a Kaffir!" What the emir wanted was a letter from Queen Victoria herself. In this he persisted, furious with Conolly and Stoddart for not being important enough to elicit the prestigious correspondence he hankered after. Soon after Lord Palmerston's inadequate letter had arrived at Bokhara, the two Englishmen were thrust into a dungeon.

They were imprisoned about the middle of December 1841, at a time when news of an event very significant for British power in the East must have come to the emir's long ears. In November had occurred the Afghan rising against British occupation, and the murder in Kabul not only of Sir William Macnaghten (political head of the British Mission) but of Sir Alexander Burnes himself.* To these outrages the British army under hesitant, doddering generals lay quiet in its vulner-

---

* I wonder if it had ever been brought to the emir's notice that Burnes had slipped through his fingers ten years earlier at Bokhara? – Burnes, who had written contemptuously of Asiatics, "Simple people! They imagine a spy must measure their forts and walls; they have no idea of the value of conversation." Were Stoddart and Conolly paying a debt incurred by Burnes?

able camp outside Kabul and made no response – took no action to exact revenge, only sought terms for a disgraceful withdrawal. In January 1842 the entire army was slaughtered at the hands of the clansman Akbar Khan as it retreated towards India. If (as Rawlinson claimed) the British position in Afghanistan had been weakened by British inaction over Stoddart's imprisonment, then Stoddart and Conolly's position after the débâcle to British arms in Afghanistan became fatally insecure. The emir could do what he liked to them without fear of British reprisal. But more than that, I imagine him to have been disgusted to find that Great Britain, upon which he had depended to enhance his own prestige, and whose sovereign he had prepared to treat as an equal, was nothing but a broken reed. He might as well have captured a couple of Dutchmen. That he had deceived himself made his rage vengeful.

Until the end of May 1842 the two prisoners contrived to keep up a correspondence, in letters smuggled somehow to the outside world, as well as to keep a journal account of their sufferings in minute characters in the margins of Conolly's prayer book. Their misery, Conolly breaking down in illness, the little flickers of hope in Satanic darkness, rend the heart of a reader. Their spirit, and indomitable faith, the true mettle of their characters under such cruelties, bring tears to the eyes. Again one thinks of modern hostages in the Middle East. Near the end Conolly writes that he and "my poor brother Stoddart" have found their "hearts comforted, as if an angel had spoken to them, resolved, please God, to wear our English honesty and dignity to the last, within all the filth and misery that this monster may try to degrade us with".

That this journal of their tortures should have survived is a miracle. The prayer book was bought in the Bokhara market by a Russian prisoner and given to General Ignatieff on his visit to the city in 1858, whence it came to be left, one evening four years later, on the doorstep of Conolly's sister's house in Eaton Place in London. I wish I had been present to see how it affected her. From mid-Victorian Belgravia's gas-light and hansom cabs Bokhara and her brother's ordeal must have seemed as remote, in time and place, as a tale of the Crusades: yet she had the details in her hand, cramped small in a brother's familiar writing in his own prayer book's margins. I wonder if she put the book in a drawer and went out to dinner; or if she went upstairs and read the children to sleep with something out of the *Arabian Nights Entertainments*.* Three others of her brothers had by this date met their deaths in the East, one murdered by a native, another as a prisoner of the Afghans after the Kabul disaster; yet it is painful to discover how ineffectively Victorian hearts were cauterised by the frequency of tragedies' occurrence in their families, and Mrs Macnaghten's heart, which carried the scars of these violent deaths, will have been comforted by the certainty that her brother Arthur faced his executioner "with English honesty and dignity to the last", as he had prayed to do, on the patch of bloody ground outside the Ark at Bokhara.

The circuit of my day alone in Bokhara brought me back at last to the Ark's ramped entrance between fortress walls. I had walked more or less everywhere about the town, into mosques and medressehs, under the remains of the covered bazaar, into its shops, round its walls, through its streets; and I was pleased with everything, satisfied to have marinated the Bokhara of my imagination in a long day's reflective wandering through Bokhara itself. Just as my thoughts had returned again and again during the day to the Bokhara Victims, so my footsteps led me back in the end to the dusty waste under the Ark's arch-hooded gateway. This was the scene for the final act of the tragedy.

I know of a Victorian painting of Stoddart and Conolly herded along in beautifully pressed uniforms and rather theatrical chains by a crowd of tribesmen waving their weapons towards a dungeon tower in the early days of their captivity. I don't know of a painting of their death scene, which took place probably on June 17th 1842 close to where I stood, but

* The prayer book was subsequently lost, by carelessness as inconceivable as the miracle which had preserved it thus far.

163

I had seen inside the Ark a drawing of the manner of execution, and from the scribble in Conolly's prayer book their physical state can be learned. Half naked, emaciated into nail-lacerated skeletons by the fever and vermin of years, chained, the two Englishmen stood, or crouched, in the midsummer heat burning on the walls and the baked earth, whilst their graves were dug in front of them in the presence of a curious crowd. The executioner first seized Stoddart by the hair, dragged back his head, and cut the exposed throat with a huge butcher's knife. Then Conolly, it is said, was offered his life if he would repeat the Muslim creed. He refused with scorn, and his throat too was cut.

The wide space below the Ark's walls was almost deserted in the evening light as I walked to and fro thinking of the scene of execution. Early photographs show a bazaar crowded up against walls and gateway, which would no doubt be the case today if Bokhara was an Asiatic not a Russian town. As it was, taking advantage of Russian emptiness under the Russian-restored brickwork of the fortress, the only people in the maidan besides myself were four or five bare-chested youths kicking a football about between goals improvised from their shirts thrown down on the ground. The scud and thump of the kicked ball in the dust, and the players' scuffling feet, ranged over the probable graves of the two Englishmen.

Walking home, I steered myself through the alleys of the old town, as I had steered all day, by keeping a fix on the Kalyan Minar. Having left this landmark of old Bokhara behind, above the domes and cupolas, I switched to navigating upon a tall modern clock-tower which I knew to be near the hotel. As I came to it, and walked by, I noticed that on each of the tower's four faces was a clock, and that all four clocks had stopped. Nothing unusual in that; but here each clock had stopped at a different hour. Four separate mechanisms packed quite unnecessarily into the tower, where one works would have driven all, and all four broken down at once? This is incompetence on a tremendous scale. I looked to the statue of Lenin nearby, but he was striding angrily away down a half-finished avenue, a hand raised in exasperation. Above him the useless clock tower advertised its malfunction across the roofs of Bokhara, its blind gaze meeting, so to speak, the malignant eye of the emirs' Tower of Death, pale and beautiful and sinister in the last of the sun. Under the rule of one or other of these two towers, native or Russian, the Bokhariots have so far suffered. I couldn't help wondering how it would have been for them if Arthur Conolly had not been put to death, but had achieved his ambition of founding a federation of Central Asian states for them one hundred and fifty years ago under the aegis of Great Britain. That was the noble game he died for. I went into the hotel looking forward to a quiet evening.*

* There was in the time of Nasrullah a clock above the gate of the Ark, the only clock in all the kingdom of Bokhara, and the story of its maker combines so many of the ingredients of one of the tales of Scheherezade that, having heard it, the listener will be inclined to view the *Arabian Nights* in a fresh light of credulity ever after. A certain Italian, Giovanni Orlando, held in the 1840s the position of overseer on the estate of a rich Russian, Z——, whose unpleasant habit it was to encourage the marauding Kirghiz to raid this estate (which bordered upon their wilderness in the neighbourhood of Orenburg) and carry off the peasantry to sell them into slavery at Bokhara. This fate one day befell Giovanni Orlando, and the report of him being a *feringhee*, an unbeliever, piqued the terrible interest of Nasrullah, who sent for the captive and threatened him with death if he would not embrace Islam. The Italian, ingenious as he was stout-hearted, would not renounce his Faith but, from the pit into which he was cast before execution, offered to construct for the tyrant a machine for measuring Time. Such a wizard-like entice- ment, promising to extend his kingdom into the realm of sun and stars, was irresistible to Nasrullah. The clock was made, and Orlando appointed chief artificer to the cruel king. In this way all went along swimmingly until Nasrullah unfortunately dropped from the minaret at Bohoneddin the telescope which the Italian had made him (a toy which had extended even further the autocrat's meddling with the starry heavens) and sent for Orlando to put the mischief right. The chief arti- ficer, by an evil chance, had been out celebrating with an Armenian toper, and came to the emir unsteady on his legs. Again Nasrullah threw him into a dungeon and abjured him to renounce Christianity or to prepare to die. Orlando would not apostatise. Even though the executioner did to him as the Green Knight did to Sir Gawain – nicked

165

III

It was clearly never going to be possible to persuade Alex that I enjoyed dawdling about towns without a retinue, doing nothing in particular. He thought my day dreary. For my evening, out of kindness, he had taken things in hand. Swinging his black handbag he caught up with me in the hard currency shop, rarely open, where I was looking for postcards. (It shows the stage of development of Russian tourism, incidentally, that a postcard will usually feature a cluster of tourists in front of whatever building is photographed, with the intention of persuading the world that lots of tourists really visit the spot: an intention exactly opposite to that of the mendacious Italian postcard of a deserted beach or of the Spanish Steps empty except for the flower sellers.) I was looking through the views of Bokhara, often taken by photographers apparently too pressed for time to move a broken-down lorry or some other casual obstruction out of the foreground of the shot, when Alex spoke over my shoulder.

"For supper we go to *chai han* outside of town, okay? Friends invite us."

"But . . . but who – ?"

"Who is no problem. You will meet. You want postcards?"

Rapidly, with that appearance of impatience or even anger which seems to sour Soviet transactions, he spoke to the depressed woman knitting behind the counter. She didn't look at him, didn't glance at me, didn't speak, but peevishly gathered together all the postcards into a pile. This pile she poked into an envelope which she slammed down in front of me,

---

the skin of his neck so that drops of blood laced his throat – nothing would move his steadfastness. Next day he was beheaded. These events, which took place in 1851, are related in *Alcune Notizie Raccolte in un Viaggio a Bucara*, by Modesto Gavazzi, who came to Bokhara with two other Italians in 1863 in order to buy silkworm eggs (and were themselves imprisoned for a time); but Orlando's existence is confirmed in other books, notably Wolff's and Vambéry's, whilst Captain Shakespear once came across him on the road to Kokand.

again without a glance, and resumed knitting. Alex said: "You can take the postcards. Now we go to supper, okay? You come in late from your walk in the town."

"You've paid for the postcards?"

"No problem."

"Well – thank you Alex. Just let me go up and wash and change and I'll be ready." I felt I couldn't cry off their wretched supper after his munificence with the postcards. Then, waiting for the lift at his side, I changed my mind. "Alex, I'm tired and I don't think I will go with you to supper."

He took a fierce drag on his cigarette. "You want to eat here?" He was crestfallen but biting the bullet.

"Yes, I will. I'm tired," I repeated, wishing that the lift would come and take me out of this scene.

"Okay, we eat here. I will tell these friends we don't come."

"Why don't you and Anatoly go?"

He smiled his superior smile. "No way!" It was as if a prisoner had offered his gaoler the night off. But he was a human gaoler, and I saw a gleam in his eye which signalled that he would accept the plan if urged. I urged.

Whether the rôle of gooseberry was pure courtesy on Alex's part, or whether he stuck to me for professional reasons, I didn't know. From that evening, though, when he and Anatoly played truant, Alex loosened up a little towards me, as if I'd been allowed to share a wink with one of the prefects behind the headmaster's back. Next morning he came and banged on my door with another suggestion, for lunch this time, as guests of an old schoolfellow of Anatoly's. I couldn't refuse lunch after turning down supper, so I accepted with enthusiasm.

Falling in with plans made for you by others, and accepting whatever results from them with stoicism, is one way of travelling, and it is a way that broadens and varies your experience of foreign scenes to an extent that following your own inclinations does not. All the same, driven at reckless speeds hither and thither about the suburbs of Bokhara in a bigwig's limo by his teenage driver, I wished myself back on my feet in the old town. It seemed to be driving for driving's sake. First we sped to an outlying park, our suave light-suited Uzbeg host beside his driver (Alex and myself in the back), where we tramped about under the trees until we met Anatoly talking to two other men by a defunct fountain. Everyone jumped into their cars and sped on. The limo's owner, who was a pleasant, saturnine, rather flashy fellow, draped himself over the back of his seat and chatted to Alex while the boy racer took on everything on the road, at last tearing out of Bokhara altogether and speeding between flat cottonfields. My Russian journey so far had aroused a good many varied feelings in me since I'd left the Travellers' Club, but this pointless, reckless drive was the first event that had thoroughly exasperated me.

Still, the minute we reached our destination, and had walked through the *chai han*'s mud yard up a step or two into a bare little back room where a table had been laid with inviting care – a still life painted on the cloth with the colours of vegetables and flowers – I was touched to the heart by such considered hospitality. Plastic curtains to the room's little windows were its only decoration; these were drawn, making the half-light seem cool after the great heat at the door. We sat down on simple chairs, and soon the picture before us was generously dismantled by hands passing dishes about the table. Bread too was torn up liberally, and vodka gurgled liberally into bowls. Such eager, attentive hospitality made the meal a feast.

Though all seven of us who had arrived in the two cars sat down at the table, three or four voices only kept up the talk which echoed between the bare distempered walls. The rest ate and drank, and kept respectfully silent. In Italy – even in Rome, in Trastevere – I have eaten in simple houses where my host himself (let alone his wife) didn't think it proper or comfortable to sit down with me, but served me and talked to me whilst I ate. In Asia everyone sits down together, liegeman with chief, in the tradition of a tribal society, but the humbler ranks don't join in the conversation. It is an egalitarianism which must have adapted itself more smoothly to a Communist society than has the European custom of separate dining rooms for servant and master, an arrangement which cannot conceal class distinction under an appearance of equality. Our teenage driver, for instance, restored himself with food and drink as freely as anyone, but he did not speak or look as though he wanted to speak, apparently content with his place below the tacitly agreed but unseen salt cellar. The invisible division does not offend the Marxist in at all the same way as it would offend him to see a chauffeur sent off to enjoy himself as noisily as he likes in the servants' hall.*

Amongst the rest of the party there was, as usual, less of conversation than of speech-making. First came the formal addresses made to me by each of our three Uzbeg hosts, which followed the well-trodden path through parterres of welcome and good wishes to the fountain of vodka at which a toast could be proposed and bowls thirstily emptied. Everyone at the table drank save Anatoly. I had always noticed him sipping a thimbleful where others drank a bottle, and today he took none, explaining to me that he suffered from a complaint of the liver – here he laid his hand tenderly on his tracksuit and knitted his face in a painful grimace – which, with bad water and the vast amounts of alcohol tipped into the system, must be an ailment pretty usual in Central Asia. Russian drinking has always appalled foreigners – "to drink [says *Murray's Guide* for 1849] seems a greater necessity to a Russian than to eat" – and the vodka which had for so long been the Russian serf's only solace came with serf armies into Turkestan, despite Islamic law, to do as much damage to the tribesmen as liquor did to the American Indians. A nation could not drink vodka for its taste, only for its effect: it is the drink of an unhappy race wanting no stops and no scenery along the road to oblivion.

I drank, and trusted at least to a remedial spin-off, for the Bokhara water, in which raw vegetables and fruit had all been well soused, has the reputation of centuries for exceptional foulness, infecting those who drink it with the Bokhara boil, a kind of guinea worm. I supped an impenetrable soup, ate

---

* "In the East, though there is much familiarity, there is little social intercourse; and, in Europe, good manners teach us to consider everyone at the same board on an equality" – A. Burnes.

quantities of bread and onion with the shashlicks, responded to a few questions, smiled a lot and drank the unavoidable toasts. I was on my feet, and halfway through my own insouciant speechlet, when I noticed with what close attention my hosts were listening to Alex's translation of my words, the fellow in the café-au-lait suit in particular pinching the bridge of his nose, eyes closed, as he frowned with the concentration of catching every syllable. I had overdone the nonchalance. I tried to look grave. I tacked on a few weightier words, but they had the effect of coal barges behind a rowing boat, and I knew that I wasn't fulfilling expectations. A "writer" in Russia, certainly a foreign writer with an entourage, is a personage in a completely different category from a writer (unless he is well known) in England. He is a delegate, a representative, an official. I hadn't thought of that until now. All I had offered was the response to hospitality of a private traveller, and they had hoped for a lecture. The man in the pale suit took the bull by the horns and asked me through Alex the burning question of the moment in Uzbekistan: "What will happen now with Mrs Thatcher?"

I pulled myself together. "I think that Mrs Thatcher will lose the next general election and never be heard of again."

A stir greeted the translation of this bombshell. "But she is best known of all English politicians!"

"The best English leader, too," I said, "but that won't save her. She'll go out and some man will come in whose name nobody outside England can remember."

"Why is this?"

"Democracy. Two more or less equal parties voted in and out on little issues at home that you've never heard of. Taxes, hospitals, things the voters think matter far more than having a prime minister people throughout the world have heard of and respect."

"So, by democracy your best leader will go?"

"Mr Gorbachev is your best leader," I said, "Russia's greatest international figure for decades, and a genius – but wouldn't free elections turn him out of office in Russia?"

"Oh – Gorbachev! He is all talk talk. No actions to help

Russian peoples." Alex opened and shut his fingers to imitate
the quack of idle talk. It was the first sign he had let show of
endorsing the opinions that he translated for me. We talked a
little about the fact that foreign policy and international affairs
are no more than an afterthought in a democracy, hardly considered by the voters. I instanced British policy towards Russia
over this part of the world in the last century: on some minor
domestic matter Gladstone was voted out and Disraeli was
voted in, and as a consequence British generals rattled their
sabres in Afghanistan, and threatened the tsar with war, where
last month the same generals had been as mild as milk in face
of Russian aggression. What looks like irresolution is really the
alternating policies consequent upon two-party government
compared to the consistency of outlook you can only achieve
with autocracy. Mind you, anything other than shilly-shally
in British policy at that time – any one consistent policy over
India's frontiers – and there would have been a war for sure in
the region between Britain and Russia in the 1870s.

"But England did not fight for us against Russia," said the
man in the light suit, slowly wagging his head. There was a
silence. I thought of the white charger said to be kept caparisoned at Geok Tepe by the Turcomans, until their city was
stormed by the Russians, in the belief that an Englishman
would appear at the eleventh hour to rally them to victory.
Then another man, more diffident, asked, "What do you think
now about future for our peoples here?"

I had thought about it a good deal. "The most striking thing
to a stranger about the people here," I said, "people in the
street, I mean, or a crowd in a market, is the variety of the
races you see mixed up cheerfully together. I've asked Alex,
and he has pointed out Tadzhiks and Uzbegs and Turcomans
and Khazzaks and heaven knows who, all in the same crowd.
Because of the mixture I don't see how you could ever draw
frontiers. I don't see how you can ever have a separate sovereign state for each race. What I can imagine is a Republic of
Central Asia – all the old territories of Turkestan together in a
federation."

"Do the British think about Central Asia as you do?"

As a private traveller I was insufficient for them. "I expect some do," I said. "There was an Englishman called Arthur Conolly who had the idea of trying to found a federation of these states about one hundred and fifty years ago. He came to Bokhara. Is his name ever heard?"

They consulted one another with glances, shook their heads. I asked, "Do you think an independent federation could be economically self-sufficient?"

Again they shook their heads, without need of consultation this time. I was surprised at their realism: other Uzbegs had spoken of Russia's theft of their wealth – cotton, wool, gold, coal and meat – as though keeping these products in Turkestan was all that was needed to make the region rich. The isolation-ist policy of the Soviet Union, magnified in its effects on men's minds by the insulation of this remote place, has generated views on world affairs sometimes almost as naïve as might have been found in one of Nasrullah's courtiers. But economic realism didn't interfere with their political ambition as it should have done; despite inevitable dependence on the Soviet Union, it was an "independent" Uzbekistan, achieved no matter how, that they were determined upon. All this time the vodka was splashed out of bottles into our bowls, and the successive, heated voices dinned off the distempered walls. I asked about the boundaries between themselves and their neighbours, cit-ing the problem of Azerbaijan; how do you settle the frontiers between nomadic peoples, the borders of Uzbekistan, say, when there are Uzbegs over the Oxus in Afghanistan, or the borders of Turkmenia when there are Turcomans in Iran?

The man in the pale suit spread out his hands magnani-mously and tipped back his chair. "We will have boundaries," he said, "where they will cause no unhappiness."

There was optimism and idealism in the talk of these men, and a passionate earnestness, which would have encouraged Arthur Conolly's hopes for Turkestan's future in his own day. To end slavery – to form a federation of Muslim states independent of both Great Powers – this policy was what might be distin-guished as "the noble game" in Central Asia, in contrast to "the Great Game" of Conolly's high-handed and arrogant successors in the field. For with Conolly's death at Bokhara in 1842 his generation of travellers in Turkestan, men with noble objectives, came to an end.*

Whilst Conolly had been agitating for the governor-general's permission to travel to Khiva, in 1839, Captain James Abbott, another of these adventurous Indian Army officers, was serving with Major D'Arcy Todd's mission to keep the Persians and their Russian paymasters out of Herat. In December Todd sent him on a journey to Khiva, knowing that a Russian invasion of that khanate was imminent, to see if he could negotiate the Russian slaves' release and thus frustrate Russia's ostensible purpose in attacking Khiva, which was the chief slave market of Turkestan. The journey offered a fearful prospect, which Abbott's rather desponding temperament made the most of. He set out, he said, "to accomplish that of which the sanguine have no hope [as] a matter of duty, entered upon cheerfully".

Cheerful he was not. I know of no account of a dangerous journey in which so many of the author's private fears and tender sensibilities are allowed to remain in the narrative. Abbott didn't attempt to construct an alter ego to serve as the hero of his book, but drew as honest a self-portrait of his true self as he could. It is this honesty which makes his *Journey from Heraut to Khiva* exceptionally interesting: in reading, say, a Burnes' or a Burnaby's account of his adventures there is always the sly amusement which we take in watching how the mock-modest hero will contrive to tootle his own trumpet in ever so roundabout a manner, but with Abbott's alarms and uncertainties and sudden changes of mood the reader feels nothing but sympathy.

In the early pages his reflective style prepares us, with its insights into his temperament, for what is to follow. To an Uzbeg unable to understand his motivation he asserts that it is the desire of fame at home in England ("there is a society,

---

* "The designs of our government are honest [Conolly wrote] and they will work, with a blessing from God."

173

a public, whose opinion is of the utmost consequence to an Englishman") which has led him into this adventure, staking his life against the chance of fame in a nearly impossible commission. On every count he is apprehensive, and remains so throughout. Having survived Khiva itself, and having obtained from the khan a letter to the tsar at St Petersburg promising freedom to the Russian captives if Russia will withdraw her armies from his territory, still Abbott's spirits fail to rise. "I left Khiva [he mopes] under the most melancholy of auspices." Soon, "amid deep snow and a mist hurried by the east wind", he writes on his birthday (his thirty-third and still a captain), "The retrospect is full of bitterness. Faculties misapplied . . . powers and affections, diverted from their right object, to waste and prey upon the heart. And what is the present, to balance the gloom of years gone by? This day will long be remembered as one of the most miserable of my life." We learn of the murder, with all their suite, of two recent travellers, thought to have been Englishmen, whose fate is not talked of to Abbott, "for your case [says a servant] is exactly like theirs". Drawing ever closer to the journey's catastrophe he is brought by a camel driver a little injured bird which "by a homeless, friendless wanderer like myself was to be regarded with peculiar tenderness" as it hops into the candlelight at the foot of Abbott's bed. "None but he, who has been similarly circumstanced, can conjecture the hold, which the little thing had taken on my heart. In the morning, my first care was to attend to my wounded guest. I found it lying dead on the spot where it had slept. I dug a little grave, and buried it there. Incidents, trifling as this may seem, affect the tone of our feelings, and I was melancholy on the death of the little desert bird."*

---

* In another touching incident at this stage of his journey Abbott presents two silver spoons to two pretty Kuzzauk girls, daughters of his host, and is at pains to impress upon the rough assembly that these spoons of his ("they bear my crest and initial, and may puzzle some future traveller") are truly made of the precious metal; he seems to have had no thought of arousing his hosts' cupidity.

Within a few hours, on the shores of the Caspian, comes an attack upon Abbott's party by a band of Kuzzauk robbers. In a mêlée in the dark he is clubbed down and made prisoner. Injured (he lost two fingers to a knife-thrust), Abbott passes many miserable nights full of painful thoughts and fears between the days of exhausted misery spent hurrying with his captors over the frozen wastes. It is an extraordinarily interesting section of his book. At last the dire event feared by all these adventurous travellers, capture, had befallen him: very few lived to write up their journals.

He is certain of death, because it is only by killing him that the Kuzzauks can hope to hide their crime in having attacked the Khan of Khiva's envoy to the tsar. "They had no choice between my destruction and their own." One of his guards, "the giant, Afris Matoor", who is forever swinging an axe or trying its edge on his thumb, fills Abbott with dread: "the hideous and ominous expression of the features . . . made me conceive a sort of horror for him", and it is certainly this creature (Abbott decides) who will deal him the death-blow. "The approach of death [he claims] was no bugbear to one who had so often confronted it, but the fate of my people was a source of constant anxiety." He records too amongst his night fears some morbid and detailed apprehensions: "I meditated deeply upon Death . . . I never could quite reconcile myself to the shape in which it was ever threatening; namely, the crushing together of the brain beneath the hatchet of Afris Matoor . . . the head when struck off retains life until the blood has discharged itself from the vessels of the brain. The eyes open and shut. The lips and muscles move." Not, perhaps, a singular line of speculation for a mind under the shadow of death, but certainly unique among the printed anxieties of one of these soldier-travellers. In the night he asks one of his servants, a man he had bought out of slavery, to convey some day to India, if he can, the message that his last thoughts were of his mother and of his home. These are the chief issues in his mind – "for I stood upon the brink of Eternity" – but he records too the minor details which wake a reader's sympathy by their clarity: on two tin trays in the robbers' possession, for instance, he sees inscribed the maker's English name, "and this sight of a record of civilised life, made me for the moment envious of the meanest animal there".*

I had cherished for years the vivid impression which Captain Abbott's account of his feelings and fears had made on me, and so, when I came to open the book again (a copy I had bought in the intervening time) I was surprised – disappointed – to find myself reading an altogether duller and more conventional narrative than I remembered. A glance at the title-page showed that I was reading a second edition. In the preface to the first edition, looked up when I was next in the London Library, I found Abbott's apology "for instances of egotism, of which I was not aware, until I saw the book in print". Further on he writes, "I conceived that the personal narrative of a traveller through the steppes of Tartary could only be interesting, by drawing largely upon his sensations and emotions: I noted roughly every thought and fancy that could yet be recovered, intending to select carefully from the mass . . . The selection has, I feel, been injudicious." That, then, was the explanation of why the second edition was a duller book than the first: the intimacies which I had liked most about it had all been thought "injudicious". When I compared the two editions in detail I found that almost everything I have cited here had been either cut out or much modified. Abbott's account of the affray with the Kuzzauks he has shortened from ten pages to five. His night thoughts in his captors' hands are trimmed of the effusions which made them striking. Emotion

* How Abbott extricated himself from captivity, and reached St Petersburg and England, is an interesting narrative; and his subsequent career as an Indian officer, earning the thanks of both Houses of Parliament and winning a knighthood for holding the Marquella Pass with 1,500 matchlockmen against 16,000 Sikhs and 2,000 Afghan horsemen – as well as having the town of Abbottabad named for him – shows his remarkable powers. Abbott was a poet, too (there is a five-stanza dedication to Queen Victoria in his book, and a *vale* of equal length), and he wrote also a novel of Eastern life, this combination of talents showing that the balance of action and reflection, which makes his travels so unusually interesting, was the natural habit of his character.

and extravagance are everywhere curbed. Where Afris Matoor's grisly features "made me conceive a sort of horror of him" they now "prepossessed me against him". The Brummagem tin trays are omitted. The author no longer stands numbering his fears to us from "the brink of Eternity" but has schooled himself into the stern mental uniform and stiffened upper lip which, from about the date of Conolly's death at Bokhara, became the *de rigueur* habit of mind required of the imperialist traveller. Perhaps most significant of all Abbott's changes, he edited out of his second edition the asperity of his earlier criticisms of English society as it had struck him on arrival in England from St Petersburg at his journey's end. He had realised that an Indian officer who wanted to make his way was unwise to compare London society unfavourably with that of "our circle in Upper India". "In the present edition [wrote Abbott in the preface to his book's second edition of 1856, when he had had sixteen years to reflect upon the incidents of his journey and to reconstruct his attitude to them] it is to be hoped that many of these blemishes have been cut out." What is lost were not blemishes. It could be said that between the two editions of the book the noble game went out and the Great Game came in.

CHAPTER VI

Khiva

I

CAPTAIN ABBOTT STARTED for Khiva from Herat, and reached it through an expanse of wintry steppe on the left bank of the Oxus. From Bokhara to Khiva is about three hundred miles, the road crossing the Kyzil Kum desert on the Oxus' right bank, and because it was summer we woke at four-thirty in the morning and left Bokhara at five. Very different from the great heat in which we had reached the city, we drove out under a cool rainy sky. We had had no breakfast, but I trusted Alex and Anatoly as to that.

To cross even a part of the Kyzil Kum – to see the Turkestan desert at ground level instead of giving it the *de haut en bas* treatment by flying over it – was one of the reasons I had wanted to drive between the oasis towns of Central Asia. So now I looked out keenly for desert to begin whilst Alex produced his usual bursts of static from the radio and Anatoly fought the steering wheel.

We were about thirty miles from Bokhara before the cultivation of the landscape into cottonfields began to falter. The soil grew sandier, waste patches more extensive, the face of nature harsher. Groves of silver-leafed poplars were left behind, and the road was no longer lined by mulberry and elm. Without altering its structure the landscape shrugged off the works of man. It became again its primitive self, level and dim wastes of sand, a hard reddish granular surface tufted with spiny shrubs, which reached to every horizon. The sand formed low undulations, or occasionally hillocks enclosing the road, and a rare pool amid marsh grass flashed gunmetal water at the cloudy, hurrying sky. In such a pool I glimpsed a pair of tufted ducks swimming, and once an ash-coloured bird of prey drifted low over the sand; but across the desert the road lay straight and empty into infinite distance, the occasional black dot on the horizon enlarging itself into a truck we met with a rush, its slip-stream clapping into ours and shuddering the car like the lance of a jousting horseman shivering on plate armour.

About eight o'clock, three hours on our way, Anatoly pulled off the road into a hollow and stopped the car. We got out and met the desert. It was cold, the sands swept by a north wind pushing bruise-coloured clouds overhead. Leaving the shelter of the hollow with me to gather fuel for a fire from the levels of the desert, the wind blowing fierce and cold through our clothes, Alex claimed that the shrinking of the Aral Sea had altered the climate of Turkestan, affecting in particular this north wind out of the Russian steppes which sharpens its teeth on the salt wastes which now rim the Aral as the aftermath of too much irrigation and of chemical pollution. Because he was expressing a view himself, rather than translating the views of others in his usual neutral tone, I was interested, and opposed his argument with the view that the Aral has been drying up throughout recorded time, and has been little affected by Soviet policies.* Did he at last consider it safe to say what he thought to me, pulling up dead *saksaoul* together in the Kyzil Kum? I hoped so. As we shouted to one another in the wind a thin fragrant smoke from a kindling fire began to blow up to us from the hollow where Anatoly was active with his preparations for breakfast, and, as soon as each of us had gathered an armful of the spiny shrub, which clings to the sand with roots like a skeleton's hands, we carried it down and dumped it by his fire.

He had laid out a delicious meal. There was bread and cold

* "The great Blue Sea of Central Asia . . . occupies but a small portion of its former extent. It fills a shallow depression which is drying up with astonishing rapidity . . . large parts of it have dried up since the Russians took possession of its shores . . . Former rivers and channels, the main arteries of prosperous regions, have now disappeared." The 1910 edition of the *Encyclopaedia Britannica*, from which this passage is taken, tells also of shells found two hundred feet above the then sea level.

mutton, there was yoghurt in one jar, sour cream in another, there was fruit and handfuls of raisins, and raw carrots which Anatoly had sliced up with the sheath knife which was always in his hand. Whilst he carefully snapped the *saksaoul* and built the fire into a crackling pyramid he told me (through Alex) of the journeys he had made by car through Russia: to Odessa, once to Moscow itself. He was a practical traveller, and the blaze he took pains to build wasn't just to warm us or beguile us. I saw that he had set a glass bottle close to the flame, and in this vessel the heat soon began to agitate the water whilst he kneeled nearby making his preparations with the teapot. Afraid that the glass would burst I watched it as you watch a smouldering firework. But it did not burst. In a few minutes the water was bubbling away in it as if kettles might as well be made of glass as of anything else, and Anatoly, drawing the bottle from the fire with a couple of sticks, deftly tipped its contents onto the tea in his pot – Big Ben English Breakfast Tea, I was proud to note. We ate and drank comfortably by the crackling flames. As always with a good picnic, we seemed for the moment to be enjoying comforts wrested from nature by our own efforts, the hot tea and good bread, and the fruit from Bokhara's gardens, doing duty for what the hunter has trapped to cook over his bivouac fire.

When I had eaten all I wanted I climbed the slope out of our sheltered hollow. Near and far the desert was infinitely dreary under a sky of rapidly moving clouds. Again I was cold. The cheerless scene, the emptiness, the knowledge that these wastes of gravel extend to distances vast even by Russia's vastness – this was just the point of view I'd hoped for, to look into a wind singing drearily over the sands which have over centuries swallowed up much blood and treasure from Russia's many expeditions sent to capture Khiva.

The difficulty of conquering Khiva was the difficulty of getting an army to the spot. On every side lie its protecting deserts. There had already been three Russian failures before Peter the Great sent Beckovitch Cherkassky against Khiva, in 1717, with ambitious plans for sifting gold from the sands of the Oxus and for turning that river back into its old course so that it might empty into the Caspian. Thirst and heat destroyed a quarter of the force: the remaining 1,000 were invited into Khiva by its khan with the suggestion that, so as to be sure of comfortable quarters for all, they should divide up into seven handy parties to be billeted in different parts of the town. Only forty Russians survived the khan's arrangements. After this massacre no further military expedition was sent until December 1839, when General Peroffski led 5,000 men out of Orenburg to march on Khiva, giving the plight of the Russian captives sold at Khiva's slave market as the excuse for his attack. He had chosen the cold season instead of the heat and drought which had been fatal to Cherkassky, but winter in the Kyzil Kum was no less severe. His 5,000 camels, unable to scrape away the snow to feed, died in hundreds. His men froze. Despite shooting a rebellious camel driver *pour encourager les autres* Peroffski, with half his camels lost, was obliged to send the tsar a message – "obstacles which no foresight can take account of run counter to the success of the expedition" – and turn back at the halfway mark, giving up hope of opening the packet he was rumoured to have been given, its seal to be broken only at Khiva, which contained a coveted decoration. Meanwhile, in Khiva itself, Captain Abbott was just then undermining the Russian *casus belli* by negotiating the release of the Russian captives, a release put into effect the following summer by Captain Shakespear when he brought all 418 of these famous slaves safe to Orenburg, and was knighted by the Queen in consequence.

It took Russia thirty-three years to put together another expedition to Khiva, by which time the knight errant adventures of Abbott or Shakespear, together with Conolly's noble game, had given way to modern armaments and modern men, to the appalling Kaufmann and Skoboleff on the Russian side, and to the equally bombastic Burnaby or Baker playing the Great Game for England. Shakespear straddled the two eras: his extraordinary exploit of marshalling the 418 captives from their owners' hiding places (he rode back overnight ten miles into Khiva from his first camp to demand of the sulky khan one particularly beautiful Russian child so far concealed) – of providing a camel to each pair and food for all – of shepherding his party over eight hundred miles across desert and sea to Orenburg – is a wonderful achievement in a twenty-eight-year-old captain, but when he came to write up his adventures some years later, for *Blackwood's Magazine*, his style had already been weakened by the woodworm of facetiousness and mock modesty which hollows out the books of the Burnabys and Bakers of the next generation. As in Abbott's revised edition we are given not an honest sketch of the traveller's mind but the touched-up studio portrait of the traveller's alter ego, the hero of a Victorian novel. Given his orders at Herat to follow Abbott into the lion's jaws, aware that the khan's triumph over Russia will have made him careless of a European's life, Shakespear pretends that his response was this: "The hazard is so slight, that the heart of a wren would be gladdened at the prospect." Compared to the true little desert bird whose injuries and death had so touched Abbott's feelings, this wren of Shakespear's is an improbable creature.*

The event which had interposed between Shakespear's adventure and his account of it was the massacre of a British army in Afghanistan. Such treatment at the hands of tribesmen seems to have surprised young men such as Abbott or Eldred

---

* What feeling or friendship existed between Shakespear and Abbott is unclear, though Abbott does drop a hint of his resentment that he should have suffered many of the trials and pains of the enterprise, whilst Shakespear walked into Orenburg with the released captives and walked off with a knighthood (Abbott wasn't knighted until 1894, by which date Shakespear had been dead nearly thirty years). There happened to be at Orenburg in June 1840 a Mr Cottrell, an Englishman setting out to look round Siberia for his own amusement, who had met Abbott earlier in the year at a St Petersburg reception (when both had been presented to the tsar) and had evidently liked him. Cottrell writes: "Mr Shakespear was expected at Orenburg two or three days after we left it . . . his letter announcing his arrival with the freed captives was written in English and was almost wholly unintelligible to the learned of Orenburg. As an English traveller is not likely to be on the spot to interpret again, perhaps in this century, it would be as well for an agent of that sort to be able to write French. We perceive that he has since been knighted, but hope that Captain Abbott has received some more solid reward for his services.

Pottinger or Shakespear – surprised them out of the innocent idealism which had supported their spirits until then. Alexander Burnes, sanguine by nature and trusting much in his powers of rapport with the wild races of Asia, was nonetheless cut to pieces in the uprising in his own garden at Kabul – in the very garden whose flowers and arbours he had shown off to Vincent Eyre as symbols of Afghanistan's regeneration under British influence – and by his murder were warned all Englishmen who had trusted as he had done. What came to grief in that ghastly retreat was self-confidence, the basis of English prestige in the East, as well as confidence in a system which, though riddled with abuses, had always appeared to answer. The camel-loads of cigars brought up through the Bolan Pass for elderly general officers to smoke at Kabul – one general's private baggage required eighty camels* – were inevitable cankers in an army made top-heavy by a twenty-five-year European peace, but they were also a sign of British trust and confidence. The status quo no doubt seemed aggravating to ambitious young soldiers like Conolly or Abbott, but tolerable so long as their own adventurous efforts at self-advancement were permitted. In the "signal disaster" of the army's destruction in Afghanistan was shattered all that self-confidence, both the good and the bad of it, as well as England's eighteenth-century tolerance and trust towards the native races of the East. It began a process of enlightenment, a loss of innocence and naïveté, which the Mutiny in fifteen years' time was to complete. A watchfulness, a contrived hauteur laid over distrust, became the attitude of the traveller towards the tribesmen in whose company he rode. By 1870 an Irish viceroy of India, a man almost without experience of office, was instructing his staff "to teach your subordinates that we are all British gentlemen engaged in the magnificent work of governing an inferior race".

What was lost was the way in which a Conolly or an Abbott

---

* General Arnold who, perhaps not surprisingly, died of liver disease at Kabul. The sale of his possessions occupied three days, his cigars fetching up to half-a-crown each.

had contrived to view themselves and their field of action in a romantic light which had given their adventures and ordeals a long pedigree reaching back into the days of chivalry. In his early pages Abbott describes how he is surprised in the dark of his hut by the sudden arrival of an Afghan chief sent to him by the Khan of Herat to lead an escort of native soldiers. "When I looked up I saw before me a figure which almost startled me by its resemblance to our best portraits of Edward the Third." Of all mediaeval kings it was Edward III who was held to be the pattern of chivalry. Thus a note of knightly adventure is struck which the narrative sustains. It is deliberately done: the arrangement of society in the East, the customs and manners of Asia, its warfare and weapons, the character of its chieftains, all echoed mediaeval Europe, and left room in the picture for the traveller to take the protagonist's rôle of knight errant in a tale of adventure. In England just then the fashion for mediaevalism was at full tide, the Eglinton tournament having taken place whilst Abbott was at Herat – and for the Windsor *bal costumé* of 1842 it was as Edward III that Prince Albert dressed himself up, Landseer's portrait of the occasion showing him in a brilliant surcoat very like a Bokhara noble's robe – so that a reader of these Eastern adventures would take the hint and picture the book's author riding through an Ivanhoe-the-Terrible landscape towards one of Smirke's grim keeps, Eastnor or Lowther, where peacock colours and the glint of armour would mingle the enchantment and menace of Maclise's paintings behind a narrator spurring into the picture out of Tennyson's *Idylls of the King*.* It is how I see them

---

* Between Khiva and the Caspian Abbott writes of a "ruined castle . . . isolated by steep and lofty precipices . . . built by demons in the reign of Ali Khaun . . . called 'the castle from which there is no return', its gate guarded by mighty dragons who have never been known to sleep". On other battlements in these parts appears a snowy-robed hermit who exclaims in marrow-curdling tones, "Return, my children, this adventure is not for you, but is reserved for a man who is yet an infant hanging from the breast." This is familiar fare to readers nourished on Otranto and Waverly, whose inward eyes will fit out the traveller in the trappings of knighthood, and colour his journey with the significance and hidden meaning of a Quest.

myself, the background of Malory's Europe giving resonance to the deeds, and sparkle to the torchlit weapons, thoughts of Camelot linking the character of the traveller to archetypes of the Round Table on their similarly doubtful and harassed journeys. I believe that a sizeable factor in the allurement to me of these Eastern travels is that the best of the narrators can number amongst their ancestors the hand that wrote the most haunting of all descriptions of a journey, in *Sir Gawain and the Green Knight*.*

Early reading of *Sohrab and Rustum* certainly never made the impression on me which *Sir Gawain* made, but Arnold's poem – or perhaps illustrations to it in an edition I no longer possess – left me with the idea that the Oxus flowed amongst a people ruled by the same notions of chivalry which Edward III's England had inherited from the *Iliad*, and I had looked forward keenly to seeing that ancient and famous river.

Once the car had turned north towards Khiva off the Chardzhou road there was a chance that the Oxus might come in sight at any moment across the sands to the west, and I watched the landscape apprehensively. The chance of a lucky or unlucky first glimpse can make or mar any of the world's wonders in your own memory. I saw the Danube first from a train creeping through a misty dawn over the long metal bridge from Bulgaria into Romania, and the Tigris first where it flows through the valley below Dyarbekr, so that no matter how debased the view I have had of either river subsequently, it is that first glint of its stream that the ring of its name puts instantly into my mind. I hoped for the best from the Oxus.

The road was still straight after we had turned north, though narrower and rougher. So violent were the thumps and buffets of the harrowed tarmac to the wheels – I travelled wedged down low in my seat or my head hit the roof every instant – that when a back tyre exploded it took Anatoly a moment or two fighting the steering to realise what had happened. Once

* A modern translator says of Sir Gawain arming for his journey, "The doublet he dressed in was dear Turkestan stuff".

he did, and had stopped the car, he was out on the road in a trice, to fall on the work of wheel-changing with the busy relish with which he attacked all his tasks, a burst tyre, or breakfast in the desert, given him as welcome chances to score high marks in an aptitude test. Alex held spanners for him and smoked – any halt he seized on for a smoke, a soldier's (and a policeman's) characteristic – whilst I walked away up the road to try and keep warm in the cold and silent sands. The work done, Alex poured water over Anatoly's hands, who dried them on a rag drawn from a cubbyhole – his car was full of the requisites which mark out the man whose car means to him what his ship means to the single-handed sailor, or his *yurt* to the nomad. The tyre he had taken off had a rent blown in its wall you could put a fist through. I asked Alex how easy it would be to find another: he showed his teeth in a humourless smile. He didn't say "No problem". We climbed aboard and battered on.

Before long, where the road climbed one of the landscape's undulations, my chance came to catch sight of the Oxus. What a chance! Across ridges of stone-coloured desert there opened a view down into a green rift. Down there the landscape softened from desert to pasture, became the grassy shore and reedy inlets of a lakeside; and the splendid shining river beyond these bays had the placidity of a lake too, an expanse of unhurried water as far as a horizon of low capes, its clouded, gleaming surface reflecting the varied light and chance sunshafts of a cloudy sky. Only far out from the shore could the immense river be seen to be solemnly moving through the desert, a current gathered amongst the Pamirs and flowing towards the Aral Sea. The Oxus! Up rushed the idea like a firework and exploded into stars, beautiful and memorable.

II

It was plain enough when the confines of the oasis of Khiva had been reached, for at that point the landscape of desert and sky broke up into squalid industrialised fragments. Even the straight desert road lost its line. We skirted quarries and crossed canals – was this slack effluent what had become of the Oxus? – we threaded between factories funnelling out black smoke and lost our way in streets of miserable apartment blocks. We reached no metropolis, entered no deeper into any town, but drove through an outskirt world pitiful in its castaway ugliness. There was not perhaps the English misery of wetness-with-wretchedness to be found in idle Tyneside shipyards or Midland steelworks decaying in the rain, but the stained concrete and rusting iron of this Soviet industrial shabbiness lacked that hint of lost imperial grandeur which flickers its elegiac light even yet over the magnificent smoke-blackened buildings of a bankrupt Liverpool, or sadly gleams on a Mersey empty of shipping. Industrialisation at Khiva looked as though it never had been a success. I was staring rather impatiently out of the car window at these surroundings, anxious to get clear of them and reach Khiva proper – "Ah, Khiva!" I had been told. "How you will love it, the whole city a museum!" – when the car stopped. Alex turned to look back at me.

"We are here," he said. We were at the kerb of a wide loathsome street. My heart sank.

My heart has sunk innumerable times on learning that the destination is no longer in some golden future – not even round a corner – but just here in the hideous present. "Khiva?" I faltered, peering out.

"Urgench."

This was a partial relief. I got out. The sun was now burning down pretty fiercely onto the concrete and dust of a long straight street clattering with trams, its skyline laced with derricks and cranes. But I had no expectations of Urgench, and Khiva is still twenty miles off. We walked into the hotel, an elderly building following the usual Soviet plan (for pre-high-rise hotels) of expanses of shiny-floored emptiness round the entrance, with dark corridors and rooms tacked on as an after-thought at the back. There is no hotel at Khiva, so at Urgench you must stay.*

It was time for lunch: we had been eight hours on the road. From upstairs came a clamour of noise. Upstairs we went, to a low-ceilinged dining room packed tight with tables, each table packed with customers. It might be said that each chair was packed tight with its occupant, too, and each outfit a tight fit on its owner. Formidable Soviet women, and big brown bewildered men buttoned into skimpy suits, crowded the room to its doors: I've never seen such a squash. Large red hands grasped bottles and filled glasses, or carried loaded forks to the mouth, and the glitter of satisfaction at food and drink was in every eye. Who were they all? Not tourists. It looked as though everyone in a rush-hour train had won a free meal. There was certainly no room for us. Thank goodness for Alex, who began to try to throw his weight about with the hurrying waiters. The windows were all closed and the heat stupendous.

When we sat down at the extra table which Alex had com-pelled the manager to set up for us in a mop-filled corner I asked, "Who are they all?"

* There are two cities named Urgench in the Khivan oasis, this one close to the Oxus, founded in the seventeenth century by an Uzbeg khan, and another, the seat of ancient power one hundred miles or so to the north-east, capital of an empire laid waste by Genghis Khan. It is not always clear which Urgench (or Coogentch or Oorgunj or Urgendj) is meant by nineteenth-century travellers such as Fraser when he writes that "Ourgunge, once capital of an empire which embraced the principal part of Western Asia, has become a ruin, and the seat of the petty power which now exists has been transferred to the mean and modern town of Khyvah" (*Khorassan*, 1833). In Count Pahlen's time (1908) new Urgench was a trading station which owed its prosperity to "the enterprise of a few wealthy Russian merchants who had . . . monopolised the commerce of Khiva" and who formed the Council which ruled a practically indepen-dent town. In this Russian Shanghai Pahlen was fêted at ten commercial houses, and "in every single one was treated to *zakuska* and iced cham-pagne . . . to this day I do not know how I survived the ordeal". Since that time (he laments in his book) the Revolution of 1917 had replaced that dubious mercantile oligarchy with "a new breed of loud-mouthed, uncultivated barbarians".

He looked round the dining room as if he had not noticed anyone in it but ourselves. "Deputies," he said briefly, his eyes returning to the tablecloth. Then, as if he might have revealed too much, he added, "Maybe".

"So many! Where are they all from?"

"From Choresm region."

"Were you ever interested in going into politics, Alex?"

"*Por*litics! No!" He laughed, filling my glass again with the Shakhrisyabz wine he never forgot to provide. Despite this token of thoughtfulness, a gust of exasperation with him veered my opinion to the view that he was after all certainly a policeman, and I resolved yet again to make no further effort to penetrate such dour indifference.

That afternoon, Anatoly having put himself on the sick list with his hepatitis, a car as well as a guide was hired for my unavoidable official tour of Khiva. The driver, a silent Kazak, pulled down his felt hat so that its brim rested on enormous ears and drove us by another straight tree-lined road through a landscape of cottonfields and mud-walled enclosures towards Khiva. Only in 1968, the neat little lady guide told Alex and me, had the first visitors been permitted to enter the city; and so careful of their trust had the authorities been that even now the tourist would find, she promised, "a museum-city" uncontaminated by the hotels and restaurants and everyday buildings which disappoint the traveller elsewhere. We could look forward to a city of mosques and medressehs and palaces sleeping in the shadow of Khiva's evil name as the central vortex of the slave trade into which were sucked all the unfortunates captured on Turkestan's borders. To the Khiva market were dragged – literally dragged at a rope's end – the Persians snatched from Khorassan, Russian fishermen seized on the Caspian, prisoners from Kokand's or Bokhara's wars: anyone, in short, whom the Turcoman brigands of the steppes could catch and bring for sale. It was a reign of terror. "No Persian [the Turcomans boasted] ever approached the Attrek without a rope round his neck"; indeed, so resigned were the peasants of the Persian border to their fate, and so dreadful was the Turcoman's name for cruelty, that the poor captives would bind one another and hand over the rope's end as soon as a *chappaw* surprised them in their fields. The old were slaughtered, women flung across saddles, the men dragged on foot after the far-trotting Turcoman horses whose stamina on a diet of chopped straw carried these raiders hundreds of miles across the steppes on their forays. According to our guide the traffic in slaves had gone on until 1970; but how it was supplied, and why it then ceased, she would not divulge. Still, all she had to tell us about this city which lay ahead sharpened my appetite, and I felt glad of every mile of elm-lined road – the elms which were carved at Khiva into fantastic tracery for doors and window shutters – which might have quarantined Khiva from the urban cancer at a terminal stage in Urgench. Who would complain of the destruction of Urgench, with the Khiva of the guide's description lying ahead?

We entered its suburbs, promisingly sparse, a scatter of flat roofs under the usual tangle of wires, many trees, and were put down by our driver in a space left clear of buildings between the new town and the old; on one side the modern age ended in office blocks and a bus station, on the other rose the bastioned walls and ramped gate arch of the Khiva of history. A number of Intourist coaches were drawn up, engines running to keep the air conditioning at work, and, where the crocodiles of visitors straggled out of the shadow of the gateway into the heat of the square, a desultory trade in *kvass* and Fanta was going forward under umbrellas to the sound of pop music. The three of us, our guide leading, left the car and approached the old city's gate, the light brilliant on a fountain's hissing spray and on the leaves of some willows in an angle of the walls. I was aware of everything, as you are when the expectations of eyes and mind fuse together into one sharp focus. It is the moment of eager suspense. You wade into the river, you lengthen your line and prepare to fish, aware of the weight of swift water, of the scent and hurry of it, hopeful that the mysterious quarry is resting on his fins deep in his own element like an idea not yet expressed.

The moment we were through the gate arch, and Khiva's first street lay ahead, trim brick lined with trim tourist stalls, I knew that the pool was empty. Whatever the general outcome of travelling in Central Asia, I knew that I had wasted my time in coming to Khiva. That required no thinking about. It was a conclusion – a disappointment – which head and heart jumped to together at once, and wouldn't jump even halfway back. I knew the pool was empty, and that I might as well reel up and wade ashore.

It is hard to put adequately the case against Khiva as the Russians have restored it. Their renovations have been exact, their accuracy in matching paint and tiles no doubt scrupulous, the tidiness of street and square is beyond reproach, the glass-case displays in scrubbed-out mosques as informative as scant material allows, the stalls selling rock music cassettes and nylon fur hats are tastefully recessed into walls in which not a brick is out of line. But what has renovation, matched colours, taste and tidiness, to do with an Asiatic city? The deadly aim of those weapons has killed Khiva stone dead. Never, at any period of its history, was this perfect suchness the appearance of Khiva. Never did every coloured tile glitter in its place on the façades, the streets were never swept like this, nor the squares empty nor the lanes silent and clean. It *is* a museum: a museum directed by an authority wilfully out of sympathy with the material it has preserved, an authority indeed with nothing but contempt for the true past of this Asiatic city.

In Disneyland you can walk through a dandy little replica of New Orleans, a brick square neat as pie alongside a Mississippi a foot deep; and this is what has happened here. Russia has replaced Khiva with the theme park facsimile. Is it spite, is it contempt: or is it fear? – is it, in a modern form, the old Russian fear and hatred of the place which tricked and slaughtered so many thousand Russians sent on successive expeditions to subdue it? In Russia's scouring and sanitising of Khiva I can make out the motives of the settler in Africa who puts a lion's skin just where he steps on it getting out of bed, or makes his wastepaper basket out of an elephant's foot – who makes into something servile the claws and tusks his instinct fears. Just as the elephant's foot must be hacked from the body, and scoured out and treated with preservatives, so have the centres of the old cities of Turkestan been severed from the Asiatic body, dipped in formaldehyde, and put down to have tourists tipped into them. It was the boast of Russian conquerors in these parts that they, unlike the British, did not interfere with native government but allowed (in Soboleff's words) "full liberty to native manners"; though it meant the perpetuation of native tyranny, their policy did indeed leave the teeming cities unchanged, their bazaars thronged, their mosques tumbledown but in full employment – left an immemorial Asia, in fact, to survive alongside the steam train and the machine gun.

But such tolerance did not survive Russia's revolution. Mass deportations and razed cities, the tsars' weapons used to break the tribes of the Crimea and the Caucasus, were now employed by Stalin in Central Asia. Citizens and races were divided and scattered, mosques profaned, caravanserais and covered markets dynamited, history eradicated. As best he was able, Stalin broke the backbone and severed the limbs of the Asiatic elephant which General Kaufmann, for all his brutality, had only ever tethered as a beast of burden to work for Russia. Now the cultural colonialism of Moscow has turned the dead creature's feet into wastepaper baskets and its carcass into a museum. Here in Khiva's dead streets and whitewashed mosques – very much like the interior of a dead elephant – here is to be seen, at last, the full retaliation of Russia for all those humiliating failures to capture the city, for all those Russians under Cherkasski murdered in its streets, for Peroffski's thousands dead of cold in its steppes, and for those Caspian fishermen sold in its market place. *Delenda est Khiva.* As the Romans did to Carthage so Russia, by her scheme of renovation, has finally laid waste to Khiva, and taken her revenge upon it.

General, vague and unhappy was my disappointment as we walked at Alex's brisk pace through brick streets and tidy squares. What had I expected? What did I want? I think I had expected Khiva to express what I wanted, Khiva itself to be the destination of the journey and so to show me in its streets

and buildings – in my feelings when I arrived – what it was
that I was looking for. The hooked salmon – the feelings of
the fisherman in that sudden connexion with a mystery –
expresses the point of fishing. But reaching Khiva expressed
nothing. It was not the destination. I felt like the Flying Scotsman in a book I've known since childhood, who escaped from
his engine shed and sped north all night under the moon's pale
rays to find in the morning that he had "reached John o'Groat's
and could go no further". And what was John o'Groat's? Nothing. The end of the line. He waited sulkily on the turntable for
his driver and fireman to pedal to Scotland on their tandem
and fetch him home from his pointless spree. I could not even
fix – not precisely enough for satisfaction – upon just what to
hate about Khiva.

Then my eye caught the large unhappy eye of a tethered
camel. In a patch of dust the scrawny beast was tied up short
to a post whilst a woman in broad tight jeans scrambled shriek-
ing up a stepladder onto his back. As she clasped his hump,
and shrieked and shrieked again for the photographer, I saw
the suffering in the camel's eye, and knew what I hated about
Khiva in Soviet hands. At my side the lady guide announced
that we would now visit the bazaar.

"Good, so," said Alex, brightening up, "now we search for
your trousers."

My mention at Samarcand of the success at home of the
Trebizond shalwars had caught Alex's interest. Here was a
tangible want of mine which, like the Shakhrisyabz wine, he
could understand. After our lunch party outside Bokhara he
had asked our host where we might find such garments, thus
setting off the whole inebriated gang on a wild goose chase
through Bokhara's bazaar and shops, the rest of us keeping
behind our leader whose white suit and grand manner parted
crowds up to every fruitless counter. The shimmering rainbow
of overdress and peg-tops worn by the Turkestan women were
not for sale. Nor did Khiva's drab little market sell the outfit.

Still, even enquiring for shalwars furnished a question to ask
of the market, gave a point to going from stall to stall; and, as
we drove away from Khiva behind the jug-eared Kazak,

myself rather weary with heat and disappointment, I wished that my purpose in coming here had formulated itself into as precise a question as the search for shalwars instead of remaining in the state of inchoate curiosity and expectation in which I had arrived at the gate. Museums, like guides, exist to answer questions. Had I known what to ask the museum-city, or what to ask my guide sitting silent beside me, a visit to Khiva might have dissatisfied me less. It is, as readers of Malory cannot forget, the failure to ask the right question of the enigma found at journey's end, which causes the seeker to remain unenlightened, and his view of the quest's true objective to be but a glimpse.

III

Next morning about ten o'clock I was dropped at the gate of Khiva by Anatoly, who was sufficiently recovered to motor off for the day to visit a sister. I had asked him to drop me not at the showy entrance at which we had arrived yesterday, but at a simple gated arch in the walls which leads into the covered market. By choosing the back door I hoped to surprise the genius loci. I had a few dried apricots with me, some bread, a tin of sardines, a bottle of water and a book: the sky was blue, the light strong, and I was ready to make a day of searching Khiva.

I had thought overnight a good deal about my expectations. What it comes to is this. Into "Khiva", into the look of the word on paper and into the sound of the syllables in the air, is packed an awareness of a hundred scenes I have read about which took place here – vivid, graphic scenes noted by the quick eye and strung nerves of travellers – and I hope to find, in the stones of Khiva, a physical setting which will trigger the imagination to unpack that word "Khiva" so that all its component scenes are unfolded to the mind's eye by a walk in its streets and squares, and all the name's intrinsic music is sustained in the town's atmosphere. I hope to feel assured that what I see is today's manifestation of the life that has always been lived in this place. On the face of an old clock you see the present hour, but you see also, and hear in its patient ticking, an unbroken continuity of time, which gives the present hour its pedigree. If you can discern that continuum, if you can rub off the ephemeral and touch the core, the journey was worth making.

I don't want to live in the past, but I want to live in a present which is rooted in the past. Only as an extension of the past does the present cease to be a chaos of unmeaning. Only continuity gives coherence. Awareness of this continuity – touching the bedrock under "the grass which withereth" – heartens us in everything. If time is a continuum, the dead are still in the picture, still active in the cognizance of the living. When you see the singular effect of, let's say, a low sun on a wooded landscape, you know you live in the same world Rubens painted: look into the face of an ivory Christ of the fourteenth century and you see the suffering of a living man: the world is constructed for us by its history, and the constructors live on in their work, as the dead clockmaker's voice is heard in the striking of his clock. I don't expect to find these famous cities of Turkestan unaltered; but I hope to find a city, even a few streets and squares, which has kept its essential bedrock identity because it has developed along lines connecting it to its origins. That was what I wanted of Khiva.

Let me give an example. When Arminius Vambéry, travelling with a caravan in the disguise of a dervish, came into Khiva in 1863 he was understandably alarmed that his alias would be discovered in this stronghold of fanaticism, so that he dwells upon executions and methods of punishment, describing how he watched in a certain courtyard whilst prisoners were segregated, some for gallows or block, and how "at a sign from the executioner, eight aged men lay down on their backs on the earth" and he "gouged out their eyes in turn, kneeling to do so on the breast of each poor wretch, and after every operation wiping his knife, dripping with blood, upon the white beard of the hoary unfortunate". Now, I don't expect to see "hoary unfortunates" – Vambéry, a Hungarian and a professor of languages, easily caught the weaknesses of Victorian writing – or even tourists taken off camels to be thrown on their backs and blinded by policemen; but I hoped to walk into some mud court whose dingy walls endorsed the veracity of Vambéry's scene. On Tower Hill as a child I had been able to smell the blood of the scaffold. Backgrounds, if there is to be any point in going to see them, must project an atmosphere in which past events are feasible, so as to nourish the imaginative appetite. I wanted to believe, in situ, in the authenticity of those hoary unfortunates, so as to understand, and even share, Vambéry's fearful view of Khiva.

Such a quickening into life of foreground figures and action by a background you feel to be authentic is a vital ingredient in the writing of fiction set in past times. To persuade even yourself of the reality of the people in your book you must believe in the copper-bottomed reality of their physical world. You need to have seen it, and sounded it out: then you may turn your characters loose in it, and hope to see them move and hear them talk. On the southern slope of the Caucasus, where the Tiflis road issues from the Krestovy Pass, lies the fortress of Ananouri. There I stopped once and walked down alone by way of castle and ruined church into the village. Street and village were undisturbed, for the main road now passes high above. Wooden houses with rickety wooden balconies line the street, a few trees shading them here and there, a child or two playing in the dust, pigs scampering through autumn gardens – a peaceful scene, the colours pale in the thin air of the mountains. The street of dwellings ends at a bridge, its approaches guarded by two chipped yellow obelisks, which spans the rapid, stony Aragvi. On this bridge two ancients in vast and floppy black caps stood screeching at one another above the noise of the river, one with a hen tucked under his arm, the other's knotty hand grasping a pail of pigswill. Beyond the bridge stretched lake water rippling into a misty distance. Now, so far as I knew, the English soldier of fortune whose adventures in these regions I was intending to write – "Captain Vinegar" – would never cross the Aragvi or ride

through Ananouri:* never mind, the components of that background had sufficient potency to summon up the Captain on
horseback riding into my own view so vividly that the old
men on the bridge stood apart to let him through, and the
children looked up from spinning their tops in the dust to
watch him clatter past. This is the world he lived in, I could
say to myself, taking down the dimensions of the scene; here
is a background with the silver cord in it of unbroken continuity with the remote past, worth any amount of driving about
the Caucasus to discover.

In innumerable places, in countless cities and scenes, you can
find that unbroken cord of authenticity – it isn't rare – but it
is not to be found at Khiva. You can't believe in any past
behind Khiva's present appearance: it is a stage-flat without
perspective. I walked through it from end to end after Anatoly
had left me at the gate, better supplied than yesterday with
questions to put to it, and there was no life in it. The authenticity of Khiva has shrunk to the dimensions of the tourist-
carrying camel's suffering eye. I walked through its neat streets
and came out of the chief gateway and sat under the willows
in a species of garden planted in an angle of the walls, and
listened to the fountain's patter.

I was aware of the many varied impressions made by Khiva
on different men, Vambéry finding a city alive with threats to
his disguise, Abbott repining over his semi-captivity in the
cold of winter, Shakespear making himself out as jolly as a
cricket whilst bounding about to collect the Russian slaves: but
I couldn't imagine any of them in the streets behind the walls.
It must then have been a dirty, teeming robbers' lair, its unas-
sailabilty confirmed by Peroffski's failure, the slave market its
chief source of wealth. "Slave market!" European hands were
thrown up to varying heights by the "horrors" of slaving and
slavery. The term *gholan*, a slave, "is not one of opprobrium
in Eastern countries", Sir John Malcolm, historian and diplomatist, gently reminds his readers, "nor does it even convey
the idea of a degraded condition". "We are certainly far from

* And I am aware that the sheet of water is artificially dammed up.

approving of this hateful trade [wrote X. Hommaire de Hell, warming up to point out Western hypocrisy] but we are bound in justice to the people of Asia to remark, that there is a wide difference between Oriental slavery and that which exists in Russia, in the French colonies and in America." This cut was very near the bone, especially to the bone of Russia's contention that she was conducting by her Central Asian campaigns only a crusade to free the slaves. The Bokhariots would admit to Alexander Burnes no offence in making slaves of Russians, for "Russia herself exhibits the example of a whole country of slaves", prompting Burnes to "melancholy reflections on the liberties of Russia, that they admit of comparison with the institutions of a Tartar kingdom", and to further murmurs about "the freedoms of Bokhara compared to the black bread and unrelenting tyranny of Russian serfdom".*

Still, slaves the poor Russians at Khiva certainly were, and, however it was achieved, it was a brilliant coup by Abbott and Shakespear to extract all 418 of them from the khan and conduct them safe to Orenburg.† No European on earth was in a

---

* The success of the British ploy in exposing Russian humbug over her slaves may be judged by the bile and virulence of Russian response: the historian M. A. Terentieff, when he has related how "Abbott and Shakespear pocketed their British pride and were saved [in Khiva apparently] by the Russian agents Nikiforov and Aitoff . . . and reached Russia half dead from cruel treatment", goes on to say that this humiliation "did not prevent Shakespear from asserting that the liberation of 500 Russian captives by the Khan of Khiva was due . . . solely to the influence he possessed over the khan . . . This English Don Quixote [Terentieff concludes] considered his prison to be a palace" from which he could negotiate with his gaoler, the khan, whilst Nikiforov (who is never mentioned in either Englishman's narrative) apparently got his way with this tyrant, who had just repulsed Peroffski's Russian invasion, by "treating him like a menial". Colonel Ignatieff, however, in his report of his *Mission to Khiva in 1858*, wrote that "it has been shown in former years how fruitless in results were the missions of . . . Nikiforov and Danilefski to Khiva", so we may discount the foamings of Terentieff.

† Burnes gives an interesting account of his interview with an enslaved Russian at Bokhara, a poor carpenter who had been twenty years a captive, well enough treated, yet saying, "I appear happy, but my heart burns for my native land, where I would serve in the most despotic army with gladness. Could I but see it again, I would willingly die."

position to dictate terms to the ruler of Khiva in 1840. Abbott's painful account of his comings and goings in the wintry streets, and of his plots and schemes to influence the khan, paint us a graphic picture of such a stronghold and such a court as Khiva at that time, indeed like a baron's stronghold of Edward III's reign. But where now are the crooked streets and narrow courts with their blank walls where Abbott lived and worried? Nowhere in Khiva as it has been restored is there the quintessential Eastern sense of enclosure, of unseen watchers, closed wooden doors, lanes like tunnels between shabby mud walls echoing your footsteps, dust and silence. It is not to be found in these clean brick streets with idling tourists their only traffic, or in the empty, functionless squares. At every mosque door – at the door of every public building – a harridan shuffles forward shouting angrily for money to let you pass into some poor array of broken pots and scraps of carving which are laid out on a trestle and called an "exhibition". With this museum-city it was impossible to imagine forming that complex relationship of uncertainty mixed with exhilaration which is at the heart of the traveller's enjoyment of a foreign town, particularly in the East.

I had been better able to imagine the Khiva in which Abbott lived and suffered from reading of it by the fire at home than from my bench under the willows against Khiva's renovated walls. Rather gloomily I spread out my picnic. Because there is no everyday life about the place, only tourism and its predators, there is no background in which a visitor can make himself invisible, as there is in thriving cities: no busy crowd concerned with its own affairs, no mothers with children resting under the trees, no old men playing draughts. Every step I took in Khiva was self-conscious. Every step I took all morning had been followed by a pair of boys, not street children but clean unpleasant boys, who stopped a few yards off whenever I paused and held out their hands and shouted "Hey! Money!" These monsters were now occupying the further end of the bench on which I had set out my bread and fruit and tin of sardines, and soon began sidling along on their bottoms towards my lunch, both of them shouting "Hey! Money!" in my face. I threw them the tin of sardines – not easy to catch an open tin of sardines neatly – and walked off. As I had done with success at Bokhara, I thought I'd try a circuit outside the walls in hopes of finding a quarter which renovation hadn't obliterated.

Undoubtedly Khiva had been one of the most dangerous cities in the world for a European to enter until General Kaufmann marched in as its conqueror in 1873. By the winter of 1875/6, when Captain Fred Burnaby of the Blues performed his *Ride to Khiva*, so much had things changed that "this vaunted exploit was of itself [in the opinion of the Central Asian pundit Charles Marvin] not a whit more remarkable than the visit of an English tourist to the capital of any Indian feudatory prince". Yet the bold captain "thanks to the enterprise of his publisher and the advertising skill of the proprietors of a certain pill, has acquired a wider renown as a dashing explorer than any other traveller of modern times".

Burnaby with his bombast and bravado came galloping onto the scene and carried off the laurels (his book went into eleven editions and made him famous for life) just at the moment when Khiva was in fact safe, but still sounded dangerous. In appearance and in style he was just what the public of the 1870s wanted in their heroes, and his book (as a critic said rather cleverly of it) "will appeal to those who usually read a newspaper". The *Graphic* called him "a big stalwart dashing wide-awake Englishman with a large heart and an open hand" full of "sound British pluck and unfailing good humour" who – a touch of Tennyson's Arthur here – "wielded a sword other men could hardly lift with both hands".

It is rather hard to like Burnaby nowadays. What a change for the worse he represents, both in himself and in his book, from the sensibilities and feeling of, say, Arthur Conolly or first-edition Abbott. It is Empire's high noon, the Great Game, and onto the pitch to play for England stamps this Heavy Dragoon, an enormous man capable of lifting a pony under each arm, his favourite weapon in an action against natives his double-barrelled sporting shotgun. Perhaps at no other period of history or literature was the Hero so odious.* Still, not everyone cheered Burnaby on: to set against the *Graphic*'s raptures is the comment of the anti-imperialist poet Wilfrid Scawen Blunt (who sang in the train all the way down to his Sussex estate on hearing of Gordon's death at Khartoum): "I felt some disgust at shaking hands with a man who has been murdering Arabs with his shot-gun . . . I have never liked him, for he has the most evil countenance one can imagine . . . a dull, heavy fellow with a dash of cunning and more than a dash of brutality." Can this be the same good fellow and popular clubman as the *Graphic* describes?

Burnaby was in truth a very much more complex creature than his book or popular opinion portrays. A linguist (he spoke good Russian), a traveller in several continents, a balloonist – and surely no one is a balloonist who is not at heart a dreamer – as well as a Member of Parliament, he is altogether a good deal deeper than the rather abominable hero he created as the protagonist of his *Ride to Khiva*. Physically, first of all, he was "of unEnglish appearance", looking in fact like "a Jewish-Italian baritone" (though possessing a thin high voice) which, says his biographer, "led him to resist attempts to procure portraits of him". Instead he drew his own self-portrait with his pen in his book, of the big stalwart dashing wideawake Englishman, a deception which took in millions. It took in an Irish heiress, too, very young, who married him "as a result of reading his book". The marriage hardly outlived the honeymoon, the bride removing herself immediately and permanently to Switzerland, her lips ever sealed, whilst Burnaby resumed tramping between his clubs and his lodgings in the heavy overcoat and muffler he always wore.

Burnaby may not have needed his valour or his vast sword to ride to Khiva, but his courage – or his fearlessness in face of death – is undoubted. Indeed he courted death, with that streak of morbidity which often underlies foolhardiness. To a

* Never more repulsively characterised than by George Lawrence in his eponymous *Guy Livingstone*, 1857.

friend he said that he always left out of the Litany the petition for deliverance from "battle, murder and sudden death". This might seem a further posed stance of the heroic self-portraitist, but, when he was killed in an action at Abu Klea in 1883, where he had no business to be (and he was said to have stepped outside the fighting square to get at the Mahdi's dervishes), a fellow officer's account ends with words which confirm it: "Alone of the dead his face wore the composed and placid smile of one who has been suddenly called away in the midst of a congenial and favourite occupation."

Khiva after the Russian conquest may have become a place where "a Blues captain of wealth and rank" like Burnaby could (in Charles Marvin's mocking words) "spend his holidays", but the city and its people and its government remained as they had always been, so that Burnaby saw the same town that Abbott and Vambéry knew. Only the danger had gone (and the public sale of slaves). Those earlier visitors had lived at Khiva as if uncomfortably close to a wasps' nest, always at risk from the furious stinging swarm at its mouth, whilst Burnaby could saunter about to examine the appearance and making of the nest amongst wasps with their stings drawn. In its close-fitting topography of streets and courts Khiva as it was must have matched a wasps' nest for intricacy and fascination. And so it lasted for almost another century after Burnaby's visit.

To have missed by a few years a scene essentially unaltered since the time of Alexander the Great irritates me dreadfully. Perhaps I shouldn't have cared for the full stinging days of Abbott or Vambéry, but what Burnaby saw would have satisfied my curiosity; and the Khiva he describes had hardly changed in the 1920s – was to last, indeed (as can be seen in the photographs in Knobloch's *Beyond the Oxus*), until the renovators invaded the town in the 1960s. In the 1960s I went here and there about the world, always travelling in order to see friends rather than to see places, but I had no friends in Turkestan and no curiosity to see Khiva. Now I am too late.

I had walked by this time from gate to gate both inside the walls and out, I had scrambled upon the walls themselves, I had pushed open every half-closed door, looked in at every window, explored every lane, every turning, every court and yard and mosque: there was nowhere left for either hope or curiosity to lead me. It was early afternoon. I found a seat near the gate where Anatoly had dropped me five hours or so earlier, a little of my bread and fruit left me, and a little water, and George Eliot her old reliable self to quiet the discontent I felt with myself and Khiva.

IV

It could have been upon a predecessor to the renovated gate arch by which I sat reading, for it was at a point opposite the town's main entrance, that Colonel Skoboleff, a Russian Burnaby, had launched the assault which exemplifies the trigger-happy attitude towards their duties of the Russian officers in Turkestan. Three separate columns, one each from Orenburg, Kazala and the Caspian, had arrived at Khiva virtually without meeting resistance in the summer of 1873. The odious Kaufmann – his appointment to supreme command in succession to the more courtly and cultivated Peroffski exhibits the same Russian degeneration in heroic type as was taking place on the English side – General Kaufmann was in command, and, having dictated terms to the khan, was just then entering the city with full pomp and swagger by its main gate. Skoboleff meanwhile, with a thousand men under him, was determined to win at this last moment the medals which only came with the bloody action so far denied him by the Khivans, and set about storming this rear gate and clearing the streets to the khan's palace with rockets and bayonets. Only when he heard the trumpet and drum of Kaufmann's triumphal entry on the other side of the city did he tiptoe back the way he had come. Medals the Russian officers were determined to have, to compensate them for the gambler's last throw of taking a posting in Central Asia, and to be sure of medals it was necessary to kill Asiatics, whether or not they had already surrendered.

Riding in at the front gate with General Kaufmann was one of the two newspapermen whose exploits in Central Asia about this time were thought by Charles Marvin (himself a journalist) to be undervalued in comparison with Burnaby's fame: this was the American J. A. MacGahan, who had indeed survived some amazing adventures on his way to Khiva. Sent by the *New York Herald* to cover Kaufmann's campaign, he had been obliged to dodge about to outwit Russian officers sent to stop him, and finally to ride for thirty days in high summer across the steppes of the Caspian from Kazala towards Khiva. In his narrative of this journey he makes an appealing and attractive impression, confessing that he had only set out on such a forlorn hope because he had spent too much of the paper's money to turn back, and entrusting himself to the mercy of the steppe Kirghiz by handing the grown-ups his rifle and settling down to romp with the children. Finally he caught up with the Russian Orenburg column as it was shelling a Khivan force across the Oxus, and, slipping through the cloud of Turcoman skirmishers hanging upon the Russian flanks, found himself welcomed after all by Kaufmann, who told him he was *molodyetz* – a brave fellow – and offered him a cup of tea. "I suppose I looked as though I needed it . . . dirty, dust-covered and ragged, my rifle, which I had carried for a month, slung over my shoulder in a bandolière, had worn my coat into holes – I presented a sorry spectacle among the Russians, who were all spruce in their white coats and caps and gold and silver buttons, as clean and starchy as though they were on parade in St Petersburg."

Once safe among Russian officers MacGahan's character seems to deteriorate, his appeal to vanish. Associating himself with the conquering force – "our cavalry", "our artillery" – MacGahan was buttered up in return by Kaufmann and Skoboleff in a way that evidently went to his head. The "condescension" of the Grand Duke Michael and Prince Eugène in speaking familiarly with him seems to have rendered him wholly uncritical of Russia's actions, and of the effect of what he describes as "the iron tread of grim-visaged war" upon the

people of Khiva and their possessions.* The fifty or so pages
of his book which narrate the massacre of the Yomuds by
Cossack troops are a heartless and somehow horribly unseemly
account of an unforgiveable episode.

Once settled at Khiva with the khan licking his boots, Kaufmann had turned his cold eye upon these Yomuds, a tribe of
the Turcoman nation which inhabited the Khiva oasis and had
fought as guerrillas for the khan. From their chiefs he
demanded an indemnity of £41,000, or about 75 pence a head,
for every man, woman and child of the tribe. There was
known to be no chance of them finding such a sum. Envoys
sent to beg for time were imprisoned by Kaufmann, who
declared that he would exterminate the tribe, and in July 1873
sent General Golovatchoff with a large force into their territory. Proud to ride with these Russians, MacGahan had halted
to survey what he can only call "a strange, wild scene"† when
he saw smoke and flame rush up from the straw-thatched
dwellings and ricks of the Yomud village at hand. Cossacks
ride through the smoke – yes, "like spectres" – firing roofs
with torches: the sun is veiled, the sky dark, and a sullen
unusual rain begins to fall, beating down the smoke low upon
a landscape of fire to every horizon. The scene is now
"strangely in keeping with this strange, wild land" as Golovatchoff draws up his Cossacks on the fringe of the desert, colours
flying, whilst the people of the villages tumble away in desperate confusion amongst their carts and flocks. "I galloped
forward to the head of the column," says MacGahan. Spurring
along the reined-in, sabre-flashing line, "I catch sight of Prince
Eugène, who welcomes me to the front with a hearty shake

* Having watched a released Persian slave steal a jewelled dagger
MacGahan draws his revolver and demands the prize for himself, wrest-
ing it from the man on threat of having him shot for a looter: when the
dagger is again stolen (he suspects the same Persian) "my only revenge
was in devoutly wishing and praying" that the man is murdered by the
Turcomans on his way home to Persia.

† He must have been right: within two years Captain Fred Burnaby
would describe these steppes in the very same phrase, as "a strange, wild
scene".

of the hand, and kindly puts me into one of his squadrons, as a good point of observation". It proves a good point from which to observe a massacre. The six *sotnias* of Cossacks charge a flying civilian population whose villages they have burned, killing all they come upon with sabre, with breech-loading rifles (American rifles, MacGahan notes proudly) and with rockets. Riding with them, himself armed with two revolvers and a breech-loader, the newspaperman shows his concern for the pitiful families by shouting out to terrified and wounded stragglers, "Aman, aman, peace, peace, as I gallop by, to allay their fears". To allay their fears! For a fortnight the Cossacks devastate the oasis, burning and murdering in all directions, and MacGahan recounts the cheery camaraderie of the Russian officers he lives with during these operations, whose attentions so gratify him: newspaper readers' liking for a human interest angle is taken care of by our reporter personally rescuing a pretty little orphan in an anecdote as sickly and unlikely as another tale he spins of his encounter with "Zuleika" in the khan's harem.

I suppose that the jarring note about the men of all nationalities who now came into Central Asia as soldiers or journalists or private travellers is struck and sustained by their want of interest in the place itself or its natives, save as a background to the rivalry between Russia and England. They have none of the curiosity or sympathy of earlier visitors. The place was the pitch for the Great Game, that was all, and MacGahan wrote like a sports journalist covering an away match, using just the same unthinking clichés he would have used to report, say, England's war against Cetewayo.* His description of Khiva after the main Russian force had withdrawn, its streets empty of everything except for rubbish left behind by the soldiers, is exactly the description of a football stadium after close of play.

---

* "It may be expected [wrote MacGahan] that I should say something of the Russian political position in Central Asia. On this subject however I have but little to say. I do not deem that the mere fact of my having been in Central Asia during a short campaign, enables me to say anything new on the question."

MacGahan had stayed behind because Colonel Skoboleff had asked for his company whilst he wrote a report in the summer palace commandeered from the khan. I feel very dubious about the private character which it bestows on the American, to have his company sought by Skoboleff, into whose white uniform, scented chestnut beard, diamond-hilted sword and pale blue eyes were to be concentrated, at Geok Tepe a few years later, all that was most pitiless and sanguinary in Russia's prostration of Turkestan. And what sort of light does it throw on Skoboleff's character, to learn that when he heard of Mac-Gahan's death of typhoid at Constantinople in 1878, he "wept like a child"? These blood-and-iron soldier's tears are of two types, the crocodile's and the sentimentalist's. The manner of Skoboleff's own death was so queer and unsavoury that I hope I shall be able to work it into this book on one excuse or another.

I had been in Khiva long enough. I took a final turn through its streets, came out through the walls by the show gate which it was impossible to imagine Kaufmann and his Cossacks entering, and walked down into the expanse of tarmac which distanced the old town from the new.

What I needed was a seat in a shared taxi back to Urgench. Yesterday's guide had told me that I would find one here. Plenty of full-grown buses sat about, some of them Intourist and some of them local, the oldest amongst them being examples of the busmaker's art in an early stage; but every bus was either completely deserted or completely full. From the step of one or two of the full ones I asked tentatively for Urgench. Stout women nursing bundles in their laps, swathed to the eyes in variously coloured wrapping, stared at me speculatively without replying. I suppose the occasion to help stray foreigners doesn't arise often enough to become a habit in Central Asia. In most parts of the world now a tourist who is in his own view attempting the feat of a lifetime is only trying to gain an objective which the locals see foreigners struggling towards a hundred times a week, so that they shepherd the lost sheep back into his right path whether they understand him or not. But the defensive hostility of a body of female

Soviet citizens looks out like an eye through the grille of a closed ticket office, incurious and uncharitable. From every seat every face repeated the slogan of Communism – "I'm all right, Jack, so bugger you" – an attitude which it has taken seventy years for the hospitable Asiatic to get by heart.

My own heart, not high as I wandered about the blindingly hot tarmac asking for a means of reaching Urgench, rose only for a moment when an idler jerked his thumb towards a dusty van baking alone in the sun. I could see that the van was packed to the windows with people. A glance within encountered the same dull and hostile glint of eyes. But when I made it clear that I was joining the ship, the crew's attitude altered at once, the women's especially. As a frosty mass separates into particles under a sunbeam, the crowd in the minibus stirred, under a charitable instinct, and separated into a collection of individuals, some welcoming and some not, but each reacting as a fellow creature to the conundrum of finding me a space. A seat was out of the question – there were already fourteen people of half a dozen races in a van with seats for ten – but the minute I was aboard I was amid the friendliness of an Indian bus, or a Turkish *dolmus*, a fraction of room squeezed for me on a wheel-arch, those nearest to me packing robes and children tighter together and smiling out of softened dark eyes. My spirits rose. If Khiva was dead, here was Turkestan alive.

In the arbitrary way of such transport the driver suddenly jumped in, elbowed himself a space to grasp the wheel, and sped us away. He was a captain very much in charge, not just of the driving but of every aspect of life aboard the van, and at his passengers' opinions he spat with contempt. He talked ceaselessly. He talked in the style which Burnes noted as common to the Uzbegs, in a high sharp tone "as though they despised or were angry with you", and murmurs of assent from those squashed closest to him was all he would tolerate as contributions from the crew. Discipline was tight. By means of his mirror he kept a close watch on doings at the back, and a fit of screaming was brought on when an old woman, with the feeble clawing movements of a dying fly, attempted to open a window. Like Alex in our Moscva, he insisted that the

van was shut up tight in the heat, and in the back the temperature was truly terrific with so many bodies crowded together
like eggs under a hen – eggs, I might say, in constant danger
of a cracked shell as we dashed over potholes at racing pace.
But we were friendly in the back together; the heartlessness of
one person to another, which I had found so uncomfortable
everywhere in the Soviet Union, was here banished, or at least
suspended, in place of an amity ready to assist with bundles
and baskets if a party was clambering out, or to smile apologies
for possessions encroaching on a neighbour's space. Yet the
communal outward gaze, when we stopped, which confronted
the hopeful passenger peering in for a place, was that same
defensive hostility which had met me at bus doors in Khiva;
and past several bus stops our driver dashed at full speed, a
derisive fling of his hand anathematising the cluster of would-
be passengers signalling from the roadside. What felt like amity
in the van, faced the world with complacency. It seems that
those citizens who have for the moment got what they need –
in our case a ride from Khiva – are like survivors who have
clambered onto a lifeboat, their sense of charity reduced by
want and despair below the point of caring for the plight of
others still waving from the water. Harangued by the driver,
drowsy with heat, our passive little society tore along the
straight road lined with mulberry and elm. Next to me, eyes
closed under her black headdress, dozed a woman with the
smile of an ivory Madonna carved on her features by sleep,
the fingers of the sleeping child in her lap occasionally clutching
my arm in an unconscious grasp which seemed to include
myself in the lifeboat's crew.

On reaching Urgench it became a great question amongst
them as to where I should be put down. I had become their
own foreigner, an infant in their hands to be passed to the
boat's gunwhale and thrown into the sea with directions for
my route ashore. The van even waited an instant, when I was
set down, and all those friendly eyes watched me set out. Then
they were gone.

I've often noticed that people in Russia don't expect things
to be convenient – don't expect a metro or a bus stop near at

hand – so that the distances to be walked in their spread-out cities are considerable. It had been so in reaching Pavarotti's recital at Moscow, and it was so in Urgench. But I liked my longish walk through the ugly busy streets of this remote Soviet town for its contrast with the disappointment of a day amongst the waxworks of the Khiva museum-city.

The pleasurable sense of being an unregarded component of a Soviet crowd, which may be felt as you walk through provincial streets, or share a minibus, is an ordinary activity which has a compelling interest for my Cold War generation. Eye and intelligence are alert to every detail. This plain Russian street, throughout my lifetime, has been the territory of the spy, and a valuable sliver of the spy's heightened awareness belongs to the foreigner who walks down it un-remarked.

I tried to express something like this to the Ukrainian school-master whom Alex had asked to supper that evening. Having walked back from the bus stop I had only been in my room for a moment or two – moments spent swatting mosquitoes, since I don't quite trust the official dictum that there is no malaria in Central Asia – when Alex's familiar hammering shook the door. "Dinner six-thirty, okay?" he shouted through it.

I looked at my watch. It was six-thirty now. "Could it be in half an hour, Alex?"

But I heard his feet slapping away down the lino corridor. By imperceptible degrees the minder takes over the minded: soon I would be leading a life entirely to suit Alex. I remembered, as I changed my shirt, how it had happened in my days as an attaché at the Rome embassy that the young prince whom I was supposed to be minding was found by my ambassador wandering about the residence before breakfast: when H.E. indicated that I must in future rise at the same hour as H.R.H., I saw to it that it was at my hour, in those days ten o'clock, that the prince henceforth left his room. Before hastening to the foyer to meet Alex's deadline I noticed that apart from a rainbow of bruises on breastbone and shins, and the flaking scars left on my nose and cheeks, the impressions of my Moscow attacker's knife, nails and shoes were almost gone, cured thus rapidly, I suppose, by the dessicated air of the Turkestan steppes. In the hall, beside Alex in his blue shirt and grey trousers, stood a tall spare man who stepped forward, when Alex introduced him as a friend of his own Ukrainian youth, and rather diffidently shook my hand. We went upstairs to the dining room.

"And what do you think of our country?"

At parties in Delhi I remember having to answer the question a dozen times in an evening, so that, knowing how I used to fabricate and vary my answers, I now try to get at the opinion of foreigners about England by a means less direct. In a society as self-confident as New Delhi's, though, the question is asked with the complacency which Khanikoff complained of in the Bokhariots,* for an Indian does not want to hear any criticism which he has not initiated; but in Russia and in Eastern Europe – I remember the earful of complaints gathered in a strange night I once spent drinking in an underground tavern in Ceausescu's Bucharest – I have found that people ask you what you think of their country only as a preliminary to grumbling about it themselves with the loquacity of the confessional.

To the Ukrainian schoolmaster's question, therefore, I replied (whilst I had the chance) by telling him what had been in my mind riding in the minibus and walking the streets of Urgench: the acute interest to me of the commonplace, in a country made as remote as the moon to my generation of Europeans by a forty-five-year-old Cold War. Even in the year and a half since I had been in Georgia the psychology of the Westerner's situation inside the Soviet Union had changed, glasnost and perestroika having become in those eighteen months household words which had altered our perception of Russia by bringing Russian affairs under our direct observation

---

* "Individuals who have been fortunate enough to be received at the Imperial Court, and have witnessed the splendours of the palaces and edifices of St Petersburg, had yet the audacity to ask, with a complacent smile, what we thought of Bokhara" – Khanikoff, *History of Bokhara*.

in newspapers and television, instead of allowing us only a picture refracted through the ice of *Pravda* and the Cold War. I told him this, and I told him that I remembered sitting on a shady bench under the plane trees in one of the squares of Tbilisi's nineteenth-century quarter, watching the children's games, listening to the old-timers clicking their dominoes on tin tables, and gazing through the leaves at the elaborate pistachio or eau-de-nil façades of the houses which enclose these squares – I sat there, incredulous that it was possible so to sit, alone and free to poke about as I liked, in the heart of a Soviet province. There was a café I used to go to, too, in Tbilisi's Lenin Square – you could sit at a chipped gilt table eating chocolate cake and drinking coffee in an atmosphere more like Vienna than Moscow – whose window gave a rear view of Lenin's mighty heel as his statue strode away to conquer fresh worlds, and I recall thinking then that the little old-fashioned café existing unregarded under the colossal statue, and myself free to sit eating chocolate cake in the little café, were all part of a complex permanence, a tolerable status quo, which Communism inside the Russian Empire had evolved for itself. But six weeks later, a few yards from that café, Russian troops, who had been ordered to put down a Nationalist demonstration, sprayed the Georgian crowd with poison gas and hacked women to death with spades sharpened for the purpose; and by now the statue of Lenin has doubtless been felled. I was wrong. There was after all no permanence in the status quo, no tolerable balance. What I saw in Georgia was the very end of the illusionist's act – the USSR funambulists on stage for the last time – before the roubles to paper the house ran out. So long as the Russian Empire was the formidable power darkening our eastern horizon, as I remember fancying that it darkened the view eastwards from the fortress of Kars, a sinister hand working the marionettes in Prague and Sofia, in Bucharest and Budapest, then to be at liberty and alone in a Russian street sharpened every perception. But that grim allure which it has for the Cold War veteran, of the shuttered charnel house, it cannot now have for an eighteen-year-old, and will soon have for no one.

The schoolmaster found it easy to imagine that he would be interested to walk through the dullest of English streets. He contemplated the idea for a moment, looking down into the waiting plate which he turned round and round with his strong hands. But Russia and himself, not England, was what he wanted to talk about. He spoke English – he was an English teacher – in slow careful words learned from books. It was also a change from Alex's impassive indifference, this school-master's earnest desire to inform me about Russia and himself. He was a gentle, intelligent man, with grievances irritating every surface of his mind. Cotton, the staple crop in the Uzbeg economy, was what he wanted me first to understand. Irrigation, intended to extend the ground available for cotton, had brought about the salinisation which had reduced tracts of the country to salt wastes: the chemical fertilisation of marginal land, and chemical crop spraying, had contaminated wells and canals; of course you don't have to travel to Urgench to hear these opinions, but there is something both touching and convincing about an ordinary citizen on the spot who repeats in his reasonable quiet tones the outline of an "ecological disaster" which world agencies trumpet from rooftops. I found it touching and urgent in his anxious mouth – a desperate whisper.

Wasn't there a good crop in prospect this year, though? I'd seen the growing cotton far and wide over arable landscapes on our trip.

Only when the cotton plant grows above six centimetres can you be confident it won't fail, he said. This season had been too cold, last season too wet: the range of temperature and rainfall is critical and the margin small. And next (he went on) the plants must be hand-pruned, the ground hand-weeded. I had noticed everywhere the small lonely groups of women in the vast landscapes, hand-weeding the cotton, symbols of toil in blowing robes stooped as close to the earth as frightened partridges, and they had struck me as an image of oppression and humility as old at least as the Bible. Yes, yes (he agreed eagerly) there is oppression in all this, in all the life these people must lead. The machines do not work. At the cotton-picking season he and his pupils must work in the fields. They must empty the schools to pick stones and pick cotton. As he told it, the tyranny was destroying lives he was responsible for. He was like the protagonist in a nineteenth-century reforming novel.

Because of this likeness I described how boys in the England of those days were obliged to miss school if hands were needed for rook-scaring or stone-picking or harvest. I said that the complaints of an elder against the German bailiff's demands in a serf village in tsarist Russia would have chimed with his own. But it was his own community only that he wanted to talk about. Take the black market, and how it operates against the poor and honest. You hear that a batch of shirts has arrived from the factory at the price set officially, ten roubles each. When you reach the shop there are none, they have vanished. They are, he said (shuffling his hands a little uncertainly as he used the phrase) "under the shelf". For ten roubles no shirts. But, you give to them twenty-five roubles, you will have a shirt. So – he spread out his hands and looked in my face with his gentle expression of sadness to make sure I had understood.

I didn't put into words what had been in my own mind when I'd compared his pupils' "oppression" with their ancestors' condition under the tsars, for his expectation of change showed an optimism I wouldn't attack. But that the two opposite systems, autocracy and Communism, should produce identical oppressions – and I mean oppressions which put stone-picking and shirt shortages in the shade – seems to me to argue that the nation in question may only be governable in one style, the style of Nicholas I and Stalin. It is the echo in Solzhenitsyn of Dostoievsky that makes me doubtful of Russia's political future. Nicholas I gave way to Alexander II, and in the 1850s and 1860s came liberalisation, the freeing of the serfs, tolerance of political expression, relaxation of the secret police, reforms to law and army. It might be Gorbachev's and Yeltsin's Russia. But then came into operation, as I have noted before, the characteristic Russian despair at reforms which failed to regenerate the whole empire and to place Russia "in one bound in the van of civilisation".* There was an assassination attempt, a Polish rising, a threat to the continued existence of the empire. The iron hand returned. The enemies of reform were given back their old places. Russia lumbered on in the chains it had always worn.

The parallel with Russia today is gloomy, and I knew besides that to discuss Russia's past with a Russian is a waste of breath, for the version of events taught to him and taught to me are so dissimilar that they make poor grounds even for a quarrel. I listened instead to the schoolmaster's distress with the present day.

Alex said almost nothing. He poured the Shakhrisyabz wine into our glasses, and followed the talk attentively enough to supply his friend with a word to make his meaning plainer, but he offered no opinion of his own. His silence, after producing this disaffected fellow countryman, was interesting. Had he undertaken to make no complaints to me in his own voice about life in Russia, and brought forward a friend whose views he shared to speak out for him? Never had Alex fed me the propaganda line of the hired guide about the triumph of industry or of agriculture whenever a factory chimney or a field appeared in view: he had simply answered my questions laconically, colouring his reply with no opinion. His voice was cynical enough, a disparaging voice, but he watched what he said and volunteered nothing. Though I knew how many hours he spent trying to ring up our next stopping-place, he made no comment on Russia's communication system. He was surely no gossip.†

---

* Geoffrey Drage: "Russia and the Period of Reform" (*Cambridge Modern History*: Volume XI, Chapter XII).

† The odious Marquis de Custine, complaining as usual of everything in his high-flown style, does have a point when he says how he was "wearied with the tact and prudence of the natives" where "gossip is a phenomenon, a rarity delightful to encounter, a thing that is missed every hour by the traveller".

V

Because of Alex's prudent demeanour I was considerably surprised by the suggestion which he made to me (a suggestion
which Anatoly's watchful face endorsed) over our tea-bowls
at breakfast next morning. Would I accept the invitation of a
group of friends – two of them schoolfriends of Anatoly – to
picnic on a lake not many miles off across the Oxus, and spend
the night as their guests in a village near the lake? The question
was put diffidently, would I agree to the plan, but Alex's voice
for the first time let a therm or two of intercessionary warmth
glow in his words, one bar of an electric fire in a chilly room,
and dark little Anatoly's sparky black eyes watched for my
reaction. I guessed the idea was his – I'd always thought
Anatoly knew what I wanted, and now in his own country he
could offer it – so of course I jumped at their plan.

It is a rare thing, when you're past forty, for the experience
of a moment so to overwhelm the mind's preconceptions that
it reconstructs your view of the country it happens in. The
strength of pre-preparation, of what you have learned of the
place in advance from books or people, ordinarily makes sure
that you only find under stones the sermons you have already
hidden there. My expectations of Turkestan were disappointed
by Khiva, but they didn't disintegrate altogether, as such a
disappointment might have caused them to do twenty years
ago, when outlook depended upon temperament, and temperament was volatile. Uncomfortable as it was (and trying for
companions) I do sometimes miss that knock-down response
to places and people which once filled the world with emotional violence and colour, and caused me to drive two hundred
miles through the night so as not to see the sun rise upon a
scene which had upset me at sunset. Wordsworth's "Lines
Written above Tintern Abbey" are pretty well incomprehen-
sible until you are middle-aged, and then almost too poignant
with private meaning to read. Despite all this, within an hour
or two of leaving Urgench I was in the midst of a scene which
did indeed flood my heart with delight, by the way in which
all its light and colour and variegated life had dramatised

around me the idea of "Central Asia" which my whole journey had been an attempt to explore.

I was standing on a knoll of grey gravel. Wind-shaken reed beds, and dykes and marshy pools, made up the landscape behind me through which we had driven by a rough road which here ended in the confusion of vehicles and the press of people below my knoll. There were trucks, old windowless buses, carts drawn by ponies, a few cars, all crammed together in the compound of gravel and blowing sand. Around the vehicles moved the multifarious crowd, hundreds strong, a gathering in this spot of men and women from every race living between the Black Sea and China. They drifted and chattered, they bought sunflower seeds from the vendor who had established his stall, and spat out husks, and smoked, and congregated on the little eminences of sand tufted with spiky grass, and drew wind-tattered robes around themselves as they gazed down from their sandhills onto the mighty river. For it was the crossing of the Oxus. This was the traffic collected from the villages on its shores, and from more distant travellers, who had assembled in a crowd to cross the Amu Darya.

I looked out over the famous river as one of this crowd with the intense feelings of delight I spoke of. A hurrying, eddying expanse of sand-coloured water about a third of a mile broad moved northward between jungle-green shores. Its surface was spanned, from a point just below my gravel outcrop, by a pontoon bridge, a metal track rocking on floats, the whole fluttery structure awash with the stream and sucking whirl-pools. But the bridge was closed to traffic; that was the delay, and that was the focus of the crowd's interest. A section of the pontoon, opened to let a boat pass, was being butted back into place by a tough little vessel smoking furiously as it battered into the rapid current. Active figures clambered on its pitching fo'c'sle, the confined waters swirled in a cataract through the breach, and there was that sense of a crisis in waterborne affairs which it is so pleasant to watch from the shore.

The sky over this low landscape of water and reedy jungle was deep blue and full of wind. Scuds of foam were dashed about the river's surface by the wind, the tug's smoke fled in wraiths, the wind whirled up the gravelly dust into spirals and dashed it down like hail showers peppering the water far and near. Most of all the wind seized on the robes and headdresses and veils of the groups of women, blue and black and rose-red streamers tattered and fluttering in the heat of the sun which burned down behind the wind; the groups they made, outlined on sandhills against the river and its distant shore, above the battered caravan of their vehicles, formed an image – a destination – which satisfied every expectation I had ever had of the word Turkestan. I had arrived exactly where I wanted to be. Did we wait an hour? Two hours? I could have waited a day absorbed in the scene.

When the section of pontoon had at last been butted back in place the bridge was opened to traffic. First the crowd on foot streamed out along the metal tracks, loading the rocking bridge with the colour which had brightened the shore where they had waited. I watched them go wishing that I was walking with them close to the water. But something about the integrity of the scene, which was its appeal – the renowned river to be crossed all in a day's work – depended upon it containing no artificial additives, which myself on foot might have been. So I thought, anyway. I walked down to the Moscva. With a great clapping-shut of doors and gunning of engines – under a cloud of diesel smoke whirled upwards – the trucks and buses now scrummed down on the line and nosed one by one onto the bridge. Our turn came. The track clattered under our wheels, licks of the river smelling of floodwater lapped our tyres, and the spongy undulations of the current rocked the car strangely. Then we were across, and climbing the sandy ridge of the shore into a green wilderness of reeds and pools and jungle which clothed the country for some miles beyond the river, almost indeed as far as the small town which seemed to be our objective.

Because of the difficulty of hearing in the back of the car what was said by Alex over his shoulder from the front I could only pick up clues to these mystery tours as we went along, but we had evidently come into this town to start assembling the picnic party. First stop was the compound of a police station where we were joined by a swarthy traffic cop in sunglasses; then, following his directions, we drove to a quiet spot in a park where everyone got out. Nearby, on a plinth, stood the statue of an Asiatic with the expression of gloomy exasperation which mullahs often wear, and this monument I made a show of admiring, walking all round it with my hands behind my back, in case our halt in the park had no other purpose. But it was soon clear that the spot was a rendezvous; hurrying towards us through the spindly trees came another short figure, this one in a suit and plastic cap, who embraced Anatoly and shook the rest of us by the hand with his vigorous, friendly clasp.

These two strangers beside me in the back – we shared the seat with a crusty confection made by Anatoly's sister, a pie of sorts, which needed careful nursing – we sped out of the little town and met at once with the desert, the Kyzil Kum, which is here a waste of sand. On we drove until a crossroads in the sands was reached, where the car stopped, doors were flung open, the radio turned up full blast, cigarette packets flung down; and a little island of noise and refuse very soon established in the midst of silence and desert. I had watched it done by Russians in the Caucasus, the picnic in forest or mountain glen beside the car whose open doors thumped out radio music, the noise of it scorching out into the surrounding scene with the destructive power of a flamethrower. But in the Caucasus I had suffered Russian picnics from the outside looking in, and had often driven off full of spleen to find somewhere you could hear the wind in the trees and the water over the stones. Here in the Kyzil Kum I was on the inside looking out, whilst around me the four of them smoked and drank bottled water and nibbled at Anatoly's sister's pie. Alex and Anatoly, amongst friends with a holiday in prospect, had taken themselves off duty and talked with the rest.

I walked away into the sun and wind of the desert rather as you go down the ladder of a convivial yacht to swim in the silent sea. Ten or fifteen miles off across the sands to the north rose a line of hills, an isolated ridge of harsh mauve rock seamed with shadow, its outline quivering in the heat. Everywhere the wind waved the fine hair of the tamarisk and rattled the *saksaoul* and stirred up wisps of sand, whilst the only touch of life in a dead landscape was the pop and scuttle of gophers between holes. Then I heard on the wind a strange double note, the oddest bird song I ever heard, the clear call of a cuckoo ringing across the desert. Talk of nightingales and the sad heart of Ruth –! No song can have excoriated the heart of an exile in this treeless waste – Arthur Conolly's perhaps, pining for his lost love in England – with such exquisite pain as the cuckoo's chimerical voice speaking of leaf and shadow in a summer wood at home. On and on it mocked, arising from no source in the sands that I could see, for as long as I walked away from my companions.*

After perhaps half an hour at our desert crossroads the gleam of a car's roof could be followed hurrying towards us out of the distant wastes. It arrived, stopped behind the Moscva in the middle of the road, and opened its doors to emit more music and another three men. There were embraces, introductions, welcoming handshakes. I wondered if I would ever sort them out. As yet they formed a group which might have been picked off an Uzbeg street at random, the traffic cop included, as I watched them milling between the two cars. Then all eight of us piled back aboard, slammed the doors and set off at speed.

A few miles on the desert road brought us to a cross-track onto which both cars swerved, wheels smoking sand, and plunged down into a green declivity of rough pasture grazed by cows which raised tethered heads to watch us dash by. The green hollow was as sudden and surprising as the cuckoo's voice. Ahead rose reeds, a wall of reeds, and above them the distant stony hills. The reeds closed around the track, met over the roofs of the cars, formed a tunnel of tiger-stripe sun and

---

* Peter Dobell, travelling in Siberia in 1813, has a curious footnote about the cuckoo: "The singing of the cuckoo amongst the mountains, where echo repeated the sad notes over and over again, had a most unpleasant effect upon our feelings and seemed like a warning voice that bade us prepare to perish in these solitary wilds. I have never since heard a cuckoo without feeling a painful sensation that I could not overcome" – *Travels in Kamchatka and Siberia.*

shadow till we stopped at journey's end. Doors opened. Everyone got out. Reeds grew gigantic all around us, the busby-
topped bulrushes waving in regiments against a sky pale with
heat, the gleam of water in shadow at their feet. Though the
reeds swayed and whispered, no wind reached us in this hot
still shelter in their midst. An inlet of lake water wound
amongst their roots to meet the bank of oozy turf onto which
provisions in many boxes were being unloaded from the cars.
Calves hung about warily, like street urchins, and nosed the
boxes.

A plank sunk in the ooze served for a landing stage, and at
the plank's farther end was moored a curious craft. Timber
laid on oil drums formed its decking and hull, and this deck
(perhaps twenty feet long) was divided amidships by a plywood screen six feet high, the forward section being roofed
over with an awning supported on poles. Round the foredeck
ran a roughly spot-welded rail, somehow a stylish finish to the
whole rattletrap vessel which gave her the top-heavy dignity
of a Mississippi steamboat as she lay in the gleamy water
against the reeds. I threw my shoes into the back of the
Moscva, splashed along the gangplank and leaped lightly
aboard.

I found the deck in the awning's shade carpeted with old
Turcoman rugs, and strewn with cushions round a tablecloth
on which the beginnings of a meal – washed carrots, bunches
of onions, loaves of bread – were already set out. From the
afterdeck behind the screen smoke rose in furious clouds and
flames crackled. I made myself comfortable cross-legged on
the deck, my back against the rail, and watched proceedings.
In a sleek little metal-hulled speedboat some of the party ferried
stores from shore to ship, handing up boxes and bags to the
afterdeck, punting back for more. To and fro it went. Most
stores went to the galley behind the screen, but the bottles – a
dozen bottles of vodka – were passed up to the foredeck, where
they were arranged on the cloth between us by a ponderously
large man smiling to himself with pleasure, who looked at me
now and then with a ruminative, gauging eye. The others
called him "Sultan". He first, of the five strangers, became an

individual as he crouched across the cloth from me, arranging the bottles into a formidable battery.

The activity soon shipped our stores, and the men came one by one over the side, prints of bare wet feet on the planks drying instantly where the sun burned down outside the awning's shade. The outboard from the speedboat was fitted to our transom, and pulled into life in a splutter of blue smoke adrift on the water. In a moment, with a grand forward surge like the progress of a swan, our ramshackle floating restaurant left shore and cars and surprised cattle, to swim into the mouth of a watery passage opening amongst the reeds.

This alley wound at the foot of reeds fifteen or twenty feet tall, and our ship, responding only sluggishly to the helm, rustled and nudged against its reed walls, the galley-fire still pouring up its steamer smoke as the whole top-heavy structure swayed gracefully along. Anatoly, keeping his usual sharp lookout by the outboard, was the helmsman and mechanic of the party; Alex had folded up his large legs with difficulty to sit next to me at the cloth, Sultan had not moved, and the others, without much thought for the trim of the staggering vessel, milled about between galley and foredeck shouting cheerfully to each other. So the voyage continued. Though we emerged now and again into a pool of clear water, always the reeds surrounded it, and always we nosed again into the wind-stirred sunlit reeds across the pool, and found the mouth of another winding waterlane leading us in time to another pool. There was no outlook beyond the close hot world of reeds and lagoons. In one of them we snagged a fisherman's net under water, and, in the activity which followed, a pleasant youngster with tow-coloured hair (much the youngest person aboard) proved very agile and quick at getting us free. He too I could now separate from the rest as an individual, watching him at work and listening to his eager, high-pitched voice. I asked Alex about the nets, and he told me that the fishing rights on the lake, which is called Akhcha-kol, the Lake of Money, are the possession of a collective to which one of our party belongs. Besides the right to fish, the collective has the right to shoot the wildfowl with which the lake teems in autumn, a fact easy to believe of these retreats among the rushes which we were passing through.

As we puttered across the still blue water of a pool of perhaps an acre, talk and argument and gesticulation was ended by Anatoly revving the outboard to maximum and driving our craft over the bubbling water until he slammed it full tilt into the reeds with a magnificent soft shock amongst the sliding parted stems. We had reached our moorings. Anatoly cut the engine, and the rustle of reeds and the lap of water resumed their quiet accompaniment to the scene. Blue water, and reeds burnished by the sun; above their restless heads the stony still-ness of the distant hills; over all the burning sky. It was a picture – and a boat – and a company – which I could no more have set out from Liverpool Street to find, than the chance scene at the crossing of the Oxus; but I recognised it as an aspect of the same destination, which luck had led me to.

Preparations upon the cloth now began in earnest. The plac-ing of vegetables into dishes and bowls, their arrangement as to spacing and colour, the setting out of simple comestibles so that the effect is profuse – I noticed the care with which this was done by these men, the same care taken over every private table I had sat at in Turkestan, to produce the generous abund-ance of a feast. A man in his fifties, long dark hair flecked with grey, squatted opposite me slicing up bread with a pocket-knife, his quick and intelligent eyes upon me as he talked to Alex. It was not the usual flat flaps of bread but oblong loaves, and I noticed that he sliced it the wrong way, lengthwise rather than across, as I never saw bread cut before. Evidently Alex was telling him about me, but I was content to sit quiet and look on. The spot was well chosen: we rested on windless water against the reeds which, now that we were settled, had come to life with a continuous susurration of the chatter and busy wings of little birds living unseen in their shade. This stirring of birds, like the presence of fish in the lake under us, added to the sense of being at rest in an oasis full of life amid the desert we had entered from the Oxus, a desert whose presence was still to be felt in the barren hills peering over the reeds at our craft. With vegetables sliced, bread distributed, eating began in the usual style of picking at the dishes on offer, whilst the silver cap was stripped from the first vodka bottle by Sultan's practised thumbnail, and liquor splashed into each person's bowl.

The first draught of vodka, taken with the strawberries I was eating, was delicious: clean as flame, it was quickly into the blood and dancing through the veins. In good spirits before, the emptied bowl left me feeling terrific. Tempted by happiness I felt the pull of the hospitality and good-fellowship of these men, the tug at my sleeve to forget caution and drink deep. If ever there was a reason to break rules, it was here on this reedy lake at the end of the world. Resolution wavered as Sultan refilled the flowing bowl. Another toast of welcome, from the youngster this time, more strawberries heaped before me, another tongue of fire lancing down my throat to discover the ichor in my veins. I hardly troubled to attend to Alex's muttered translation of successive speeches; it was the friendship and bonhomie of the speakers that I cared for, which shouldered aside the language barrier. Indeed, a sense of amity came across purer without translation, the guttural flow of their toasts a vernacular like the stir of the reeds and the chuckle of water against our craft, the tongue of the country speaking hospitably.

From behind the screen, out of the galley, now emerged a dark-skinned creature in shorts, his eyes bloodshot, a dish of smoking shashlicks in his hand. Several were heaped onto my plate, the mutton tough and fat but full of flavour, and, whilst we worried the taste out of the burnt meat with teeth and fingers, the clamour of talk and toasts and drinking rattled along. It was then about two o'clock, and from that hour until seven in the evening a constant supply of these burdened skewers of scorched mutton, and of stews or soups, was rushed to our cloth by the sea-cook toiling behind the screen. Whole flocks of sheep were reduced to white bones sucked dry and tossed over the ship's side by the hearty appetites aboard. The cook though shabby was not servile: he adopted the air of a host who has elected to do the cooking, as an Englishman might put on an apron and superintend the barbecue at his country manor; and yet, deeper engrained than this claimed equality, there was something more fundamentally humble about him than about the others, which made me wonder if his turn ever came to sit at the cloth whilst another member of the collective worked in the smoke and heat of the galley fire.

For the floating picnic was a regular occasion. The ship had been elaborated for today's cruise – the screen and railing erected – but these men came when they could to the lake, and knew and loved the place. They fished here, and shot the migrating wildfowl in autumn; they made a group of friends so well used to one another's minds that their conversation had the integration of talk in a play, each part a stance well known to the others, the arguments following familiar lines. For myself, cross-legged against the rail and listening to the give-and-take of Turki and Russian between these old friends, I had the comfortable feeling of being incorporated for the moment into their society with very little said on my part. Strong identities had very soon separated each of my five hosts out of the confused group I'd first been aware of at the desert crossroads – it seemed days ago – and each became an individual I warmed to as we ate and drank and talked and the sun burned down on the glistering water outside the awning's shade. Apart from the cook behind his screen there was Sultan, already a little sleepy, and the falsetto youngster who had freed us from the fishing net, and the sturdy traffic policeman in his shades: most interesting, though, and most distinguished, was the man in his fifties across the cloth from me, who gave the impression of harassed nervous energy contained in a narrow fine-featured head which he held aslant like a listening hawk. He was a doctor. In the conversations I had with him, whilst he listened to Alex's translation of my words, he kept his eyes all the while on mine with a burning intentness which questioned the value and probity of all I said.

We talked of course about politics; the world seen from this Central Asian province. The youngster was voluble, Sultan ("tired eyelids upon tired eyes") slow and caustic, the police-man excited. Throughout their lifetimes all of them, even the doctor, had been deprived of the basic information on both sides of a question which makes rational political discussion possible – for the unofficial aspect of all issues had been as speculative as the dark side of the moon – and there was a kind of intoxication (for the policeman and the young man at least) in having sudden access to adverse news. These two took a relish in the mere badness of the news, as well as making the assumption that all news unfavourable to central authority must be true (a trait I have noticed amongst Marxists in England). There was, too, in the young man's urging (for instance) that farms and businesses should be privately owned, that same simplistic streak which weakens exactly opposite proposals by English Marxists for nationalising land and businesses here, a naïveté which nullifies the arguments of hotheads everywhere. The doctor pointed out insuperable problems: what title to property would the seller have, of a collective or state-owned farm, which would serve as adequate security for private capital to buy the property? In the way the young man brushed objections aside I was reminded of my host at lunch outside Bokhara, who had promised that Uzbekistan's frontiers would be drawn "where they will cause no unhappiness"; and as I listened to the doctor overwhelming optimism with difficulties I understood why his face was strained and taut with anxiety in contrast to the youngster's eagerness or Sultan's sleepy cynicism.

Political discussion of the lake's ownership turned to talk of the fishing to be had in its waters, on which we had now lounged for some hours over the sucked bones and emptied dishes of our lunch – vodka bottles as they were emptied Sultan threw over his shoulder into the reeds – and I was asked if I'd like a spin in the speedboat to explore. I jumped at the chance. Well, I didn't quite jump as I intended, but got rather carefully to my feet whilst Anatoly (active as ever due to his liver forbidding him vodka) sprang down into the little metal speedboat which lay alongside, and began mounting the outboard. The doctor, who had also risen to his feet, and stood beside me looking down into the sunlit water, impressed me earnestly with the affection and high regard which he and the others had for Anatoly. From Khaurism he had gone to Tashkent, the far-off capital, and there he had prospered. His friends were delighted at the chance that had brought him back today. He spoke full of concern for Anatoly, with a kind of worried tenderness in his eyes. Standing barefoot beside him at the rail in the sun's heat the frankness of what he said to me made me share his situation. I saw Anatoly and his distant career in Tashkent from this lake in Khaurism. More, I felt I understood for a moment what it was like to be a concerned and thoughtful citizen of Khaurism in the midst of the present Soviet upheaval. The doctor's urgency and gravity took me out of the grand-stand watching the race and drove me a lap beside him at speed on the track.

Then I went over the side into the little boat, took my seat on the thwart and gripped the hot metal gunwale as the prow lifted with the drive of the outboard. Away we peeled from our moored flagship, her rail lined with our companions, an exhausted vapour still rising from her galley fire, till reeds hid her as we twisted from pool to pool, the speedboat now leaping forward into open water, now subsiding in a gurgle of wash as we slowed for a tight turn into a reed alley. The heat among the reeds was fierce. Now and then the traffic cop, who was the only passenger besides myself, lifted a cork float to examine a few dripping, sparkling yards of net drawn up from a deep clear pool. Here and there a scaly fish of three or four pounds with whiskers like a cat's struggled in the mesh, and was detached to leap and twist in the slop of the boat's bottom till I knocked its head on a paddle.

We had fished up perhaps half a dozen when we broke through a wall of reeds and found ourselves scudding over wide wind-rippled water which stretched as far as a low green shore. Anatoly opened the throttle. The bow lifted, the spray flew. I watched the white arches of spray hiss on the speeding blue water, and the dazzle of the sun, and I felt the heat, with the mesmeric effect recalled from happiness long ago, in fast boats off the coast of Italy or France, a yacht and a lunch party under its awning moored behind, ahead the evening and dinner in the dusk of a lamplit terrace above the sea. Because I haven't lived such a life for twenty-five years, memory's images, suddenly evoked, have the magical intensity of dream pictures, sharper than reality. The open bay we crossed at speed was two or three acres of water ending in a low shore and a ridge of sand rising between the lake and the ever-present sterility of the desert hills to the north. (But through the spray-arches I still saw more clearly the outline of Monte Argentario across the Tyrrhenian sea: is no present reality, not even the vividness of this remote lake in Turkestan, sufficient to expunge nostalgia?) On the shore ahead were a couple of stone huts and a boathouse. As we headed in fast for this settlement, hull banging the waves and spray flying, another speedboat put out and headed towards us in its own bursts of spray. We circled one another; the two helmsmen cut their engines; from the vigour of speed both boats lapsed into logs wallowing side by side in their own wash-waves. Whilst the traffic policeman strung our fish on a line and threw them to the boy crouching in the other boat, its skipper, a curious thin old creature standing up in the stern in a fur hat complete with ear muffs, screeched out broadsides of Uzbeg at Anatoly, who kept his engine puttering as if poised for flight from the ancient mariner's tirade. And indeed we didn't stay.

Back at the flagship bathing had begun, the heads of Alex, the youngster and the cook all lolling on the glistening water like victims of execution on a silver dish. But, though it was now five o'clock, the picnic aboard was by no means over. Smoke rose again from the galley. On his side of the screen I believe Sultan had never moved, masticating the gristly meat of as many shashlicks as were set before him, sinking a bowl of vodka now and then at one voracious draught, a picture of the impassive Turk which (I was now told) he indeed was. I told him of my own slight experiences of Turkey, which increased his affection for me from mere words into positive gestures. "Phleep, Sultan: Sultan, Phleep," he repeated a dozen times when I sat down in my old place, a moment later seizing my hand across the cloth and dragging it under his damp walrus moustache to sprinkle it with kisses.

The bathing party climbing aboard in their underpants –

228

Sultan's show of brotherhood – our own return from the refreshing dash in the speedboat – these things, and the sun slanting westwards, put an end to all formality amongst us. I had of course already made a speech of thanks, possibly two, but those now seemed coldly spoken long ago in the light of toasts now being proposed and the atmosphere of fraternity now binding shipmates together. The young hothead gabbled out some excitable phrases, striding about the little deck in a way that made the whole vessel pitch and roll: Sultan, his heavy head sunk on his chest, muttered sleepily and gestured with the hand not busy slopping liquor into our bowls: the doctor spoke again. Alex must have told him of the attack made on me in Moscow, for the burden of his speech was to regret that Russia should have greeted me with a knife at my throat, and to offer the friendship and hospitality of Khaurism in hopes of correcting my ideas. I had come to a remote spot amongst unimportant people (he said) but, if I'd been attacked in this district whilst the guest of anyone present, no one in the neighbourhood would have sheltered my attacker, who would have been discovered and punished at once. He raised his bowl, and all drank with hearty cheers.

I wanted only to respond with the affection I felt for these kindly men whose attention was now upon me. Alex, smoking away at my side, waited to translate whatever words I could find in the rose-coloured mist drifting through my head. I thought it best to speak from my seat. First I said that the traveller finds that no place is remote where he falls in with such friends as I had found here – Lake Akhcha, I said, was the lake nearest to my home, and they were all my neighbours. Then I picked up a distinction which had interested me in the doctor's speech: he had allowed that no host could ever guarantee that his guest wouldn't be attacked by a murderer, but the true host (as he had promised of this community) wouldn't shelter the attacker by their indifference and neglect, as the National Hotel in Moscow had done. It seemed to me at that moment, though my thoughts were a little unclear, that here was the distinction which divides the honest hospitality of a community from the grudging bargain to put a roof over his head, so long as no responsibility is incurred, which is all a stranger can buy for himself in a city. I told them that it had been necessary to be neglected and ignored by the National Hotel, before being welcomed aboard this remarkable craft, for me to understand at last how true hospitality may be distinguished from false. I would have told them more, but I found words a little hard to sort out, and some of them apt to trip up, so I reached for my bowl and toasted them in another bumper.

The response was warm. Cheering and stamping, renewed slopping of vodka into eagerly held out vessels, my hand again seized across the cloth by Sultan and drenched in kisses: the mood aboard was a jolly one. In my case, perhaps in theirs too, vodka had only released into words sentiments that were sincere. They had taken a gamble, throwing a party for an unknown foreigner, and their party had been a success. Through the clamour I heard Alex translating a toast flung at me by the young firebrand: "You are a good man, Phleep, a good man!" I couldn't help laughing at this, and laughing very probably aloud.

About seven o'clock I stepped ashore into the mud, delightfully cooling for the feet, and helped load the cars with what remained of the picnic. Above us the radiance of sunset flooded the upper air and the stony hills with colour which had been lacking in the heat of noon, and even gilded the heads of bulrushes, whilst water and shore grew rapidly dark. "A good man" –! What made me laugh was that this had been a popular phrase at school to describe a clubbable, likeable sort of fellow, good at games, on the fast track upward towards success, and it had a kind of Rip-van-Winklish ring to it, heard forty years later on the lips of a drunk Uzbeg in the Kyzil Kum. Players of the Great Game in these regions certainly drew portraits of themselves in their narratives togged out as "good men" – swells, sportsmen, popular at the clubs – but the type is rare now, having depended upon the swagger of empire and social class. Perhaps even at school there was always an element of self-disguise about a "good man", like the bonhomie of naval officers assumed so as to rub along with all sorts in the ward-room; certainly the dark characters of Burnaby or Valentine Baker, both outwardly archetypes of the genre, were most inaccurately ticketed by the "good man" label they tied on themselves for public show.

With reflexions such as these diverting me from paying full attention to events, a certain disconnection blurs my memories of the rest of that day, which was by no means ended with the drive of a few miles through the dusk to a settlement of low whitewashed buildings under trees. Here we got out, and strolled to and fro on a terrace up a few steps from the gravel lane which was the thoroughfare of the village. The air was cool and sweet, daylight fading upwards, dusk under the trees. I remember feeling extraordinarily cheerful. On the terrace was a child's tricycle, a little tin affair with pedals attached to the front wheel, which I determined to take out for a spin. Restraining hands feared that I would ride over the steps, or crash into a wall, or come to some other mischief, but I brushed them aside and with knees up to my ears and bell ringing, rode amongst the Uzbegs in a style that made them skip for shelter.

We were called indoors. A high bare oblong room had a table set in its centre, open windows giving onto a courtyard full of roses. Again we sat down to the spread of Uzbeg hospitality. Apart from table and chairs the only furniture in the room was a large wall-cupboard with glass panels, its shelves crowded with crockery, crowded indeed with all needful possessions, amongst them a fully decorated Christmas tree. Round the door of the room peeped children's faces, but no child entered, and no woman entered, though a heavily shawled pair of female arms handed in to one of the men a platter of shashlicks which he carried to table and put down amongst us. Besides vodka, various liquors now circulated. How long we sat eating and drinking – who was our host – how many we were – even whether I made any more speeches – are questions which I do not find that memory answers. That I was there and wished to be nowhere else is all I can remember.

Outside after supper it was night, cool soft darkness among the whitewashed buildings under the trees as I walked to and fro in the village street responding heartily to suggestions made to me through Alex that I should soon come back bringing wife and children. It seemed an excellent plan. Euphoria, which had made me feel so comfortable and easy with these men, took a further step and convinced me that wife and children would wish themselves here instantly, if they could only see this ideal spot for a family holiday. We would ride the Turcoman horses into the desert, fish in the lake; I would learn Turki and take up the life of a brother to these men. I remember embracing them one after another. I remember the satiny red petals of roses put into my hand. I think we then parted.

I awoke pretty early next morning and lay quiet, recollecting with pleasure how I came into such surroundings. I was under rugs on a sleeping mat on the floor of the large white room where we had eaten supper. Violent snores showed where Alex was buried in rugs elsewhere on the floor, and I could see the outline of Anatoly further off. I remembered now having come into this room to find it transformed in the time we had spent walking in the village street, its table and chairs whisked away by unseen hands, mats and bedding spread for us on the floor . . . but, think as I might, I could not recall the actions of putting myself to bed. Hadn't I taken a cutting of one of the courtyard roses at some stage? Here in my shirt pocket was the cutting, pushed into one of the little plastic bags I carry about for the purpose, so this much was true . . . I lay on my back piecing together other memories of the previous day, and I noticed that a *trompe-l'oeil* Tuscan pillar had been painted into each corner of this otherwise undecorated room, its capital appearing to support the architrave. The elegance of this embellishment completed my satisfaction in the place, as if a string quartet had struck up Mozart in the courtyard, and I lay waiting contentedly for the others to wake.

That early morning hour was to be the best part of the day, until evening at least, for it considerably checked my gaiety to discover when I got up that I wasn't completely sober, a thing that never happened to me before (though I have not before tried the experiment of drinking two bottles of vodka at a picnic). Both Alex and Anatoly were likewise a good deal subdued at breakfast, meat-filled pastry and bread and honey prepared for us in the room we had slept in. In the hallway on the way out to the car when we were leaving were mingled several much wrinkled, much shrouded women dipping their headdresses to us, and I grasped and shook any hands I could see peeping among the folds of robes – dry thin hands as bony as thorn trees which had done all the work of hospitality unseen – and thanked the muffled and turned-away faces as best I could. We left at once, the settlement under its grove of trees soon vanished into the desert behind us, whilst ahead lay three hundred miles more of desert to Bokhara. We had turned for home.

VI

At home, making plans on my atlas, I'd intended to go south from Khiva to Merv and Ashkhabad; but the frontiers of Russia's republics are faintly drawn on English maps, as they are in most English heads, and I had found when I reached Tashkent that my invitation, issued by Uzbegs, would not allow me into neighbouring Turkmenia where Merv and Ashkhabad lie. I had listened to Mr Eshtaev's dismissal of both towns as not worth visiting, and had rationalised my plan's curtailment rather as Colonel Valentine Baker had rationalised his on the Persian side of the same frontier in 1873: "Although we had failed in our attempt to reach Merv, I felt that we were doing much more useful work exploring the Kuren Dagh" (a range of hills of no strategic interest then or now), Merv having been visited by "several Englishmen".

Ten years later, in 1883, Russia's annexation of Merv, once "Queen of Cities", was to be her final appropriation of Central Asian territory until she attacked Afghanistan in 1979. Last wicket to fall in the Great Game, the taking of Merv completed the conquest of Turkestan, which the sabre-rattling of Burnaby and Baker, and of dozens more russophobes both military and political, had neither prevented nor delayed. These last stages of the game appeal to me a good deal less than the romance of the early years, and "Merv" hasn't the ring to it of "Bokhara" or "Khiva" in my ears, but nonetheless these late-order bats-men, a Baker or a Skoboleff, though rather abominable in their imperial swagger, do still transfix a modern reader with that bulging choleric eye of arrogant effrontery which ruled the world in the 1880s. They were "good men" in the most unpleasant sense.

The Central Asia they travelled in was a very different prop-osition to the storied kingdoms under tyrants' thumbs which Abbott or Conolly had tiptoed through. Railways, for one thing, had cut in half the journey from home. Burnaby, con-sulting train timetables, kept in mind throughout his ride to Khiva the need to be in England again before his leave was up, and here beside the frozen Don we find Valentine Baker making his way home: "There, puffing and blowing, came an engine and train; . . . those two rails of iron ran in one uninterrupted track to Calais, and we already felt at home." The iron rails made it possible, too, to bring to these "wild lands" the comforts of home, chairs and good big tents, and salmon rods and a supply of claret, and evening dress in which to dine at Teheran "with a pleasant party of our own countrymen" which made their travels already "seem almost like a dream". In the Persian border highlands by Baker's day it was a simple matter to keep in touch with St James's: "While the tent was being pitched, a letter-carrier arrived from Meshed, bringing us a bag of . . . old numbers of the *Pall Mall Budget*; which latter, by-the-bye, is a capital paper to have sent to you when on a wild foreign expedition."

How wild is the foreign expedition, if you can sit reading the *Pall Mall Budget* in your camp-chair, a Purdey breechloader across your knees, whilst some of your "people" put up your tent and look out your evening things and open a few bottles of claret? Mind you, Captain Abbott would have done the same thing forty years earlier if he'd had the chance: there was never any question of the traveller imposing upon himself any restrictions as to comfort or luggage: restrictions were imposed by necessity, and the traveller made himself as comfortable as possible, employing all the aids and inventions of the day. There was no idea of repining, as some do today, over the passing of old dangers and old miseries. Baker's reaction to the train is refreshingly spontaneous and natural, if you compare it to Ruskin's bewailings over the Lakes' railway.

The spontaneity with which these "good men" of the 1870s and 1880s welcomed the advantages put their way by European progress becomes rather devious when their position vis-à-vis an enemy needs to be described. Look at that generation's vocabulary when they come to write about blood sports; smokeless powder, breechloaders, split cane rods instead of greenheart poles, drawn gut leaders instead of horsehair – such advances in efficiency made the killing of fish and birds a much easier and less uncomfortable pastime than it had been in the 1840s: but it is now, in order to sweeten conscience against these advantages, that sporting authors begin to use language which suggests equally matched opponents engaged in a duel of wits for one another's life. The humble brown trout of the Hampshire streams, which Colonel Hawker used to catch from his horse's back, was elevated about then into "a foeman worthy of our steel" by many a bulky, knickerbockered angler crawling amongst the tussocks of the bank, just as if the fish had developed modern weapons too. An artificial code of self-restraint was erected between the sportsman and his quarry, so that the age-old wish to go out and kill a few animals could be re-presented as a match between peers: "dry fly only" became the Hampshire rule, as a way of preserving man's self-esteem rather than as a way of preserving trout. These restrictions, a kind of chivalric code controlling the methods of killing wild creatures, made up rules of "honourable behaviour" entirely for the satisfaction of the sportsman's conscience, for it makes very little difference to a Hampshire trout whether he's basketed by Halford's upstream dry fly or by Hawker's downstream wet. The mediaeval code which allowed a French seigneur of the day to warm feet chilled by a cold tramp in the blood of freshly killed peasants, forbade him as a point of honour to use more than one peasant per foot; but the peasantry, like the trout, were not asked to help frame the code.

For the same purpose, to imply that level ground existed between the adversaries, Burnaby and Baker's generation tried with similar tricks of language to redress for conscience's sake the imbalance which modern weapons had put into European hands vis-à-vis their native opponents. A drawing in the *Graphic* shows Burnaby reloading his twelve-bore shotgun at the battle of El Teb exactly in the stance of a man facing driven grouse; his biographer describes the action (in which 2,000 Arabs were killed by Martini rifles for a trifling British loss) as "a tough fight but a fair one". "Tough" and "fair": the words couldn't be better chosen to convey a blurred sense of tournaments and sportsmanship. Similarly Valentine Baker gives off a great glitter of dauntlessness as he swaggers along: "It would have been bad indeed if we three Englishmen, quite handy and ready, could not have held our own against any such desultory attack as we were likely to meet with." What was "handy and ready" was their armoury of breechloaders, a possession which would have cheered up poor Abbott very considerably when facing an attack of those same "desultory" tribesmen on the truly equal ground of swords and muzzleloaders in the winter of 1839.

It is possible that Colonel Baker nursed a secret fantasy of the messianic rôle he might play in Central Asia – he had a nature full of surprises, as the sequel shows – and that this ambition had brought him to the spot. The journalist Charles Marvin, writing of the threat to India offered by Russia's conquest of Khiva in 1873, suggests that "perhaps it was with the idea of arresting this movement that the three English officers – Colonel Baker, Captain Clayton and Lieutenant Gill – made their way to the southern side of Central Asia. It is certain that if the fears of England had been realised, the presence of two good cavalry officers and one of the engineers on the spot would have been exceedingly opportune, and Baker and his companions might have made as grand a stand against the

Russians, as Butler, Nasmyth and Ballard had done on the Danube in the summer of '54." Hints of this ambition to be the man who saved India surface here and there in Baker's book, *Clouds in the East*, which describes a journey otherwise objectless and ineffectual. *

The practical military idea, of raising the native tribes against the Russian invaders, was made romantic by the gloss of legend hanging about it. There was the tradition that at Geok Tepe, a fortress of the Tekke Turcomans on the plain below the Persian mountains where Baker was making himself ready, a white charger was kept saddled to carry a fair-skinned deliverer who would appear from the West. Questioning "one of the greatest of the Tekke warriors" who was "anxious to know whether England intended to let them be swallowed up by Russia", Baker enquires: "What do you wish from England?" "We want to be under England [he replied], that is the great wish of the Tekkes."† And how could such an end be accomplished without troops? We find Baker lent an escort of border irregulars whom he is soon calling "my cavalry" and whose leader he reports as saying, "Why not take us with you? Give us a little pay and we will follow you . . . wherever you choose to lead us, and fight for you as hard as you like." "There were some splendid fellows among them [adds Baker wistfully]; if only they had been drilled and disciplined . . ." In an appendix he says of them, "Should they ever come under European officers (a result which might easily be brought about) these 120,000 magnificent horsemen, guarding as they do that great sea of desert, which now isolates Russia from India, would form a splendid frontier force. If they be conquered, however,

---

* Baker's two fellow officers, whom he describes with his usual condescension as "sticking to me so manfully", shortly met with fates which demonstrate, far more typically than Baker's own débâcle, the risks of military life in those days; Gill being murdered by the Bedouin, Clayton killed at polo.

† Can these be the same people who will be saying to Colonel Grodekoff in two years' time, "Would to God the time might be hastened" when the Russians will come, for "the English we do not like at all"?

and brought under Russian rule and leading, Afghanistan will ever lie at their mercy."

So Colonel Valentine Baker waited, in the mountains of northern Persia, with a hope in his heart that the white charger in Geok Tepe was saddled for himself, *chevalier sans peur et sans reproche*. The call to arms never came. Under Russian rule the Tekke Turcomans did indeed fall – and the Irish journalist Edmund O'Donovan watched Skoboleff storm Geok Tepe from a spur of those same mountains eighteen years later* – but the advance which the russophobes predicted, on Herat and India, never materialised. And by the date of the fall of Merv the showy and popular Colonel Baker of the Tenth Hussars had become a sort of shadow-image of himself in the person of Baker Pasha, soldier of fortune to the Sultan of Turkey, leader of an Egyptian rabble defeated by the Mahdi; but, as an English officer and a gentleman, disgraced by the term of imprisonment which he had served for assaulting a twenty-two-year-old girl in the railway train from Liphook to London.

Our morning's drive south-east across the desert towards Bokhara was hot and tedious. No landscape looks half so interesting once you have turned for home. The road seemed rougher, Alex's attempts to tune the radio more cacophonous. We stopped about midday at a dusty pull-in where trucks and a few cars had been run under the shade of some trees around a mud compound. Inside a malodorous timber hut food was slopped onto plates, soup or stew, grey slithery meat, alongside the round flat loaves of bread. I had appetite for nothing and went out to wait at a wooden table. The elms which shaded it shaded also a viscous pond seething with mosquitoes, as well as other trestles at which men lounged. I noticed that Anatoly had left his wallet and car keys on our table; petty crime hardly exists – a crumb of comfort, like Mussolini making the trains

* "When the stronghold was captured a splendid white charger, richly caparisoned, was found in a stable, which the defenders had kept all along for the English commander" – C. Marvin.

run on time, to set against the enormous criminality of government. If Uzbekistan became independent, and democratic, you
couldn't leave your wallet and keys on a table any more. We
hardly spoke. Neither Alex nor Anatoly could eat their soup
or stew, whichever it was, rancid-looking fluid not unlike the
pond water, and we soon left it to the flies and went back
to the car. As Anatoly regained the highway, and his usual
breakneck speed, Alex turned to me and asked,

"Bokhara, or Samarcand?"

"Haven't you booked us in at Bokhara?" Samarcand was
three hours further at least. I had been counting off the miles
of this desert journey.

"No problem. We find room at Samarcand also."

Evidently they had made the decision. I was irritated. "Do
as you like," I said.

He turned back, and I heard him murmur to Anatoly, in a
tone of satisfaction, "Samarcand."

Why did I give in? I had counted upon Bokhara. I settled
down to stare at the sandy cottonfields which now began to
struggle for a foothold in the desert, and at the rough black
tarmac which flickered ahead to the heat-hazed horizon.

The conundrum of Colonel Baker's débâcle is an intriguing
one. In 1875, aged fifty and by now quartermaster general at
Aldershot, he caught a train at Liphook for London. Between
Walton and Esher a distressed young woman, a Miss Dickinson, was observed clinging to the outside of a carriage door;
she sobbed out (when the train was stopped at Esher) that she
had been attacked by the military gent in the compartment,
who could indeed offer the guard no sound reason for the fly
of his trousers being agape to the top button. At Croydon
Court on August 2nd – it was a show which "attracted more
interest than any political event of the day", and the judge had
the street cleared on account of the bank holiday crowd's noise
– Baker was convicted of indecent assault, sent to prison for
twelve months and fined £500. The judge didn't spare his feelings, either, calling it "a brutal assault inspired by animal passion" and condemning such men's "habit of licentiousness".

Baker was dismissed from the army, "Her Majesty having no further occasion for his services", and, after his release from gaol, served the sultan against Russia – notably commanding a handful of irregulars in a brilliant engagement against heavy odds at Tashkessan – thence finding his way to the command of a force of the Egyptian police, a rabble of 3,500 which, faced with 1,000 of the Mahdi's men, threw down their weapons and offered themselves for slaughter. In these last ten years of life (he died of angina in Egypt in 1887) what were his thoughts and feelings? Did his wife and two daughters stick by him? Was he cut by English society in Egypt? Can he ever have recovered his self-esteem from the judge's damning strictures on his character under the vulgar gaze of that bank holiday crowd? His subsequent book, *War in Bulgaria*, tells us nothing. In *Clouds in the East* he had constructed for himself the self-portrait of a dauntless and wintry knight of old: the effect of the Croydon courtroom, and of twelve months in gaol, on such an image – whether he believed in it himself or not – is devastating.

Was it some momentary madness, I wonder, that took hold of his mind in the train, making him kiss Miss Dickinson repeatedly and "attempt to raise her clothing", or was this violence all of a piece with the usual actions of a violent and brutal creature disguised as a gentleman? The whole man, and his life and character – watched no doubt by hundreds of men of the time just like him – a whole attitude and section of society (as the judge made clear) was on trial at Croydon. When Baker's counsel tried to make out that Miss Dickinson (one of whose three brothers was an army officer) had led him on with suggestive conversation, the judge cut short that line of argument.* He would allow Baker "no shadow of excuse". Here was this imperial swell, formidably armoured by class and convention, a thoroughly alarming figure to most of the people in the courtroom, who seems suddenly to have acted

---

* The judge did suggest that single females should avail themselves of a "Ladies Only" compartment, though confessing that the company was not likely to be so "lively" as in a mixed compartment.

in the very way – unmanly, unchivalrous, wanting in self-control – of which his public character would be most contemptuous and condemnatory. Perhaps it wasn't out of character. We don't know how he conducted himself towards slave girls and concubines in the East, though we know that he had spent a good deal of his youth in Ceylon; and we know too that his brother, the African traveller and hunter Sir Samuel, is supposed to have bought his wife in a Turkish slave market in Wallachia.

The Mahdi's defeat of Baker Pasha's Egyptian policemen near Tokar in February 1884 was made a good deal easier by the dervishes having armed themselves with Martini rifles taken from the 10,000 or so Egyptians under Hicks Pasha whom they had slaughtered at Kashgil the previous November. In this disaster had fallen Edmund O'Donovan, correspondent of the *Daily News*, who had witnessed from a mountain top the final fall of the Tekke fortress of Geok Tepe in 1881. A bloodthirsty *coup-de-main* under General Skoboleff, the storming of Geok Tepe was the last military action of the Great Game, for, although Merv wasn't annexed until 1883, that fortress fell without a struggle, its ruler Makdum Ali having no more inclination to fight the Russians after his visit to St Petersburg than had Cetewayo to fight the British after he had seen London.

The Turcomans of Geok Tepe had already once repelled the attempt of a Russian army, under General Lomakin, to storm their fortress; but now "the White General", Skoboleff, had arrived to take command. O'Donovan had been living about the Russian camp near Krasnovodsk on the Caspian for months picking up news, on excellent terms with the then commander General Lazareff (a curious soldier who had been a tailor until he was twenty). Lazareff, however, died of a fever, and the new commanding officer ordered O'Donovan out of Krasnovodsk "by the seven o'clock steamer". O'Donovan left, but not by steamer. He rode out of camp to creep painfully through November swamps into Persia, whence he could watch from beyond their jurisdiction the assembling of the Russian force.

Edmund O'Donovan was more than a resourceful and ten-
acious journalist; he was (judging by his book *The Merv Oasis*)
a most likeable and well-informed Irishman, tall, good-looking
and amusing, who, at thirty-five, had already been imprisoned
in Dublin and in Limerick as a Fenian, had been a prisoner of
war to the Prussians in 1870, had fought for the Carlists in
Spain and reported the Balkan rising against the Turks in 1876.
There was continuous amusement to be had for a restless spirit
outside Britain in those times. Although he complains in his
wry, dry manner of the hardships of his daily life, and under-
scores the peril of his position, it is very clear how he relishes
the fun of the thing. "I could not help thinking [he writes of
his captivity at Merv] what some of my friends at home would
think could they see me sitting among the crème de la crème
of the prime brigands of Central Asia, far, far away from
the remotest chance of succour, unknowing how long my
detention might last, and entirely dependent on myself as far
as my ultimate fate was concerned." He never loses his vigilant
eye for beauty, in a Persian city or a desert storm or a range
of Eastern mountains; nor does he lose the alertness of mind
which analyses impressions and compares them with others
drawn from experience, however long the ride or cold the
wind: but I don't doubt that what attracted him most to the
dangerous life he led was expressed in those last words quoted
above, that it left him "entirely dependent on myself as far as
my ultimate fate was concerned". Thus it was a cruel end to
such a life, to find himself trapped helpless in the rout and
slaughter of Hicks Pasha's broken army at Kashgil, where his
resource and self-reliance were of no use. His dead face would
not have worn the smile that Burnaby's wore, of a man called
away from a favourite occupation.* In north Persia, though,

---

* There is an account in Father Ohrwalder's book (*Ten Years Captivity
in the Mahdi's Camp*) of how O'Donovan's servant Gustav Klootz, a
German, deserted Hicks Pasha's force before the fatal battle – due to
"certain socialistic tendencies" says Ohrwalder charitably – and was
brought in front of the Mahdi, where he at once apostasised to save his
life and told all he knew of the disorder and low morale of Hicks' army.

he was in his self-dependent element: when he reached Sabza-var, beyond which Valentine Baker had thought it too danger-ous to advance, he at once pushed on into the Turcoman country towards Merv, alone save for a Kurdish servant shaking with fright. A cable from Skoboleff refusing him per-mission to join the Russian expedition against Geok Tepe had determined him to throw in his lot with the Turcomans, what-ever the risk, and to watch the Russian advance from their viewpoint, which must at all events have been the viewpoint which appealed to his Fenian past against the might of Russia; for I doubt if Skoboleff's patronage could ever have turned the Irishman's head and his views as it had turned the head of the American journalist MacGahan at Khiva. To Skoboleff's refusal he cabled back *"Au revoir – à Merv"*, for he was determined to reach the Queen of Cities before the Russians.

Skoboleff would run no risk of his assault on Geok Tepe failing as Lomakin's had done – he was an ambitious creature with his eye quite probably on the governor-generalship of India, once he had persuaded the tsar to take India from the British – so that he amassed men and matériel by rail at Kyzil Arvat, halfway from his Caspian base towards his objective. Then in the first weeks of 1881 he moved against the Akhal Tekkes' fortress. On the very day of his assault it happened that O'Donovan

ascended the top of the Markov mountain, which rises some 6,000 feet over the Tekke plain, and is not above twelve miles from Geok Tepe. With my double field-glass I could easily make out the lines of the Turcoman fortress, and the general position of the besiegers . . . I could plainly see, by the smoke of the guns, that the attack had begun in earnest, and I watched its result with intense anxiety . . . after what was apparently a desperate conflict it was evident that [the Russians] had forced their way. A crowd of horsemen began to ride in confusion from the other side of the town, and spread in flight over the plain. Immediately afterwards, a mass of fugitives of every class showed that the town was being abandoned by its inhabitants. The fortress had fallen, and all was over with the Akhal Tekkes.

It is wonderfully appropriate that we can watch the fall of the last wicket in the Great Game through the double field-glass of one of its best commentators watching from his press box on a grandstand of mountains above that bumping pitch; art lending history a hand, as the amateur historian wishes it would do more often.

Skoboleff was as merciless in his pursuit and slaughter of the Tekkes fleeing from Geok Tepe as Kaufmann had been at Khiva. Twenty thousand were massacred in the three days' license this "genial king of men" allowed his Cossacks, in accordance with the view which he expressed in conversation with Charles Marvin: "I hold it as a principle in Asia that the duration of a peace is in direct proportion to the slaughter you inflict upon the enemy. The harder you hit them the longer they will be quiet after. We killed 20,000 at Geok Tepe, and the survivors will not soon forget the lesson." This "hard-hitting, fair-fighting hero" – for thus Marvin translated the pitiless characteristics of the Slav into sporting language for English readers – had another side to his nature in common with Colonel Baker (whom he admired) and with Captain Burnaby, besides these robust views as to punishing Asiatics: he was "not happy in his married life" (in his biographer's phrase for it), living apart from his bride after a single day of union, whilst his death was to take place in circumstances so shady, and so carefully concealed, that I am left supposing that he succumbed to a heart attack in a male brothel.

He was right about the lesson of Geok Tepe: the massacre broke the Tekkes.* In a very few years, at Merv itself (which O'Donovan had penetrated at the risk of his life) "the postman goes his round, the policeman guards the shops" and, says Marvin, "Central Asia is abolished".

* It broke Skoboleff too: he was removed from his Central Asian command to Minsk, and thence, within a year, exiled to his country estate for making inflammatory anti-German speeches. He died in Moscow on his way into exile.

I had not reached Merv, or stood on O'Donovan's mountain grandstand above Geok Tepe, and I regretted it – regretted it with the touch of sadness put there by the near certainty that I never will reach them now. I remember standing once on a promontory of the Turkish coast a few miles from Trebizond, and catching sight of the snow peaks of the Caucasus far off across the Black Sea, and making up then for the regrets of the moment (I had no papers for Russia) by assuring myself that I'd reach those mountains some day by another route. And I did, eight or nine years later. Last night the euphoria of the picnic had made Turkestan seem the very place to return to for a family holiday, but today I was sober. When, in the midst of the desert, the car reached a T-junction with a signboard which pointed one way to Bokhara and the other to Samarcand – there was nothing else on that weathered board but the two celebrated names – I knew that turning my back on Bokhara and Merv now, as we did, was turning my back on them forever.

The evening mountains guarding Samarcand were very welcome as an end to that day's driving. Arrival cheered me up sufficiently to encourage a stroll about the town in the declining light, and, because it could be reached without entering noisy streets, I chose to walk to the Gur Emir, which contains the mausoleum of Tamerlane, along a lane already made dark by the shade of mulberry trees. The lane opens into a square, busy with boys throwing up sticks into a large old cherry tree to knock down its fruit, and across the square rises the arched entrance of the Gur Emir. I walked into its courtyard. Evening light warmed its stone, its tiled façade, the green leaves of trees; and above the courtyard the twilight glimmered in the greenish, shadow-pleated cupola which hung in the sky like a lantern beaming softly. Against the wall of the courtyard which held the last heat of the day an official in a blue uniform sat comfortably on a bench, keys and peaked hat laid down beside him, whilst at that moment the last visitor, some great man or other, lackeys hurrying in attendance, was striding away from the shrine on brand-new sneakers, so that when I entered I was alone.

It is a numinous space, the chamber of tombs. Gleaming alabaster and sculpted mihrabs reflect a light dimmed by domes and shadows. At the vault's centre, guarded by the ivory-coloured tombs of his imam and of his descendants, there glows the slim jadestone of Tamerlane himself. This sepulchre is compelling, and humbling, with the magnetism of a true shrine. Here, surely, the cult of Turkestan nationalism – the rebirth of this ferocious warlord as "father of his people" – will root itself. Here is the heart of Central Asia. Though the merry cries of the boys flinging sticks into the cherry tree came in to me, there was in the mausoleum a profound silence – a listening stillness – which seemed to me alert for the tocsin of revived nationalism. "Central Asia abolished" by the Russian conquest? I doubt it. The fierce little warring kingdoms were done away with by the Great Game, it is true; perhaps it will be Conolly's nobler game, the idea of a federation of Central Asian republics, which will be the next fixture in Turkestan. Standing by Tamerlane's tomb I was pretty sure I heard a heartbeat.

CHAPTER VII

Return Journey

WITHIN A WEEK I was aboard a plane leaving Tashkent for Moscow. Still the mysterious Eastern mountains of Kirghizia and Chinese Turkestan did not reveal themselves except as misty shadows below the wing, and I gave up hope of ever seeing them clear. Tashkent – all Central Asia – fell away below into an irrecoverable past along with the threesome then motoring back into their city from the airport, Anatoly at the wheel, Alex beside him, Mr Eshtaev no doubt in the centre of the back seat. For Mr Eshtaev himself had come to see me off, unfolding around his presence an atmosphere of influence like a red carpet for his own neat footfalls, just leaning forward sufficiently to murmur in the ear of an official who immediately unlocked a door through which the four of us had passed into what I took to be a VIP lounge, his demeanour preserving that superior impassivity of the man who has mastered the system. I pictured them silent in the car driving into Tashkent, for I had no idea what they had made of me and my tour; but I felt affection for all three, and much gratitude. If Alex was a policeman, it was clear from our truant night in the village near Akhcha-kol that he was one who knew how to wink. Their presents distended my baggage; I'd had to give away possessions wholesale to make room for them all, shoes to a chambermaid, *Praeterita* to a surprised desk clerk who had once asked me *sotto voce* if I had any English magazines. And Mr Eshtaev had offered me a trip into these mountains fading below the plane, to Dushanbe or Kokand, wherever I wanted to go. Was it the conventional gesture of the luncheon host who asks you to stay to tea as a means of reminding you your time is up? Was it a real offer? What power had Mr Eshtaev?

247

The door which his influence opened for us at the airport didn't after all lead into a VIP lounge, it led into the same shabby room everyone waited in, but allowed us in a few minutes before the rest of the crowd.

The offer of a tour to Ferghana was made at a lunch I'd been taken to a day or two earlier, the last "official" event of my visit. For a final fling of their hospitality the venue was brilliantly chosen – I put it down again to Anatoly's perception – as a demonstration of how old and new rub along side by side in Turkestan. From the suburban road we had penetrated the usual blank mud wall by the usual timber doors. Inside we found a single-storey whitewashed cottage, a flourishing courtyard garden shaded by fruit trees, and a vine arbour under which our table was set. But the surprise was the view. One margin of this rustic plot was unenclosed, bordered only by a rushing stream which separated the garden from a field beyond. The field was an unmowed waste of thistles, and just over its further hedge rose the tower-blocks of modern Tashkent. We were a hundred yards from those concrete ramparts which enclose every Soviet city with their grey uniformity, a hundred yards from the hunger of cranes and bulldozers building more; but in the shade of our garden across field and brook the birds sang sweetly from the trees and the sunlight dappled down through the vine onto our tablecloth spread with dishes of scrubbed vegetables. I was delighted with it. In the current of the stream an irrigation wheel creaked round, lifting water into a reservoir whose outlet fed channels running hither and thither about the kitchen-garden; but the reservoir was today full of clear eddying water emptying itself back into the stream, for it was in use only to cool – Oh dear! – a magazine of vodka bottles. I looked about the little garden much interested in what flowers it grew, chrysanthemums and gladioli amongst the beans and potatoes, vines forming the arbour we were to sit beneath, a fine row of pomegranates which were mounded over each autumn in rushes and earth against the frost. A room was added to the cottage every time a son of the owner married, into which the new family moved, and it was one of these sons who served us with soup and shashlicks when the time came to eat, hurrying in and out of his as yet unpainted room whilst smoke poured from the yet unglazed window.

When the rest of us had been strolling and talking for some time amongst the vegetables and flowers, the door from the road opened and Mr Eshtaev entered amid a general stir, walking up to me with a honey-tongued greeting. Courtiers fell in around their principal. We very soon sat down to eat.

In conversation with Mr Eshtaev – and he and I talked, through Alex, for most of the meal – it was impossible to avoid the idea that he was stalking an objective; his careful speeches and watchful eye were like the little runs and pauses of a man chasing an escaped parrot with a butterfly net. It made me cautious in what I replied, as even a parrot ignorant of its fault is made cautious by pursuit, but I had no idea in the world what he was after. I knew that I owed him a great deal, but I doubted if I was possessed of the currency in which he wished to be repaid. He was after the wrong parrot, but I knew that the parrot who makes this protest will only persuade its pursuer of its cunning and duplicity, never of its innocence.

TURON, the trade association he headed which had replaced VAAP as his vehicle, appeared to be his personal declaration of independence from Moscow. Sick of Moscow's VAAP commandeering all prestige and hard currency and jaunts abroad, he had responded in combative style by setting up TURON: to some enquiry from the Moscow-based Kirill Ukraintsev he had asked sharply, "Are you sure you still exist?" – rather a chilling question in the Soviet Union. He outlined TURON's plans. Meetings with Western companies were needed to attract investment capital and win outlets in the West. In the field of tourism, for example – the butterfly net crept closer, but I was still the wrong bird – Mr Eshtaev pictured TURON breaking free of Intourist and converting old Central Asian dwellings into small hotels, developing sites along sympathetic lines, offering to visitors the hire cars and packages of the West. He knew of the National Trust House Forte Company. He assured me that he had informed himself of the ways in which the West's tourist industry differed from the lumbering dull-witted methods of Russia's. I wondered as I listened how far any of his ideas had got, how detailed and developed they were. The motivation seemed to be antagonistic. The impetus towards liberation came from hatred of Moscow. For the destruction of the Aral Sea – for the want of pure water which in Choresm causes an infant mortality from hepatitis of 10.2 per cent – for the theft of raw material wealth – for the rebuilding of Khiva as a Disney theme park – for everything untoward in Central Asia, Moscow was to blame. As the vodka circulated tongues found fiercer words to echo their chief's resentments. It is the respectable who are most angered by disorder; anarchic values, which mean that fifteen boxes of matches would today buy a sheep, put an angry ring into the voice that told me this fact. "Fighting" was mentioned, if not toasted, and a bellicose camaraderie in support of Mr Eshtaev was the mood colouring our little Eden of old Turkestan threatened from over the brook by the towers of Soviet Tashkent.

The lunch party lasted until late afternoon, by which time, and in that convivial atmosphere, I hoped that the parrot-hunter had laid down his net. On our way back into Tashkent we stopped, Alex and Anatoly and Mr Eshtaev and I, at a medresseh in the suburbs which was being prepared as new offices for TURON. It was an impressive HQ for the campaign against Moscow. I admired the cool shady cells which were to be offices, wondering, as I walked round the bunker amongst Mr Eshtaev's janissaries, what his ultimate ambition might be. I couldn't help him with it: he had mistaken my standing. At lunch, having learned no doubt by experience how to secure a Russian writer's assistance, he had offered to publish any quantity of my books simultaneously in Russian and Uzbeg at Tashkent, but, having nothing to offer him in return, I could only promise to speak to my agent, and reflect on how publishing-as-bribery must bewilder would-be readers in the bookshops of Tashkent, if the shelves are filled in this way. As we parted on the roadside at the medresseh's gate Mr Eshtaev asked me through Alex – he never spoke a word of

English, though I could see in his eyes an understanding of much that I said – if his present had pleased me.

The present, with which Anatoly and Alex had come hammering at my hotel room door the evening before, had not been associated by them with Mr Eshtaev, so at the time I had thanked themselves for it. Anatoly, having given me the package, took it back again to unwrap it himself, as eagerness sometimes makes children unwrap the presents they give you, and out of the brown paper he unfolded one of the beautiful glazed cotton robes still worn by the old men in these parts, a shimmering blue with a thin black stripe, which he immediately put on my back, tying round my waist the shawl which was part of the outfit, and standing back to admire his work. I was delighted with it, and thanked them: they bowed and left. Probably I should have known that this *khelat*, like a dress of honour presented to travellers by the khans of old, would have come from their chief, whom I could only thank rather lamely and belatedly in the road outside his command post in the converted medresseh, before he stepped into a car and was driven away.*

Anatoly had chosen breakfast on the road to Tashkent a few days earlier as the occasion to present me with a jar of Samarcand brandy and a ceramic flask holding a pint of a ferocious liqueur distilled in that city. We had stopped beside a river amongst parched hills where Anatoly, quick as ever, sliced up vegetables bought before dawn that day in the Samarcand market, and Alex washed fruit, and I walked out by way of spits of gravel to the water flowing by many channels through the valley. Poppies gleamed everywhere, and the wild roses of Turkestan. The sound of the river filled my ears. I enjoyed for the last time the feeling of being nowhere in

---

* Tipped-in to my copy of Wolff's *Bokhara* is a holograph letter (dated a few days after his return from his mission) which details the presents which he had received on his journey: a robe of honour from the King of Bokhara heads the list, then come shawls and Turcoman dresses from other dignitaries, and an emerald ring from the Prince Governor of Tabreez. All of them, by a special dispensation obtained by Captain Grover from the Lords of the Treasury, are duty free.

particular in the midst of Central Asia. After our picnic breakfast Anatoly had offered me his knife, the knife so much in use
at all our picnics, because I had once admired it. But I had
watched how carefully he kept the weapon clean and sharp,
and I had seen him with his frown in the markets picking over
the knives for sale and rejecting them all as blades of inferior
water, so I wouldn't take it from him.

Alex's presents came later. One morning when we were
back in Tashkent the two of them had collected me from my
hotel, the Moscva's back seat already well filled by Anatoly's
wife and daughter, and had taken me to the chief market of
the city. Through the crowded alleys and stalls, using the
women as our bloodhounds, we set out to hunt my plaguey
shalwars, mentioned in an evil hour, which Alex had refused
to forget. It was Sunday, busiest day of the trading week. The
crowd was dense, the heat terrific: I cursed every shalwar ever
sewn. None were to be found, neither in the market nor in a
department store miles off to which the ladies dragged us,
sterns wagging and noses thoroughly to the ground. It was
clear – it had been clear for all the weeks of this fruitless search
of Alex's through every market he came upon – that people
who want shalwars buy the stuff and make up the garments
themselves, so that I begged my friends as earnestly as I knew
how to give it up. Anatoly's wife, stout and merry, was darting
about the shop upstairs and down, a terror to keep up with,
and only the taller more languid daughter was able at last to
whip her mother off the line and let us go home. But there
was to be a sequel.

When Anatoly and Alex called for me next morning to take
me to the airport Alex put a brown paper parcel into my hand
the moment I was in my familiar seat behind them in the
car. Both of them watched me open it. Out slithered in their
cellophane packages two pairs of shalwars glittering and shimmering as if made from the rainbow. They had guessed my
daughters' sizes, bought the material, engaged a sempstress.
The car started and we drove off towards the airport, collecting
Mr Eshtaev on our way.

It was a green oasis composed now of many scenes and

kindnesses which I watched drop away below the plane bank-
ing against the Tien Shan Mountains that morning to level off
for Moscow 2,000 miles to the north-west. I watched deserts
and salt wastes pass below for an hour and a half; then came
the first clouds dappling the fringe of European Russia, till
gradually the swelling colour, the greens and browns of forest
and plough and pasture, became the background to life in
Europe and not in Asia – to that provincial life depicted by the
Russian novelists of the last century which exerts an appeal
almost like nostalgia, so homely and familiar have translations
(perhaps falsely) made it seem. When I had been on my way
to Tashkent, driving from Moscow to the airport, the road had
crossed a sluggish brown river between steep banks, willows
shading the water, children fishing, a corner of rustic landscape
whose very dulness and ordinariness had seemed to promise
the direct experience of stepping into that country scene, background to so much Russian fiction, refuge of so many Russian
hearts, extolled in so many Russian memoirs.* Crossing the
river, feeling its pull, I had remembered that Lena and Isaac
had asked me to their family's dacha a mile or two through
woods and fields from Abramtsevo, the very chance I wanted,
and I had kept the promise of it before me during my weeks
in Turkestan like the cherry you keep till last to make up for
having eaten the cake. I would ring Lena tonight from the
National Hotel, where TURON had booked me a room, and
arrange to go with them to the dacha. So I had the comfortable
feeling that the trip was not finished yet, when the plane landed
and I stepped out into the cold dark air of a Moscow June.

*   *   *

* A passage in Gogol's *Dead Souls* is worth quoting as a typical generic
expression of the Russians' profound attachment to their land: "Russia!
Russia! How wretched, dispersed and uncomfortable is everything about
you . . . there is nothing to captivate or charm the eye. But what then
is that unattainable and mysterious force which draws us to you? Why
does your mournful song, which is wafted over your whole plain and
expanse, from sea to sea, echo and re-echo without cease in our ears?
What is in that song? What is it that calls and weeps, and grips our heart?
Russia! What do you want from me? Why do you gaze on me so?" etc,
etc. (Translation by George Reavey.)

I was wrong. The trip was over. About the same time next afternoon I was on another plane taxiing to the runway whilst the captain in fruity British tones welcomed us aboard a BA flight to London. At this, cheering and clapping broke out the length of the plane. I was amazed: I never heard such an outburst since, aged ten, I was on the bus leaving Bilton Grange for the station at the end of term. And I was mortified that I would have joined in, too (if I hadn't felt so abominably ill), with the relief of being quit of Moscow: very different from my feelings at leaving Tashkent.

When I had reached the National Hotel the day before, a stocky bully at the desk, Soviet woman in her element, had denied with satisfaction that any booking had been made for me from Tashkent. So much for TURON's influence in the capital. After that first brief access of pleasure flushing her grey jowl, the desk clerk was deaf to my case, only grunting out (before turning her back forever) that there wasn't a hotel bed to be had in all Moscow. I rang Lena's flat and her daughter, just home from school, told me that neither father nor mother would be there before eight o'clock. It was then about four in the afternoon. I rang Kirill Ukraintsev. Kindly, he promised to come round.

I sat on my bag and read George Eliot for the hour I waited. I had chosen the National again because, despite resident assassins, its style makes it less repulsive than other Moscow hotels. But in that hour even this residual appeal had evaporated. To one side of me a succession of people lost their temper in the telephone box, to the other an equal number swore at the Pepsi dispenser, programmed to swallow coins without disgorging a drink. In and out of the foyer through unguarded doors drifted the riff-raff off the street, their activity centred on the hard-currency shop which glittered like a brilliantly lighted *Titanic* steaming full-ahead for the iceberg. Moscow couldn't hit the iceberg soon enough for me. My feelings were already such as to make a man cheer in the plane leaving it.

*　　*　　*

I reached the Travellers' Club about seven o'clock next evening, and the porter gave me the key to the same room amongst the rooftop architecture of Pall Mall, now gilded in a June sunset, from which my journey to Khiva had started out. It had been a hot day – a month of heat had parched the roadside fields on the way into London from the airport – and I sat in a fine dusky room downstairs, sipping soda water in a deep chair below a window open onto the roses of Carlton Gardens. On the plane the usual excellent airline dinner had been served, but I had drunk only soda water and eaten not a thing.

The bed which Kirill's perseverance had eventually found for me in Moscow, the last to be left unoccupied in the city, was a bunk on a boat moored on the Moscow River at the outermost limit of the metro, an airless cupboard on the waterline for which I was charged 150 dollars.* Kirill had brought with him to the National a companion with the figure and terse conversation of a night-club bouncer, a meaty eighteen-stone crammed into leather blouson and jeans, who had made light work of carrying my bags to these watery outskirts. For thanks I had presented him with a bottle of vodka which someone had somewhere given me, and Kirill with Anatoly's jar of Samarcand brandy. Instead of putting the bottles in their pockets and making off, as I expected them to do, they drew up chairs to the cabin table, took off their blousons and drank the lot, both bottles. It took them an hour. Kirill talked in his agreeable insouciant way, I listened, and the minder, sucking his walrus moustache, his glass gripped in a mighty fist, watched us through eyes like the arrow-slits in a stone keep. Was he on duty? Did Kirill expect me to be attacked again? I drank as little as possible and wished they would go away. When at last the bottles were empty I walked with them to the metro and back alone in the fading light amongst the concrete and colourless lilac of the waterside park. On board I ate some

* I thought of Laurence Oliphant's complaint, in the 1850s, that in Russia you were obliged both to rough it *and* to pay the price of a first-class hotel in Paris.

supper, a poor meal indeed, and went to bed. At three in the morning I was wakened by sea-going thumps and cries as another boat docked clumsily alongside my bunk, and in the unhappy hours which followed I was obliged to admit that the supper had poisoned me. Kirill's minder should have been in the galley, watching the ship's cook. Had the boat been cross-ing the Bay of Biscay I couldn't have been iller. By morning I hadn't the bounce left even to try and ring Lena, so that, when I found I couldn't stay on the boat another night because the cabin was taken, I capitulated to Moscow and rang BA for an afternoon flight out, determined now only to be well enough to catch it – and, of course, to keep smiling. I had succumbed to what Galton, in his *Art of Travel*, calls "the bad habit of looking forward to the end of the journey".*

On the plane I'd eaten nothing, sipping soda water cautiously all the way to London, and by nine o'clock in the evening I felt almost recovered, well enough to walk out of the club into Pall Mall. I walked to the top of the Duke of York's Steps, which gives you a picture-postcard view of London, Big Ben and the Houses of Parliament showing Gothic pinnacles above the trees of St James's Park. Then I looked back the way I had walked. That view, across the piazza round the Duke's col-umn, of grand cool classical façades glowing in the dusk – the Atheneum, Pall Mall, Regent Street – is not quite the obvious "souvenir of London" of the other view, but in its dignity and its order, at least as it struck an eye fresh from Moscow and Central Asia, it is a prospect setting out the principles of a European architecture – and much more than an architecture – which descends to us from Periclean Athens. I mean that such a space as this square among these rather noble buildings

---

* The most thorough and frank expression of weariness with an East-ern journey must be this: "We are anxious to have done with travelling in Mohammedan countries, and again to enjoy the comforts of Italy and Switzerland . . . the want of inns, theatres, museums, picture galleries, libraries, promenades, evening parties, and the ever-handy and comfort-able caffé, are privations which a European must ever regret" – Irby and Mangles, 1823.

takes into account the dignity of a common life, in the manner of *stoa* and *forum*, in a tradition of democracy by which the art of building is used to further human amity, and to gratify the human wish for self-respect, rather than being put to use as part of the machinery of absolutism and oppression, as is the tradition of Egypt and Mesopotamia and Russia. Here amongst the London planes around the Duke of York's column, in a dusk already lit by London lamps, stand stone figures of the Indian viceroy Lord Lawrence, of Colin Campbell the imperial soldier, of Scott of the Antarctic. At their best these men acted according to principles of integrity and justice, and of courage and truth, descended like the architecture of their London surroundings from the Athens of Pericles. It is the architecture of the European mind. The spirit of Arthur Conolly would be at home here, with that of many an unknown name who played the "noble game" across the world.

I had gone to Central Asia to see the "bumping pitch and the blinding light" where a number of matches in that series were played. The view can easily be held that Conolly and his successors didn't succeed: says a recent writer, "There is little or nothing to show on the map for all their efforts and sacrifices." Perhaps the map is the wrong place to look: no map, after all, shows a Periclean conquest of England. As I walked to and fro in the violet London dusk, as usual at the end of a journey nursing the feelings of the Flying Scotsman after his adventure – "Above all he could not forget the shining rails as he had rushed along them in the moonlight, and he knew that he would give anything to do it again" – I heard that kicked football scud and thump in the dusty maidan under the walls of Bokhara's Ark, and watched a pack of Uzbeg boys scuffling for the ball between goals pitched on the very ground which had soaked up Arthur Conolly's blood. It might be said that wherever football is played, the English succeeded in their "noble game". I had been misled by Newbolt's verse into expecting cricket, that's all.

AFTERWORD

In January 1993 I came on a news item datelined Samarcand which put into my mind the prediction I had made two and a half years earlier beside Tamerlane's tomb in that city: "Here, surely (I then wrote), the cult of Turkestan nationalism – the rebirth of this ferocious warlord as 'father of his people' – will root itself". The lines which caught my eye in Hugh Pope's piece for the *Independent* ran like this: "Uzbekistan's source of inspiration is to be Tamerlane, the ruthless fourteenth-century Mongol raider . . . Guides taking visitors to his solid-jade tomb have been told to present Tamerlane as the first Uzbeg hero." Interviewed on this subject in the same news item was a man I had met at the Writers' Union in Tashkent, who was quoted as saying, "Of course we are going to use the legend of Tamerlane; he fought for the independence of Turan (Turkic Central Asia)."

In this book there are numerous signs of the imminent upheaval which, when I was in Central Asia in the early summer of 1990, was about to engulf the Soviet Empire and bring about its destruction. Uncertainties increased month by month. In August 1991 came the hard-liners' attempted coup which, though itself a failure, fatally weakened Gorbachev's position vis-à-vis the non-Communist reformers under Yeltsin. Gorbachev fell. By the end of 1991 the Soviet Union itself had fallen to pieces, and throughout its vast territory, which had been acquired and assimilated over many centuries, the genie of nationalism was all at once let out of the bottle. The speculative talk I had heard amongst men eager for independence suddenly became a real issue they had to face. I wondered how much the need for a tenable and practical

259

policy in power might have tempered the excitable idealism of nationalists-in-opposition. The Writers' Union official I have quoted went on to give an example of such pragmatism. In this "Afterword" I will consider the effect on Central Asia's future of the events since 1990.

To depict Tamerlane as a "raider" fighting for "independence" might seem rather to stunt the image of the world-shaking titan who, in 1400, controlled an empire reaching from the Mediterranean to the Ganges and from the Volga to the Persian Gulf. Nonetheless, Tamerlane is no bad role-model for the man who would rule an Uzbekistan strong enough to head a federation of the five Central Asian republics and to direct their policy on the world stage. Such a state would need to be an oligarchy if not a despotism; and we find the same Writers' Union official,* in his interview, urging that democracy in Uzbekistan be postponed: "We are saying to the opposition, please wait some years. We have no proper army. We have no strong borders. First we must have independence, then democracy." These might be the words of a twentieth-century Tamerlane – of Stalin – excusing himself for murdering or imprisoning whoever opposes him, and justifying his interference in neighbouring states (as Uzbekistan is accused of interfering in Tajikstan) in order to destroy opposition to the status quo.

Since it is not the first time this century that the name of Tamerlane has been invoked by a would-be ruler of a Pan-Turkic empire, it is instructive to look into the case of Enver Pasha, the Turkish adventurer who called himself Tamerlane's successor during the Central Asian civil war of the 1920s, to see whether there are parallels with today's issues. In 1917 the

---

* The Tashkent Writers' Union became a favoured upward channel for ambitious politicians as a result of the literary aspirations of Sharaf Rashidov. This startlingly corrupt Communist Party chief of Uzbekistan for twenty years until his death in 1985, who had been President of the Tashkent Writers' Union, was the author of a single novel, later expanded by a team of writers (as Rashidov's power grew) into a multi-volume masterpiece translated into all the main languages of the globe.

overthrow of tsarism had the effect of "liberating" the little dependency of Bokhara, very much as the collapse of Moscow's control has liberated the Asiatic republics today. The emir found himself with absolute power. Somehow his little army defeated the Bolshevik force sent against him, and, for a time between 1918 and 1920, unimpeded by a tsarist Resident at his court, the emir was able to return to the medieval barbarities of his ancestors' rule, hurling his victims from the Tower of Death, crushing treasure out of his subjects, altogether showing the world what life in Central Asia might have been like if the Russians had never interfered with it. But in 1920 the emir's troops were defeated, and he fled to Afghanistan. A Bolshevik government was set up in Bokhara, and to the city was sent Enver Pasha, expressly commissioned by Lenin to cohere and unite the many factions fighting one another within Central Asia at that time.*

Enver Pasha, forty years old and married to the daughter of the ex-Sultan of Turkey, had already led a full life, playing his part as a prominent Young Turk in the campaign to modernise the Ottoman empire, commanding armies against the Allies in the First World War, massacring Armenians – losing an entire Turkish army in the mountains around Kars – but ultimately he was unsuccessful as the opponent of Kemal Attaturk in the contest for supreme power in post-Ottoman Turkey. Indeed he had been condemned to death by a Turkish court in absentia, and had escaped to Russia, where he so impressed Lenin with his plausibility that he contrived to have himself sent to Bokhara. Within days of arrival he had defected to the enemy.

Enver's master plan was to become ruler of Turkey by attaining power over a Pan-Turkic empire based in Samarcand which would control Asia Minor as one of its provinces. To this end he joined the *Basmachi*, the guerrilla-patriot force

---

* A vivid low-key account of the terror and barbarism of the Bolshevik civil war in Turkestan is given in *Mission to Tashkent* (1946) by F. M. Bailey, a British secret agent who lived through extraordinary adventures in the region.

united (for the moment) in their opposition to Moscow and the Bolsheviks. His bid for power prospered. Calling himself emir of Turkestan – son-in-law to the Caliph as well as claiming to be the reincarnation of Tamerlane – commander-in-chief of the armies of Bokhara and Khiva – for a year he united all the dissident forces in Central Asia and won every battle. But the *Basmachi*, like the half-brigand *Klepht* "patriots" who had all but destroyed the Greek bid for independence from the Turkish empire a century earlier, could not be held together: by the August of 1922 his army had dwindled to a handful. The claimant to Tamerlane's throne was defeated and killed.*

The existence of the *Basmachi* encouraged the ambitious Enver into action, but the factionalism of the *Basmachi* – that centrifugal force inevitably at work within an alliance of "freedom fighters" with their differing objectives – sabotaged his plan. Similarly, destructive differences would as certainly disrupt an alliance put together today in support of a modern Tamerlane, if an individual successor to Enver Pasha's ambition should arise; and it is clear from current events in Osh, where horrible outbreaks of violence have killed hundreds in quarrels between Uzbeg and Kirghiz, and elsewhere that the enthusiasm with which the factions would butcher one another once they fell out would be no more restrained today than it was in the 1920s. But if the present Uzbekistan government (rather than an individual) should claim collective identification with Tamerlane's imperial policies and priorities, putting "independence" before democracy and the possession of a "proper army" before civil rights, the government would have weighty advantages over, say, the emirs of Khiva or Bokhara when they found themselves similarly liberated by a revolution within Russia in 1917.

---

* In case the impression has been created that Enver Pasha was a romantic mountebank, the story should be borne in mind (it is told by T. E. Lawrence in *Seven Pillars of Wisdom*, 1935) of Enver Pasha delaying his staff until he had heard the satisfying explosion of a prisoner's head, after he had pushed the man into the furnace of a ferryboat to roast him alive. "They always pop like that," he said.

In population, Uzbekistan is much the largest of the five Asiatic republics, having twenty million inhabitants out of the region's fifty million total. It is geographically central, and within its borders lie the famous cities of Samarcand, Bokhara, Khiva and Tashkent, so that it seems to be the heartland of the region. Most important, the government has all the stability of continuity with the Communist era, for it is the same Communist government (renamed National Democratic Party) with the same president at its head, Karimov, who had himself re-elected to power by the ballot of December 1992. The form of government is despotic, as governments in Central Asia have been without exception since time began. "Central Asia [writes a Russian commentator] is still at the feudal stage in the realm of politics"; that is to say, "the mechanism of interaction works in one direction only, from the top downwards".* If by retaining power the Tashkent neo-Communist government can secure economic and social stability, they are likely to attract the support of Turkey, and Turkish investment, to sustain an Uzbeg hegemony within Central Asia. "My country [President Karimov is quoted as saying] will go forward by the Turkic route." Thus would come into existence, if not quite the empire of Tamerlane, then at least a Pan-Turkic sphere of influence reaching from the Mediterranean to China with Sunni Islam as its unifying ideology.

To achieve this, neo-Communist governments would have to be supported by Tashkent in Alma Ata (Kazakhstan) and in Ashkhabad (Turkmenistan), whilst liberal democratic forces causing instability in Dushanbe (Tadzhikstan) and in Bishkek (Kirghizia) must be ousted. Active Uzbeg military support for neo-Communists has already pushed Islamic militants and democrats out of Dushanbe. But the Tadzhiks are an obdurate problem, potentially a source of unending trouble to a Pan-Turkic Sunni empire, for they are not of Turkic but of Persian race, speaking Farsi, and for these reasons are much more open than their neighbours to infiltration by Iran's militant

* Marat Akchurin, *Red Odyssey* (1992), the stark and shocking account by a native of Tashkent of his journey through Russia in 1990.

fundamentalism. Tadzhikistan, at the bottom of the list of the ex-Soviet Union's fifteen republics for productivity and prosperity, is a "unified" Central Asia's weakest link.

Nor are the Tadzhiks and their beliefs neatly confined to Tadzhikistan, any more than the Uzbegs are to be found only in Uzbekistan, or the Kirghiz only in Kirghizia. Nowhere in Central Asia do political borders coincide with divisions of race and ethnicity. In this confusion lies the chief difficulty of keeping the peace among independent republics within a federation led by Uzbekistan and supported by Turkey. For the inhabitants of Central Asia are originally all nomads to whom borders are irrelevant, and amongst whom, as migrating shepherds or itinerant merchants, the cities are shared: Samarcand, for instance, is historically as much a Tadzhik city as a city of the Uzbegs. Tsarist imperialism respected the frontierless nature of Turkestan, making of it one Governor-generalship without internal divisions. The Bolsheviks drew the straight lines across maps which now divide summer pastures from winter quarters, or cut off villages from their source of income, or make the age-old community of Tadzhiks in Samarcand into a ghetto of foreigners open to persecution or massacre.* Added to this brutal bureaucracy was the system of "plantations" – an idea inherited from tsarism – by which troublesome tribes were driven from their homeland and forced to settle in distant provinces amongst suspicious indigenes: in 1941 Stalin moved one million German settlers from the Volga into Kazakhstan. But, whether the races of Central Asia are mixed by nature or by man, political borders are chains laid on their freedom of movement which are bound to chafe. "We will have boundaries where they will cause no unhappiness," an idealist had said to me over lunch at Bokhara. Easy enough, full of vodka and without the power to execute his ideas; but now, with frontiers a reality between indepen-

---

* Gustav Krist, who first knew Central Asia as an Austrian prisoner of war of the Russians in 1916, describes in *Alone through the Forbidden Land* (1939) how he accompanied the Kirghiz shepherds on their last nomadic migration before Soviet rule confined them.

dent states, he will have realised that no such innocent border can exist. And even if there were no borders at all within a united Turkestan, there would still be neighbours; Afghanistan a Pandora's box across the Oxus, the militant Shiite Islam of Iran across the Attrek, and to the north the homeland of the still powerful Russian minority.

The eagerness and shared opinions (or at any rate the good-natured disagreement) which I heard expressed in political discussions had always been the outcome of a shared opposition to the Communist status quo. The Writers' Union official, for instance, whose anti-democratic views are cited above, took (when I met him) a strong line for Uzbeg nationalism which, in those circumstances, implied not only freedom from Moscow but a self-determining democratic rôle for the Uzbeg citizen. In power, he takes the view that democracy is less important than stability; and, though the continuing Communist régime may be run in part by Uzbegs, it remains the régime of Moscow, Russian-taught to Russianised apparatchiks. Not that a handover by tsarist rulers (had they kept power till now) would have resulted in an independent Uzbeg democracy at Tashkent: we have only to consider what corruption and tyranny was uncovered by Count Pahlen's commission of 1908 to realise what would have been the state of affairs in a Turkestan governed by tsarism until today. Nor do I believe that a Central Asia undisturbed by foreign imperialism would have developed into a collection of democracies, or even of tolerably well governed despotisms: we have the examples of Bokhara, as savage a tyranny in 1920 as it had been in the days of Tamerlane, and of Afghanistan, described in a recent London *Times*' leader as "a patchwork of warlords and rival fiefdoms, all existing as they have for centuries against a background of continuing low-intensity warfare". Of course, conquest by an outside power must disrupt the development of native government. We do not know for sure how far Bokhara or Kabul might have ameliorated their own systems had their emirs' tyrannies never been backed by the Russians or the British. Nowhere in the world has their been the pure experiment in self-developed government with which to compare states that are the outcome of imperialism.

Suppose though that England, not Russia, had carried off the trophies of the Great Game, and had annexed Central Asia to her Indian empire. What might post-independence Turkestan have been like, with its two-house elected democracy on the British pattern, an open opposition to the government, and all the paraphernalia of Westminster transplanted into a Gothic brick parliament building in Samarcand? Unfortunately we can guess accurately at the result, from the evidence of misgovernment, or of no government at all, in almost every ex-British possession now controlled by native power-seekers in Africa, as well as from the tragic post-imperial polarisation of religious groups in the Indian subcontinent. Pre-independence idealists can hardly be less distressed by the post-imperial world than they were by the days of empire.

Not the idealist, not the democrat, but the hard-headed Uzbeg who has learnt his way about Russian corridors, is the man to prosper in present day Tashkent. Evidently the president of the Writers' Union is such an operator; and I would be surprised if my host Mr Eshtaev were not another. His switch from VAAP to TURON, from the Rashidov-favoured world of books into fresh fields of commerce vital to future power, looked at the time of glasnost and perestroika to be shrewd and opportune. Possibly – I hope it is not so – he cut out too high a profile for himself too early as a free-market entrepreneur, before it became clear that Karimov and the Communist Party were to continue in power. TURON's prospectus of activities, when I saw it in 1991, had taken for granted the feasibility of joint commercial ventures with foreigners, along with the opening of Central Asia to international trade in private hands. It does not seem that the problem of how to regard private capital has so far arisen on a scale to trouble a neo-Communist government; the capital risked up till now in Central Asia appears to have been invested by foreign governments in hope of securing not profit but political allegiance.

A vast investment is needed by the state if not by private enterprise. Somehow, an economy which was fashioned by Moscow into the classical dependent-colony status – having a

negligible manufacturing capacity – must find outlets for its
raw materials (for its cotton above all) which will earn the
hard currency needed to diversify. Saudi Arabia, for instance,
has undertaken to provide large amounts of cheap oil to Turkmenia. The danger is, that the Turkman's loyalty might be
bought by this cheap oil, so that instead of holding together
with their neighbours in Central Asia, they are obliged to act
as catspaws for the interests of Saudi bankers and hardline
(Wahabi) mullahs. Each one of the Central Asian states is vul-
nerable to similar foreign subornation: it is the road to frag-
mentation and disaster.

This is most probably the road Central Asia will take. However, in this present day revival of the Great Game for Asia's
heartland, Turkey may still prevail, and Sunni Islam might
become the unifying ideology in a Pan-Turkic sphere of influence. What is needed in order to achieve this stabilisation of a
large swathe of the globe is that Turkey, with its European
Community aspirations as its anchor in the West, should be
enabled to find for an Uzbeg hegemony in Turkestan the
sources of hard currency and manufactured goods which could
be paid for with Turkestan's cotton and coal until the Asiatic
economies can shake off the colonial status to which Soviet
imperialism has relegated them. This seems to me the ideal.
If it requires the stability of the neo-Communist governments
of the Central Asian states in order to achieve this outcome –
and if the neo-Communists can sufficiently change their spots
so as to work together for the good of the countries they
govern – then I prefer President Karimov to the alternative.
For I would rather try to bring up a family in Tashkent, where
the statues of Marx and Lenin are still on their plinths, than
in the ruins of Tbilisi where the statues have been overthrown
and the Communist Party headquarters gutted and burnt. And,
although I will never do it, I can imagine taking my family to
that village near the lake where I spent a night as the guest of
Anatoly and his friends, and finding it in undisturbed peace
whatever the turbulence of the cities. Alex might not be there
– I don't think it would take much of a disturbance to shake
him loose from Uzbekistan and send him back to his native

Ukraine – but I would expect to find Anatoly amongst his friends and relatives in the houses under the dusty trees. That sanctuary where they catch fish in summer, and shoot ducks in winter, and make merry in all seasons – that remote village in the heart of Central Asia to which he took me – stands in my mind for the strength and assurance behind Anatoly's character, and I believe that it will outlast the present crisis as it has outlasted all previous crises.

Captain Grover and the Bokhara Victims

Captain Grover's concern with the affair of Stoddart and Conolly, and the manner of his employing that concern as an
instrument, in the end, for pursuing a vendetta against the
Foreign Secretary – outraging Stoddart's closest relatives by his
warmth – is a cautionary tale to show how even a philanthropic
instinct may become an obsession freighted with all manner of
private motives, until at last it is destructive of its original
benevolent intention. What had happened was this. In July
1843 that oddest of Anglican clergymen, Dr Joseph Wolff, had
written to the *Morning Herald* offering to travel to Bokhara
(which he had once visited before) in order to discover if Stoddart and Conolly were yet alive, as he believed them to be.
Captain Grover, a friend of Stoddart, then called a meeting of
interested persons who formed a committee to accept Dr
Wolff's proposal and to pay the expense of his journey. Grover
too disbelieved Saleh Mohammed's circumstantial account of
the two men's execution (a version of events accepted by the
government, which in consequence allowed Stoddart's two
sisters an annuity) and was already smarting under the Foreign
Office's rejection of his two conditions for travelling to Bokhara himself, viz: that he should be furnished with an official
letter characterising his mission, and that he should be author-
ised to wear his uniform for the journey.

In October Wolff set out from Southampton to beard the
tyrant at Bokhara – "any stranger witnessing his departure
[wrote Grover] would have thought he was taking a trip to
the Isle of Wight" – where he was himself imprisoned and
brought within an ace of the headsman's knife by the treacherous *nayib* Abdul Sameet Khan. But he escaped, and in April

269

1845 came home satisfied that Stoddart and Conolly had indeed been put to death in the manner described from hearsay by Saleh Mohammed, "commonly called Akhoonzadeh".* In the interval of Wolff's absence Captain Grover's grievances began to obsess him. He would not accept that Stoddart and Conolly were dead, in part because such a conclusion put the Foreign Office in the right and himself and Wolff's mission in the wrong. The lofty manner of the Foreign Office towards him rankled most bitterly, and with his soreness and mortification was mingled financial loss – he had provided £400 out of his own pocket to extricate Wolff from the *nayib*'s toils at Bokhara – as well as a suspicion that he had been passed over for promotion on account of official displeasure.

Goaded by his vexations he began to pepper the Foreign Secretary with letters. He had already proposed that a British army, with himself in command, be sent to conquer Bokhara and depose its "ummeer" – to which Lord Aberdeen replied that "he does not anticipate that he will have any occasion for troubling Captain Grover in the matter" – and his conduct now becomes a flurry of blows aimed at Aberdeen's head and honour. Reams of Army and Navy Club writing paper are employed in carrying satire and invective to the Foreign Office, until Lord Aberdeen must have sighed again with weariness when he recognised the captain's eager hand telling him, for instance, that "I rejoice exceedingly that my £400 have been the means of restoring to Her Majesty such a subject

* This is the same Saleh Mohammed, son of the principal *cazi* of Herat, whom Captain Abbott had characterised as "a handsome and gentlemanly man, and far better informed than the generality of his countrymen". Wolff, who didn't place much reliance on his testimony, nevertheless candidly admits (in his *Travels and Adventures* published many years later) that by the time he reached Teheran en route for Bokhara he was already convinced that Stoddart and Conolly were dead, but could neither admit it nor give up his journey for fear of being thought a braggart and a humbug. Grover was so determined to disbelieve all evidence of their death, and so prejudiced, that he admits expecting to hear his reader exclaim "Stop a minute, Captain" as he beats his hobbyhorse over the fences.

as Dr Wolff; and I regret that it never occurred to me, when first I became anxious about poor Stoddart and Conolly, to render myself personally liable for any expenses an attempt to recover Queen Victoria's ambassadors might have cost the nation, as it would probably have procured the restoration to liberty of those unfortunate envoys". It is bitter stuff. Grover, the "poor half-pay captain", presents himself to the reader as honest John Bull confronting a double-tongued Ministry which had abandoned its two envoys and was now intent upon covering the tracks of its treachery. He describes his book as "the plain, unvarnished statement of a mere soldier who, at the age of 15, was serving his country . . . during that period which most men have the good fortune to be able to devote to study", and in its pages he shows us himself strolling into Monsieur C's Salle d'Armes at Paris where, against his will, he is obliged to pick up a foil so as to allow "the professor" to demonstrate upon him an English captain's helplessness against an opponent versed in the art of fence. "I took the proffered instrument. M. C cried 'A vous!' and in an instant my foil bent upon his plastron." When advised that his manoeuvre was contrary to the laws of fencing he replies, "Monsieur C, I cannot discuss with a dead man the 'cérémonies d'usage', I have killed you in a manner perfectly satisfactory to my feelings" – and the reader has no difficulty in understanding that the corpse at Grover's feet is Lord Aberdeen's, his perfidious heart pierced by an honest quill. A further grievance of the captain's was the want of public recognition of Dr Wolff's mission – "if [wrote a satirist] he'd come back from India after cutting 20,000 throats, why, he might have had a round of dinners, diamond-hilted sword, wine-coolers as big as buckets, and so on; as it is, I fear nothing can be done for him" – but it was at the meeting held at Exeter Hall, in May 1845, to welcome Wolff home from Bokhara, that Captain Grover's own Committee for the Bokhara Victims fell to pieces in unseemly uproar. After Wolff had spoken (by his own account of it "for several hours") there arose the Reverend George Stoddart, Colonel Stoddart's only brother, who decried Wolff's characterisation of his relative as "harsh and intemperate", who went on to absolve Lord Aberdeen of all blame, and finally "had no hesitation in declaring" that Captain Grover "had made most cruel and false assertions" against his brother and the Foreign Office. Another Stoddart relation, a Captain Randall (forty years in the army and still a captain), came forward to testify to the family's satisfaction at Foreign Office treatment of themselves; and then, with the traveller J. S. Buckingham's mention of government pensions allowed to Stoddart's sisters "in the firm belief of his death", the cat was out of the bag: "if the matter was disturbed again, the pensions [£75 per annum to each sister from the Queen's private purse] would be suspended". The row grew more furious. Whatever the hisses and shouts of "Shame!" the Reverend George refused to withdraw his assertions or to apologise, and stamped off home to write to the newspapers repeating his attack on Grover and his book "with all its malignant accusations". The date and manner of death of "the Bokhara Victims" became ammunition for partisan broadsides in the *Norfolk and Norwich Chronicle*. Instead of the anguish of the victims themselves dwelling in our minds, the affair fades out of earshot amid the querulous and self-interested voices of unattached captains and country clergymen squabbling over their "honour".

BIBLIOGRAPHY

The reading I have done over a good many years in connexion with the Great Game, and Central Asia, and Russia itself in the nineteenth century, has all been browsing rather than "research": I have only taken down from the shelves of the London Library or the second-hand bookshop works which looked interesting and amusing. The date of publication given in the bibliography is not necessarily that of the first edition.

ABBOTT, Captain James, *Journey from Heraut to Khiva, etc*, 2 vols (1st edn 1843, 2nd edn 1856)

AKSAKOFF, Sergei, *A Russian Gentleman*
Years of Childhood
A Russian Schoolboy

ALDER, Dr G., *Beyond Bokhara, the Life of William Moorcroft* (1985)

ANON, *Sketches of Russian Life*, edited by Henry Morley (1866)
From the experiences of Robert Anderson, an Englishman long resident in Russia, who was hurt in a railway accident whilst in England, and who communicated these vivid sketches to the editor during his convalescence.

ANON, *Recollections of Russia during 33 years residence, by A German Nobleman* (1855)

ANON, *Journal of a Nobleman*, 2 vols (1831)
A French émigré's account of travels from Moscow to Vienna to attend the Congress of 1814, pompous and snobbish but containing fascinating details of country house life in Russia and Poland as well as an account of Odessa during the plague of 1812.

BADDELEY, J. F., *The Russian Conquest of the Caucasus* (1908)

BAKER, Valentine, *Clouds in the East* (1876)

War in Bulgaria, 2 vols (1879)
Colonel Baker's trial is covered in *The Times*, August 1875. I know of no account of his life.

BREMNER, R., *Excursions in the Interior of Russia*, 2 vols (1839)
Striving to be fair-minded despite frequent arousal of his irritable patriotism – "Russia has become powerful, but it is solely by permission of Britain" – Bremner provides the most detailed account available of how Russia appeared to an observant foreigner in the 1830s. Outraged at peasant miseries in Russia, he reminds himself that he has seen "during the present autumn [1838] in the rich and prosperous county of Inverness, scenes of wretchedness, exceeding all we have ever witnessed, either in Russia or in any part of the world". The comment which separates him most widely from today's visitor to St Petersburg is his opinion that "the Hermitage boasts one of the most celebrated pictures in the world, Paul Potter's 'Cow'"; but the modern traveller may well share the view he comes back to, that "Russia is a country which by universal consent is the most troublesome and fatiguing that can be visited".

BURNABY, Frederick, *A Ride to Khiva* (1876)
On Horseback through Asia Minor, 2 vols (1877)

BURNES, Alexander, *Travels into Bokhara*, 3 vols (1839)
Cabool (1842)

CAMBRIDGE MODERN HISTORY, 13 vols (1911)

CHARQUES, Richard, *A Short History of Russia* (1956)
A lucid narrative which doesn't contain a dull page.

CLARKE, Edward, *Travels in Various Countries in Europe, Asia and Africa*, 11 vols (1816–24)
But I have quoted from *Life and remains of Dr Clarke*, by his friend William Otter, 2 vols (1825)

COBBOLD, Ralph, *Innermost Asia* (1900)
On a shooting expedition in the Pamirs Cobbold became very thick with the Russian consul at Kashgar, which throws an interesting light on the last stages of the Great Game. "Whilst journeying in innermost Asia I was deeply impressed by three facts. They were: the barbarous insistence of the Russian governmental system, the brilliant success which invariably attends Russian aims, and the puerile weakness

displayed by the British Government in the protecting of this country's interests."

COLE, J. W., *Russia and the Russians* (1854)
Not over-sympathetic towards its subject. He quotes the last words of the Décembrist Ryleieff at his own bungled execution: "Accursed country, where they know not how to plot, to judge, or to hang."

CONOLLY, Arthur, *Journey to the North of India*, 2 vols (1838)

CORY, Arthur, *Shadows of Coming Events* (1876)
The Eastern Menace (1881)
Colonel Cory, of the Bengal Staff Corps, takes an apocalyptic view of the Russian threat, and mistrusts every form of defence save the sword. "Not all the science of the Syracusan philosopher, who boasted that he could move the world, availed to save him from the sword of the rough soldier of Marcellus." Fiery and choleric is his contempt for the "inaction" party, and in English society he suspects what he called, in a chapter heading, "The Weakness Within".

COTTRELL, C. H., *Recollections of Siberia* (1842)
A running battle with Captain Jesse's *Notes of a Half-pay in Search of Health*, upon whose observations and opinions Cottrell heaps his scorn. In the neighbourhood of Ekaterinburg he comes upon "a Mr Jacobef, a gentleman of Petersburg, perhaps, in absolute ready money, the richest man in the world".

CREAGH, James, *A Scamper to Sebastopol* (1873)

CROCKFORD, Doris, *The Flying Scotsman* (ND, but *c.* 1938)
A romantic story of a railway engine's bid for freedom from his irksome duties, and of how he came in the end to accept compromise between what he wanted and what was expected of him.

DE CUSTINE, Marquis, *Empire of the Czar*, 3 vols (1843)
A book of pompous and affected generalisations.

DE HELL, X. Hommaire, *Travels in the Steppes of the Caspian Sea* (1847)
An observant Frenchman and his wife – to whom the pen is sometimes handed – both of them anathematising most of what they come upon, yet finding, as French persons will, "a singular thing, and one which must strike a stranger

strongly, is the moral influence which France exercises in all countries in the world".

DE LAGNY, Germain, *The Knout and the Russians* (1854)

DOBELL, Peter, *Travels in Kamtchatka and Siberia*, 2 vols (1830)
The most kindly and well-disposed towards Russia of all these travellers, and himself evidently a brave and resourceful man. "Too much praise cannot be bestowed on the humane system adopted by the Russian government in saving the lives of criminals and transporting them to Siberia . . . Blush! Ye countries of longer civilisation, that Russia should teach ye the celestial principle of reforming depraved morals."

EDWARDES, Michael, *Playing the Great Game* (1975)

EDWARDS, H. S., *Russian Projects Against India* (1885)

EVANS, G. de Lacy, *On the Designs of Russia* (1828)

EYRE, Vincent, *The Military Operations at Cabul* (1843)

FADIEIEFF, Colonel, *Letters from the Caucasus* (1861)

FERRIER, J. P., *Caravan Journeys in Persia, etc* (1856)

FRASER, J. B., *Journey into Khorassan* (1825)
Travels and Adventures in the Persian Provinces (1826)

GALTON, Francis, *The Art of Travel, or, Shifts and Contrivances Available in Wild Countries* (1860)
A book which combines curious practical lore with the indulgence of a wide streak of eccentricity: two and a half pages of such forceful prose on the subject of tea-making, for instance, that I never now make a pot of tea that his experiments are not in my mind.

GARDINER, Alexander, *Memoirs*, edited by H. Pearse (1898)
A soldier of fortune whose adventures throughout Central Asia it would be impossible to match in fiction, however extravagant. In old age "he had wild moods of talking, letting the corners of dark things peep out, and then shutting them up again, with a look behind him, as if life at Jammu had been both strange and fearful".

GAVAZZI, Modesto, *Alcune notizie raccolte in un viaggio a Bucara* (1865)

GIROUARD, Mark, *The Return to Camelot* (1981)

GRAY, Francine du Plessix, *Soviet Women, Walking the Tightrope* (1990)

A devastating analysis of the attitude and condition of Russian women. The chapter on the female apparatchik in Uzbekistan, and of the administration which produced it, is a masterpeice of restrained irony.

[GRENVILLE MURRAY, E.], *The Russians Today* (1878)
Of the dozen or so gossipy books he wrote about foreign countries, it was only to this volume critical of Russia that Grenville Murray thought it unwise to affix his name.

GRODEKOFF, N., *Ride from Samarcand to Herat* (1885) (translated by C. Marvin)

GROVER, Captain J., *The Bokhara Victims* (1845)

GUROWSKI, A., *Russia As It Is* (1854)
A Pole in America, he sadly concludes that "the reckless, ungovernable and politically egotistical spirit of the nobility has destroyed Poland beyond recovery".

HARE, Augustus, *The Story of My Life* (1900)

HERZEN, Alexander, *Memoirs*, 6 vols (1927)

HOPKIRK, Peter, *The Great Game* (1990)
A lucid narrative incorporating all that is known of the political history of the episode, amply decorated with detail of the characters involved in it.

IGNATIEFF, Colonel N. P., *Mission to Khiva and Bokhara in 1858* (translated by R. Michell) (1876)
Behind Ignatieff an unwieldy train of soldiers and sailors blundered about the Ust Urt region alternately alarming or angering the native rulers with their clumsy attempts to spy on the two khanates and to navigate the River Oxus. Ignatieff next led a mission to Peking, and, as ambassador at Constantinople from 1864, promoted – by means of what the 1910 *Encyclopaedia Britannica* calls his "shifty ways" – the Russo-Turkish war of 1877. The failure of that war to satisfy Russian ambitions caused his fall from favour despite the charm and dangerous plausibility which had impressed themselves on the British ambassador at the Porte, Sir Henry Layard.

INGRAM, Edward, *The Beginning of the Great Game in Asia* (1979)

IRBY, The Hon. C and MANGLES, J., *Travels in Egypt and Syria, etc* (1823)

JESSE, W. (Captain, unattached), *Notes of a Half-pay in Search of Health*, 2 vols (1841)

KAYE, John, *Where Men and Mountains Meet* (1977)
The Gilgit Game (1979)
KAYE, Sir John, *History of the War in Afghanistan*, 2 vols (1851)
Lives of the Indian Officers, 3 vols (1869)
Sympathetic and informative biographies of many empire-builders, Arthur Conolly and Alexander Burnes amongst them.

KHANIKOV, M., *Bokhara* (1845)

KNOBLOCH, Edgar, *Beyond the Oxus* (1972)
An account of the archaeology, art and architecture of Central Asia, this is a clearly written and instructive book which is illustrated with tantalising photographs, taken only twenty-five or so years ago, of the monuments and cities of Turkestan in just the state of neglect and decay in which I had imagined finding them.

KOHL, J. G., *Russia and the Russians*, 2 vols (1842–3)
Kohl made himself very much at home in Russia, supported in this by his calculation that, of the 600 top jobs in the country's government, 130 were held by his fellow countrymen, of whom he said that "of all the nations in Europe the Germans may justly boast of the most general share of education and intelligence".

LABENSKY, K., *A Russian's Reply to the Marquis de Custine* (1844)
An attack on de Custine as clumsy and facetious as de Custine's attack on Russia.

LAL, Mohan, *Travels in the Panjab, Afghanistan and Turkistan, etc* (1846)
A gifted and personable *munshi* brought forward by Sir Charles Trevelyan, who accompanied Burnes on his journey to Bokhara, and subsequently to England.

LE MESURIER, A., *From London to Bokhara* (1889)
Colonel le Mesurier explains in his opening remarks on his journey that "the grand tour 'de luxe' to the East from Paris to Samarcand and back by Constantinople had not then been organised by the International Sleeping-Car Company": nonetheless, his trip was through an absolutely tamed Central Asia.

MACGAHAN, J. A., *Campaigning on the Oxus* (1874)

MACGREGOR, Sir C. M., *The Defence of India* (1884)

MACLEAN, Sir Fitzroy, *Eastern Approaches* (1949)
A Person from England (1958)
[MALCOLM, Sir John], *Sketches of Persia*, 2 vols (1827)
MALLESON, Colonel G., *The Russo-Afghan Question* (1885)
The colonel's unwieldy pen relates much interesting matter: how, for instance, "the ragged sons of the desert" saved Kaufmann's Khiva column by disclosing the whereabouts of wells of "the precious fluid".
MARSH, H. C., *A Ride Through Islam* (1877)
MARVIN, Charles, *The Disastrous Russian Campaign Against the Turcomans* (1880)
The Russians at the Gate of Herat (1885)
Reconnoitring Central Asia (1886)
An amazingly prolific and combative journalist, Marvin had learned Russian during six years spent with his father, who was an engineer in that country; he then passed into the Foreign Office, where, as a clerk employed to copy a secret treaty with Russia in 1878, he memorised the text and regurgitated it to the *Globe* newspaper, which printed it. Arrested, Marvin was released because he had committed no offence then known to the law, and began his career as a polemicist against "the Russian threat". One of his books was written and published within a single week, and sold 65,000 copies. He was dead at thirty-five.
MAYO, 6th Earl of, (*Mayo, Disraeli's Viceroy*, by George Pottinger) (1990)
His appointment as Viceroy of India seemed to Florence Nightingale "an instance of our incurable frivolity about India"; a frivolity only rectified in the case of Lord Curzon, the single instance of the appointment of a first-class man to rule India.
MOORCROFT, W. and TREBECK, G., *Travels in the Himalayan Provinces and in Hindustan, etc* (1841)
Veterinary surgeon to the Bengal Army, Moorcroft was the first Englishman to cross the Himalayas. His journey to Bokhara in 1819 was undertaken to search among the Turcomans for stallions to improve the breed of cavalry horses in India. He died of fever or poison at Andkhoi in 1825. Moorcroft was badly served by the belated and slipshod editing of his

journals into this laboured volume by Horace Wilson, for his name and fame were eclipsed by his successors in the field; by Burnes, for instance, who had been quicker into print with a more lively account of his travels. "Those who followed his example [wrote the *Atheneum*] carried off honours that were justly his due."

MORGAN, G., *Anglo Russian Rivalry in Central Asia* (1981)

MOURAVIEFF, N., *Journey to Khiva in 1819* (1871)

MUMMERY, A. F., *My Climbs in the Alps and Caucasus* (1895)

NEWBOLT, Sir Henry, "Vitai Lampada"
He wrote also "He Fell Among Thieves", a romantic account in verse of the murder of George Hayward by tribesmen near Darkot in 1871.

O'DONOVAN, Edmond, *The Merv Oasis*, 2 vols (1882)

OHRWALDER, Father Joseph, *Ten Years' Captivity in the Mahdi's Camp* (1893)

OLIPHANT, L., *The Trans-Caucasian Campaign of the Turkish Army under Omer Pasha* (1856)

PARKYNS, Mansfield, *Life in Abyssinia*, 2 vols (1853)

PAHLEN, Count K. K., *Mission to Turkestan 1908–1909* (translated by N. J. Couriss) (1964)
Travelling as the tsar's inspector with a certain disdain for the provinces ("one is constrained to meet a type one would not allow over one's threshold at home"), the count records a Central Asia little altered since the days of the previous century's Great Game. Close to the Afghan border he comes upon "an immense quantity of supplies in preparation for a possible advance into India". He even found an English spy pretending to mine coal near Osh, and, stranded amongst the sandbanks and mosquitoes of the Oxus for seven terrible days on a riverboat to Khiva, he suffered the identical tortures of Colonel Ignatieff's mission exactly fifty years earlier.

POPOWSKI, J., *The Rival Powers in Central Asia* (1893)

RAWLINSON, Canon G., *A Memoir of Sir Henry Rawlinson* (1898)

RAWLINSON, Sir H., *England and Russia in the East* (1875)

SCHUYLER, Eugene, *Turkistan*, 2 vols (1876)

SHAKESPEAR, Sir Richmond, *Journey from Herat to Orenburg in 1840* (published in *Blackwood's Magazine*, June 1842)

SHAW, R., *Visits to High Tartary, Yarkand and Kashgar* (1871)

SKOBOLEFF, M. D., *Personal Reminiscences, by Nemirovitch-Dantchenko* (1884)

His ferocious character had been nurtured by an English nanny and a cruel German tutor. England exasperated him: "Who can say what England's policy is? Yesterday it was Lord Beaconsfield, today it is Mr Gladstone. Parties holding diametrically opposed views come to power every five or six years." "One curious trait about Englishmen: when they wish to exhaust the language of compliment and outdo all the superlatives of praise which they have disposed upon a foreigner they say, 'He might be taken for an Englishman'." There is an intimate portrait of this highly unstable soldier in the artist Vassili Verestchagin's *Autobiographical Sketches* (1887), where he is depicted as repeating shrilly, as the alternative to his own plans "Or we shall die gloriously".

SLADE, Adolphus, RN (Slade Pasha), *Travels in Germany and Russia* (1840)

SMITH, Albert, *A Month in Constantinople* (1850)

An account of "the East" by an irrepressibly vulgar John Bull, useful corrective to the high-flown attitudes of what the Army called "TGs" (travelling gents). On a visit to the Whirling Dervishes "the desire to hit them hard in the face became uncomfortably dominant"; from the fountains he describes the water as trickling "slow as vinegar from an oyster-shop cruet"; and he endeared himself particularly to me by summing up the topography of the Golden Horn thus: "Scutari is to Stamboul, as Birkenhead is to Liverpool". A similarly debunking and homely note is struck by Thackeray in his *Cornhill to Cairo* (1846).

SPALDING, Captain H., *Khiva and Turkestan* (1874)

A translation of Russian points of view, taken from Russian sources, supporting a general opinion that "in the broad spaces of Central Asia, Russian power and civilisation must develop themselves inflexibly and unceasingly", and that it is "vain to think of offering opposition to this".

SPENCER, Captain E., *Turkey, Russia, the Black Sea and Circassia* (1854)

An abstract of his several other books of travel which the captain rushed out to meet the Crimea War market. According both to X. de Hell and Laurence Oliphant, Spencer never set foot in Circassia, though he wrote two volumes of *Travels in Circassia* and illustrated them with a frontispiece of himself and Count Vorontsoff landing on its shore.

STEWART, Colonel C., *Through Persia in Disguise* (1911)

STONE, B. (translator), *Sir Gawain and The Green Knight* (1974)

STUART, Lt-Colonel, *Journal of a Residence in Northern Persia* (1854)

TAYLOR, Bayard, *Central Asia* (1893)

TAYLOR, W., *Scenes and Adventures in Afghanistan* (1842)

TERENTIEFF, M. A., *Russia and England in the Struggle for Markets in Central Asia* (1876)

Violently anti-British, he attributes to British diplomacy a more coherent and Machiavellian policy than ever was the case. His account of the miseries suffered by Indians under British oppression, whilst they await deliverance by Russia, reads like a Marxist tract.

VALIKHANOFF, Captain, and VENIUKOFF, M., *The Russians in Central Asia* (1865)

Translations by J. and R. Michell of Russians' accounts of their travels in Central Asia. Valikhanoff was the son of a Kirghiz sultan who, when he became an officer in the Russian Army, was able to travel covertly gathering intelligence throughout Turkestan. When I mentioned him in conversation at Tashkent, he was abused as a traitor by the Uzbeg I was talking to. His mordant and supercilious account of the people of Central Asia could well have been written by a British traveller. "The hunting for vermin in each other's persons affords them agreeable pastime for their leisure hours, without which they would be at a sad loss for amusement, the ladies especially showing a great predilection for this savoury occupation." The backwardness and ruin of Central Asia he attributes, again in a thoroughly British style, to the Muslim faith.

VAMBÉRY, Arminius, *Travels in Central Asia in 1863* (1864)

History of Bokhara (1873)

Life and Adventures, Written by Himself (1884)

The Coming Struggle for India (1885)

Vambéry's narratives aroused much scepticism, Terentieff

referring to "European travellers who have proved that his travels in Central Asia are pure fabrication"; and his *History of Bokhara* is utterly demolished in a thirty-page Russian review reprinted by Schuyler in his *Turkistan*. Yet the viewpoint of this lame Hungarian is always interesting to juxtapose with the views of Englishmen and Russians.

"WANDERER" [W. T. Lyall], *Notes on the Caucasus* (1883)

WOLFF, Rev. Joseph, *Narrative of a Mission to Bokhara* (1846)
Travels and Adventures, 2 vols (1860)
Made intrepid by his zeal for circulating the Word, like Borrow in Spain, Wolff walked blithely and carelessly amongst dangers, and wrote from the heart. He never speaks of making converts, and was probably no more successful than the excellent Swedish missionary spoken of by Cobbold at Kashgar, who had wrested one soul from Islam in a lifetime of hardship, or the Rev. Stallybrass, met with by Captain Cochrane amongst the Buriats of Siberia, who had converted none.

WOOD, Lieut. J., *Journey to the Source of the River Oxus* (1841)

INDEX

Abbot, Capt. James, travels to Khiva,
173–4; waylaid by Kuzzauks, 175;
change of heart between editions of
his book, 176–7; subsequent career,
176n.; release of Russian slaves at
Khiva, 181; mediaevalism, 184;
260n.; *bibliography*
Abdul Sameet Khan, servant of
Nasrullah, 151, *appendix*
Aberdeen, George Hamilton Gordon,
4th Earl of, 148; view of Col.
Stoddart's status, 149;
correspondence with Capt. Grover,
260
Abramoff, General, 112
Afghanistan, fatal advance of Russia
into, 117
A German Nobleman, 122, *bibliography*
Akhcha-kol (lake), scene of aquatic
picnic, 220–30; and subsequent
night nearby, 230–3
Aksakoff, Sergei, 15, 16, 22n., 48,
bibliography
Albert, Prince, fancy dress, 184
Alex, *see* Issaev
Ananouri (Caucasian fortress), 196
Anatoly, driver and companion
throughout journey; meeting with,
97, 99; prepares breakfast, 132, 180,
251; liver complaint, 169; changes
wheel, 186; esteem of friends,
226–7; presents from, 251
Aral Sea, shrinkage, 60, 61, 179n.
Aralsk, Fort, 61
Arnold, Matthew, *Sohrab and Rustum*,
185

Arnold, General, cigars auctioned at
Kabul, 183n.
Attaturk, no Stalin, 132–3
Auckland, George Eden, Earl of, 156,
160
August coup, 259

Baker, Colonel Valentine (later Baker
Pasha), 4, 6, 59, 119; a "good man",
231; 233, 234; messianic rôle among
Tekkes, 236–8; débâcle, 239–41;
after prison, 243–4; *bibliography*
Baker, Sir Samuel (elder brother to
above), purchases bride, 241
Bariatinski, General, 84
Basmachi, patriot-guerrillas (1920s),
261–2
Bentinck, Lord William Cavendish,
"masterly inactivity", 63
Berezikov, Eugeny, dinner at his
Tashkent flat, 80–2; 96, 121, 137
Bezak, General, 84
Blunt, Wilfrid Scawen, unfavourable
view of Capt. Burnaby and General
Gordon, 201
Bokhara, approach to, 137–8; Ark
with guide, 139–40; summer palace,
141; festival of Uzbeg music, 143–5;
Ark alone, 148–50; condition under
later emirs, 152; old quarter, 153–4,
157–8; scene of execution, 164;
lunch party outside city, 167–72;
"liberation of" (1918), 261; *appendix*
Bokhara, emir of, *see* Nasrullah
Buckingham, J. S., 262
Burnaby, Capt. Frederick Gustavus,

2, 4, 13, 119; mock-modesty, 173; character and exploits, 200–2; "good man", 231; shoots driven natives, 236; married life, 201, 204; death, 202; *bibliography*
Burnes, Sir Alexander, 61, 65, 92; disguise, 118*n*., 146*n*.; 148, 150; peevish tone to Conolly, 157; death, 161; etiquette, 169*n*.; 173; sanguine view, 183; slavery, 198; *bibliography*

Cherkassky, Beckovitch, expedition against Khiva, 180–1
Cherniayeff, General, 65, 86
Clarendon, George William Frederick Villiers, 4th Earl of, and 4th Baron Hyde, retort to Gortchakoff, 85
Clarke, E. D., 7, *bibliography*
Clayton, Capt., 236, 237*n*.
Cobbold, Ralph, 98*n*., *bibliography*
Cochrane, John Dundas, RN, (*Narrative of Pedestrian Journey through Russia and Siberian Tartary,* 1824), 1, 2
Conolly, Capt. Arthur, 65, 76–7, 85*n*., 118, 144; character and history, 154–7; enticed to Bokhara, 159–61; last days, 162; prayer book, 163; death, 164, 257; *appendix*; *bibliography*
Cottrell, C. H., 1, 2, 122; translates Shakespear's letter at Orenburg, 182; *bibliography*
Creagh, James, 10, *bibliography*
Crimean War, 83*n*.
Curzon, George Nathaniel, Marquess Curzon of Kedleston, 135, 269

d'Arcy Todd, Major, 173
de Custine, Marquis, 122, 136, 215*n*., *bibliography*
de Hell, Xavier Hommaire, 198, *bibliography*
de Lacy Evans, Colonel, gloomy scenario of England's collapse, 63; *bibliography*
de Lagny, Germain, 10, 14; Russian police, 39; 45, 122, *bibliography*
Dickinson, Miss, assaulted by Colonel Baker, 238–40

Dobell, Peter, reviles cuckoo, 220*n*.; *bibliography*
Dostoievsky, Fyodor, 214
Eshtaev, Ulugbeg, host at Tashkent, 66–70; poor health, 73; attends alfresco supper, 96, 98; oversees farewells, 247; presides over lunch party, 248–50; gift of Uzbeg robe, 251; hard-headed operator, 266
Eugene, Prince, massacres Yomuds, 204–5
Eyre, Vincent, 183, *bibliography*

Fadieieff, Colonel, 136
Fitzgerald, Edward, 71
Flying Scotsman, The, 193, 257, *bibliography*
Fraser, James Baillie, seized by tribesmen, 64*n*.; 118, 188*n*., *bibliography*

Galton, Francis, 256, *bibliography*
Gavazzi, Modesto, 166*n*., *bibliography*
Gawain, Sir and the Green Knight, 185, *bibliography*
Geok Tepe, 238, 241, 243–4
Gill, Leiutenant, 236, 237*n*.
Girouard, Mark, 4*n*., *bibliography*
Golovatchoff, General, 205
Gorbachev, Mikhail, hooted off rostrum, 6; 25; opinion of in Bokhara, 170; fall of, 259
Gortchakoff, Prince, circulates Note, 85
Gray, Francine du Plessix, 153*n*.
Great Game, The, nature of, 3–4; origin of term, 65, 177; explanation to Uzbegs, 76–7; distinguished from "noble game", 172, 177; revival of, 267
Grenville Murray, E., 122, 137, *bibliography*
Grodekoff, Colonel N. L., 117–19, 237*n*., *bibliography*
Grover, Capt., 77, 146–7, 151, *appendix*, *bibliography*
Gur Emir (mausoleum of Tamerlane), 245–6

*See bibliography under M. D. Skoboleff for mention of *Autobiographical Sketches* (1887) by Vassili Verestchagin, etchings of whose drawings illustrate J. A. Mac-Gahan's *Campaigning on the Oxus* (1874) *q.v.*, and one of which is used to illustrate the cover of the present work.

ABOUT THE AUTHOR

Philip Glazebrook was born in 1937. His books include *Journey to Kars*, which describes a lonely journey taking him through the Serbian and Greek provinces of the old Ottoman Empire, and through the ruined classical cities of Asia Minor as far as Turkey's frontier with Russia and the fortress of Kars. These travels furnished the picturesque background for his two novels of Levantine adventure set at the time of the Crimean War, *Captain Vinegar's Commission* and its sequel, *The Gate at the End of the World*. He lives with his family in Dorset.

KODANSHA GLOBE

International in scope, this series offers distinguished books that explore the lives, customs, and mindsets of peoples and cultures around the world.